Out of the
FIELD

Published by Mindstir Media, LLC
45 Lafayette Rd | Suite 181| North Hampton, NH 03862 | USA
1.800.767.0531 | www.mindstirmedia.com

Printed in the United States of America
ISBN-13: 978-1-7339571-7-5
Library of Congress Control Number: 2019908159

MINDSTIR MEDIA

Out of the FIELD

*A Memoir full of Family Betrayal,
Homelessness, Survival, Forgiveness and Love*

written by
LARRY A. LEE

A human life is never over, someone only abandoned it.

Chapters

A special thanks to:

Emilie, Stacey, Jaime, Josie, and Latanga.

1

23 Lovely Street

My decision to fight my father saved my life. One day, at the age of seven, I had enough of the way he'd treated my mother and brother over the previous two years. Branded in my mind, I can still envision and feel the emotions from the moment when he came home drunk. It was a bone-chillingly cold New England evening in Unionville, Connecticut, in 1968. A patch of snow and ice covered the back steps, for it had not been shoveled in days. The sun melted what it could in the daytime, and in the evening what remained froze again. My mother was weak from contracting infectious hepatitis from dental work two years back. On that particular day, she slipped and fell while trying to take out the trash. She bloodied her knee against the jagged ice as she landed on the unshoveled steps.

I saw small tears trickle from her eyes throughout the day. Immersed in my love for her, I walked over and gave her an unexpected hug. The power of my hug always made her smile. I noticed her alone, preoccupied in her pain. That day, I watched the current of emotions in her body and mind shift as the looming storm moved nearer.

Just like any other day, my father stumbled home when he was done drinking with the boys at the No, He's Not Here Saloon. He carried on the family's tradition. A long line of Irish drinkers stood amidst the noises and chatter in local taverns or bars every day, and each of them took an oath to uphold the life that had been passed down by their ancestors. They were content and happy being drunk while the whole world changed around them. They spoke very little and even less as they grew older sitting on the barstool.

The moment I heard the creaking sounds of the screen door swinging open on the breezeway patio, fright waves flashed distress signals to my brain. Instantly, I ceased playing and tried to blend into my surroundings in an effort not to be seen. Once my father was inside, I hid from the energy emanating from inside him. I waited to see if it was safe to come out from behind the protection of furniture. I always stayed away from my father when he came home so I could assess his behavior. I never rushed up to give my dad a hug, and I didn't miss him at all. It was easier to avoid him rather than engage the unpredictable madness within him. The horror of my father's outbursts changed the way I observed life and people in general. My watchful eye developed because of the primal fear this man made me feel.

The pink elephant in the middle of the room stared me down. I created a monster inside of me to combat my father. Every day, I lived in the small puddles of light shaded by his dark inclinations. My innocence was mottled by his actions. He was simply a cold and cruel man who had lost his way. His presence brought a strange and eerie silence that stifled the words, the colors, and the feelings of my mother's loving home. The gloomy calm masked the deep, forceful, turbulent fronts between my parents.

It was the calm before the storm that had been brewing for some time, since the last time. It started out as a simple conversation between a wife and a husband. It was in the stillness of distress that the harsh climate inside the house began to change. Their conflicting thoughts and values collided and began to swirl like an ominous dance with death. Suddenly, the storm erupted. Churning distress set in, and its destructive emotion engulfed my home. My mother's warm, passionate voice crashed and spun into my cold father's deaf ears.

"Ronnie, why can't you come home right after work? I never see you sober anymore," she snapped.

The storm's explosive thunder clouds continued to shift, grow, intensify, and reposition with each word spoken. My drunken father's voice roared back, "I make money! I'll spend it any way I want. Nag! Nag! Nag! It is just a few drinks with friends!"

Within seconds, I watched the love of God leave my home. My mother didn't back down. She thundered back, "I need you home to take care of your responsibilities. What about your sons? They never see you!"

In the lightning bolts of words she yelled, the volatility of the tempest exploded in the outpouring of circling reactions between my two parents. From pale-white to rosy-red, my mother was in peril, inches from my father, and she was unleashing gusting gales that blew the words of truth at my dad's ego. "You're a drunk! You selfish bastard!" she shouted.

Out of the FIELD

Being hard-pressed against shame, he refused to see the man he had become. In his mind's instability, he unleashed a downpour as he impulsively and recklessly shoved my mother away from him.

She stumbled backward, slamming into the kitchen table. She fell to the floor. Weakened by her infectious hepatitis, she still had the heart of a prizefighter beating within her. She found the strength to get back up. Caught in an updraft of adrenaline and feelings, she began to defend herself from my father's attack. She pushed. She advanced. She screamed, "You fucking asshole!"

Her reaction knew no boundaries except truth and righteousness. My mother's passion slammed hard into the unseen rage of my father. The cracking of the thunder was heard throughout the house as the lightning strike of his hand slapped her across her face. I witnessed her sudden shudder as she crashed to the floor. Terror inscribed her face. The thoughts about what kind of man she had married weighed her soul downward. Her eyes cried out for help.

Hunkered down, in the shadows of the furniture, I saw and heard every word spoken. Crouched down in fear, I watched both the tension and the tone of their words slash the flesh from their bodies.

I beheld the moment my father slapped my mother, and the child in my heart strengthened into manhood and shouted, "No!"

My soul found the courage to conquer my fear of my father that day. My instinctive feelings were to protect my mother at all cost. Fear let me discover rage was a powerful emotion, and I moved forward behind its shield.

Abuse makes monsters, and I freed mine from a place where ghosts and bad things live. With no regard for myself, I charged in and launched my fifty-pound body like a rocket toward my father's knees. I didn't break him; I bounced.

He erupted, "You little shit!"

Too small to be her hero that day, dazed from the collision, his powerful workman hands reached down and picked me up like I was nothing. He tossed me across the wood floor toward the wall. "Stay down, you little bastard!"

My eyes opened slowly to see my mother yelling and pounding her closed fists against my father's chest while she screamed, "You're a fucking asshole!"

Not far from me, Robert, my five-year-old brother, stood in the corner crying relentlessly from the horror he'd witnessed. I gathered myself in my mother's love and grew bolder. I charged back in to set her free and howled, "Ahhhhhhhhhhhhhhhhh!"

Fear didn't know me that night, for the purity of my heart defended what it cherished most in this world. My mother's love strengthened me, and in her affection, my fate was sealed. She prepared me to push forward and not accept the suffering and harm passed down by my father. I'd created something bold and new from madness, and it would push back on my family tradition. My heart defied everyone who stood over me. In a world full of baby gods and bullies, an adolescent protagonist found strength in the freedom of love.

From the floor, I turned and looked at them for a brief second. Swept away in the desolation of the storm, Robert was still in the corner shaking in fear and sobbing uncontrollably. He was terrified and paralyzed by his unknown self-interest when he saw my father's malicious actions. In the corner, he was no longer under the umbrella of our mother's love and protection.

He tried to catch his breath, but fear wouldn't let him. His heart beat faster than his lungs could inhale. Gulping for air, shaking ceaselessly, he was kidnapped and held hostage in a moment with no thoughts, immobilizing terror controlling his mind and body.

Subsiding into surrender, my mother slid to the floor. Among the scattered debris, a deluge of tears flowed from her eyes. Ragged, she held the broken pieces of her soul together while she wept. She shook nervously in fright at the thought of what her husband had become.

I got up off the floor and walked by my father while he poured himself a glass of whiskey. As I passed him, on the way to my mother, his cold, dark black eyes relentlessly stared down at me. A spine-chilling apprehension of his evil surrounded me. Like a submissive animal, I didn't look him in the eye because of his dominance. I'd always looked out of the corner of my eye when interacting with him. At an early age, I learned how to numb my emotions and use the power of his denial to my advantage. The days of Santa Claus and the Easter Bunny were dead to me.

My imagination took me to a place where the sun shined brightly on my face. My soul knew I was another. Someone remarkable lived inside of me, for a challenge merely required an answer. Thought made me stronger than my oppressor. Ambition sparked the liberties inside of my young soul.

The suffering of my life had just begun.

Observing my father, I saw an ugly and mean man. He had shot glass eyes of insolence and a heart of empty will, and he was a destructive force to all those he gazed upon. He had so many different faces that I couldn't recognize him from one day to the next. He told so many different lies that I quit listening to him. A mere child, I looked at the stranger who fathered me and knew I could never trust him.

As I comforted my mother from the storm's damage, I helped her to her feet and walked her to her room. I whispered the sweet loving words, "Love you, Mama," only for her ears.

A weak smile crossed her face.

Traumatized by my father's actions, she sobbed and shook the whole way. Nothing he would ever do could stop me. I put on my winter jacket. All my efforts were out of love. I went outside and grasped the snow-covered shovel. By the white haze of the moonlight, through my hatred, I toiled, dug, and chopped away all the ice and snow from the walkways around our house. Finding solace with each chopping motion, my tears froze before they hit the ground, and I shouted at God about my father's abuse, "Why God? Why me?"

My young mind lit the match to the light of reflection. Life seemed overwhelming and impossible, but when I looked into the improbable, I found concealed in the doubt and skepticism the foundation of faith. My self-dignity fought my father's indifference and neglect. The purity of my heart and mind allowed me to believe in the power of God. The gift of observing facts and understanding conclusions christened my eyes with intuition. The strength of my love was born in the defiance of human despair.

It was a gift my young mind couldn't yet fully understand. The liberty of my eternal consciousness coupled with the fiery tongue of my youth made for a spirit-filled evening. Keen-eyed, I complained to God about the dry rot in people's souls, and I didn't know how people let it get there. I thought, "Shame on them for what they become."

It was while I was releasing my thoughts toward heaven my father looked at me through a window in the door. He laughed at me and said, "Get to work, boy. It's going to be a long evening."

I turned my head and whispered, "Fuck off, old man!"

I continued to shovel the snow, and my thoughts were only about my mother and brother inside. It was at that moment I realized that there were no knights in shining armor coming to save me. All alone, I saw the unwritten code of silence in my family members' eyes. It was an eternal moment in my soul when I recognized I had to champion my life. At seven years old, I saw beyond the smokescreen words others spoke. The truth was smothered by a lie. I prayed to God not to be like my father, and I didn't know the power of prayer.

♥

As the days of my life continued to pass, I could never please my father and lived beneath the volatility of his daily eruptions. My contempt for him was formed from constant exposure to his mind's slow decay into madness. His cruelty was everywhere. He forced me to deny myself. Hatred made it easy to stop asking why. A blind man, he never saw the faces of his children. His selfish and wicked actions marked my soul. As a child, injustice made me look more in-depth into human denial. The stunted lives of my family embodied a bygone era. My uncles and aunts were horribly limited.

My only relationship was with God. I vented to Him to keep my sanity. I saw a choice ripple and expand negatively through others' lives. As I kicked the ashes of the day with my feet, suffering opened my mind to see that actions didn't match the words spoken around me. As a child, I looked at the world with old eyes.

I couldn't stop the daily incoming missiles, but I dodged them from behind my missile-proof heart and retaliated, never forgetting what I was fighting against.

My father envisioned living his life through me, for he had the idea I'd play Major League Baseball. He wanted to return to his glory days through me. The shadows of my deceased ancestors lurked under my father's skin. A forced vision, its authority kicked the shit out of me every time I tried to think for myself. It was the friction of our relationship, I learned to smile and not to expose my canines unless provoked.

Internalizing rage became body armor to protect me. I knew no one could match my heart. I learned to play a game other than baseball and pushed back the deadbolt. I unleashed the chain holding back my mind. I wouldn't let my family define me. I opened the door to my imagination and became something new every day to survive. No one told me the game

Out of the FIELD

I was playing couldn't be won.

Since the time I was five, he forced me to play catch with him while he drank his whiskey. He told me stories of all the baseball games he played in as a youth. Slowly, I was ordained in the bitterness of his lost hope. His small-town vision suffered from a broken heart. My father loved the game of baseball more than he loved me. He was a star athlete in baseball, football, and track, and he was class president at Farmington High School. A southpaw, my father pitched and played outfield. His ability to throw a baseball was his gift. In the box scores and the articles written about him, I learned his drive to succeed, and it was forced down to me.

"You know, Son, the Dodgers drafted me. I couldn't play for them because my dad passed. I had to pitch in and take care of my brothers and sister."

"That's cool, Dad. Are we done yet?"

"No, you have to practice every day, Son."

I looked at him and threw the ball back, hoping it would hit him in the face. It was baseball that made it tough for him to see me as his child. He only talked about his past, and his only thought was, "It might have been different if..."

His unfulfilled dream couldn't be ignored, nor could he accept his life. He made me play catch with him for hours. At the end of each session, I could barely clutch the ball. My glove hand was swollen and red from the constant pounding. I felt the hands of my ancestors around my neck, holding me back. I refused to be reduced by another man's dreams. My father's eyes showed no emotions. Good as dead to me, my only move was to rebel.

♥

The next year he decided to coach a junior baseball team, and I had no choice but to play for the bastard. He didn't care about anything, for he was heartless, vicious, and vulgar. He wanted to win. My greatest disappointment in life was that he was never able to see me as his son. Being wide-eyed and full of wonder, I stumbled around his playing field rhyming words and kicking yellow dandelions into the wind.

Like a bird of prey, he saw everything. One practice, I didn't put my glove all the way down to the ground to catch the ball, and the ball rolled between my legs. Half-drunk and thoroughly out of his mind, his thunderous voice roared, "If you do not want to use your glove then you will use your bare hands! Take your glove off, now!"

With stern eyes, I stood there and looked at him. My heart challenged him. I threw my glove to the side and disguised my fear. I questioned him in front of every one of my teammates and mumbled to myself, "Whatever, old man."

He saw my lips move and shouted, "What did you say?"

My intense eyes gave him a "fuck you" look.

I unleashed the monster inside my heart to protect myself. Standing in silence, a chanting warrior, I looked at my enemy. Focused, I observed every one of his movements. I produced a magnetic field to repel his imposing anger. It was his madness against my defiance. It was an epic battle between a father and a son. At that moment, I didn't see him as my father, but as a man who was trying to hurt me.

Scared to death, but determined, something profound inside of me overtook my conscious movements when he tossed the ball up. The ball bounced off the bat, and it sizzled and spun across the infield. I could see the energy of the ball ripping pieces of grass in two. Broken fragments of grass flung toward the sun. Nearer and nearer, the moment came to fruition, as the vigor to defy my father gave me the courage to put my hands down to catch the first ground ball.

As the force of the ball hit my fingertips, a surge of energy ripped through my hands. I boomed, "Oh yeah!"

I puffed out my chest, spit on the ground and threw the ball over his head. It was a full-scale conflict now. He howled, "Catch this one, smart-ass!"

The second one came a little harder, but I caught it too. Once again, I threw an uncatchable ball toward the catcher.

"Here's one more for you, smart-ass!" he shouted.

The third one sent immense burning anguish through my fingers. It was the fourth one that felt like a buzz saw that rolled through my hands. My father's moral decline neutralized my force field. After that one, I realized he was just nuts.

My knees were bent and ready, and a tear trickled from one eye. I looked over at the fathers watching, and none of them said a word.

I mumbled to myself, "Cowards."

My heart exploded with desire and defied his insanity. He wasn't the

Out of the FIELD

man he thought he was. Doggedness drove me onward, and it made me stronger than I ever imagined. He never did let up, even when he saw me crying. Numbed by the pain, I wouldn't let him win. Wounded, I used my legs to aid me. I was still in this fight as long as I was breathing.

I accepted the fact he was a madman trying to hurt me, and I knew there would be more battles to come. Fear made me tenaciously resilient. I outlasted him, as finally, my father shouted, "Get back in line."

As I walked over toward my teammates, I cradled and comforted each throbbing hand with the other. When I looked into my teammates' eyes, they looked away. Frustrated and angry, I kicked my glove, and my father saw me. He yelled at me, "You better pick it up now or else you will run all night!"

At the back of the line, one of my teammates whispered to me, "I'm glad he isn't my father."

I whispered back, "Yeah, you got lucky."

His demeanor went unchallenged by everyone except me.

♥

As I dared to dream beyond my family's tradition, I opened the imagination of someday and ten million thoughts. I looked for the reason why life was so cruel. The solitude of my abandonment drove me to ponder the still-framed events of each day. My mind always roamed somewhere between humanity and divinity. As the two worlds clashed, I began to have little patience for both God and my family. I looked to God for my strength, praying every day. It seemed to me that my prayers were white noise in a universe gone mad. I voiced to God, "Where does someone like my father come from?"

"Who and what caused him to be this way?"

"Why was he trying to hurt me?"

"Why doesn't he love me?"

"Where is God in all of this?"

I grew up a prisoner of his expectations and experiences. I lived in fear of this man.

As a child, I saw the ugly side of loyalty, for it cannot see the truth objectively. Inopportunity emancipated me. I found something stubborn, ambiguous, and ambitious lived inside of me. It was rebellious. It was lifesaving. It was the understanding that life was the sum of all the small choices we make each day. My mom inspired me to fight for my life.

2
A Mother's Goodness

My mother, Anne Marie Holiday, met my father while she worked at Hartford Electric Light Company (HELCO) as a switchboard operator. My dad was an electrician for the company. It was a skill he learned in the navy. In the 1950s, young women were expected to marry and start a family by the age of twenty, and my mother was no exception. However, her father passed away from World War I mustard gas wounds when she was only a year old. Without a father figure to protect and guide her, she quickly succumbed to the yearnings of her romantic heart. A dream of a loving and loyal husband and bright blue-eyed children with ice cream noses captured her heart.

Feeling bright as the sun, she lived in the warmth of God's love each day. Underneath the umbrella of her bliss, I felt whole and loved eternally. She was the antidote to all that was unknown and scary. She was the one who taught me how to talk to God. By taking us to church, she showed me the goodness in people. Each Sunday, she took my brother and me to church while my father slept off his hangover. In church, I learned to pray to Jesus, treat people with respect and dignity, and share my cookies with others. As a child, my mother taught me the principles of an unprejudiced world.

She was a gentle lioness whose only concerns were two boys. Her daily teachings, board games, storytelling, and reading opened my mind to the magic of emotions and the color in the tone of words. She handed me sympathy, and in it, I found her quiet grace. She taught me to laugh, and in laughter, I found the joy of being alive. She was passing on her inherited disposition for life, and in it, I found memories that aided me through my days. It was her love that made me wealthy and warmed my soul with the endless possibilities of being my mother's son.

As I started to lose my mom to her illness, she lived at Hartford Hospital. I missed her gentle hand and caring eyes. Life made me feel unlovable. My father always brought home his cold reality and speckled it with his hidden horrors. At the age of eight, the distinction between right and wrong helped me discover myself. There were a billion pleasant ideas of peace and noble ambitions in my mind. I didn't have one decent thought of my father. As I pondered his lack of principles, my faith and understanding helped me uncover the insight and riches of my soul.

Alone, with no one in this world, a thousand times a day my young poetic eyes saw life stop and redirect itself in the will of a motive. In a moment of change, thoughts and wisdom entered my mind. My observations were endless and romanced the truth seldom seen. I wouldn't waste my talent. I wouldn't let my father take from me what was not his. I began to scribble my thought and rhyme words on a page or in my mind. My keen eyes dismantled a cruel and controlled world. My faith grew from the lies and mistrust of others. The silence in everyone's life made me a seeker of truth.

♥

I watched my father drink whiskey like it was water and was continually amazed at the invincibility of his ego. In the hideous fanfare of his mind, the late stages of alcoholism began to break down and destroy every aspect of his life. The poison he drank fostered the complacency of failure. He sat among his ancestors at the bar while they played cribbage for a penny a point in purgatory. He acted and rehearsed his role every day at the No, He's Not Here Saloon. At the end of each daily performance, his encore was to drive us home. As our automobile drifted between the lines and the oncoming traffic, I sat in the front seat waiting for the moment of impact or death. I could hear the oncoming horns in the distance when we crossed the double yellow lines.

I yelled at him, "Wake the fuck up, old man!" The tone in my voice slapped him back into reality.

He startled out of his blackout and right back into life. He shouted at me, "Watch your fucking language!"

I never knew if we would make it home alive. Every journey home was a roller coaster ride full of emotions. Unpredictable, terrifying, and blessed in its design, I learned not to fear death because of my father's fear of living.

Out of the FIELD

♥

My father intended Robert and me to be just like him. We grew up in bars around town while my mother stayed in the hospital for months at a time. I called it night school. I excelled in street smarts and resented the controlled thinking of public education. We studied all hours of the night. We waited for him to stumble back from oblivion and into his car. Our undergraduate classes were from ages five to eight. He left us in the car while he drowned his soul. With nothing to do, I studied people to pass the time.

Picking up conversations through body language, I saw a clearance sale of bodies and voices selling drugs and pleading for love. Eyeballing their actions, they told me their story of disregard and shame. Every minute, someone or something changed the scene of maddening vice in front of my eyes. I saw in the vast confusion of life, a billion unfinished thoughts washed down the sewer hole. The unpremeditated art of life embraced the renaissance of wonder in my mind's eye.

Professor Lee held classes year-round. The weather didn't influence my lower education. Winter or summer, there were no breaks or family vacations. My father didn't care about us, so we waited in the car. He only cared about getting drunk with his buddies, and he never cared about the cold New England winters. The love and security of my mother warmed my heart. She inspired my resistance. She illuminated my young soul from the coldness and disenchanted thoughts of despair. Frozen cold like a manhole cover, my poet's eye searched for warmth where the sun never shined. I merely squirmed about in the car to keep from freezing. I couldn't feel my fingertips or toes at times. Night school's tortuous moments were not for my pampered classmates. I filled my monster with a blizzard of cold raging thoughts to stay warm.

After a few years with the underachievers, Robert and I were accepted into night school's graduate studies. We sat at the back table in the bar. We drank soda and ate cheese-covered popcorn for dinner. I watched the baseball game on the television. Bored out of my mind, I studied modern mankind's deconstruction. Barflies looked to ease their emptiness with someone they called "Lucky."

Dollar bills exchanged for beer chasers and whiskey on the rocks. The smoke gathered at the ceiling, and the smoke up top circled from the flux of patrons coming and going. I couldn't help but notice this was in sharp contrast to the love my mother showed me. Comparing the patrons to my classmates' families, I determined they were missing love, conversation, laughter, and a family. I watched and listened to bikers advocate for drugs, alcohol, and violence, and barflies fondled into desire. Working-class men stumbled in and stumbled out. I heard my father talking to other racist men about "niggers, hippies, and spics." From my seat in the bar, life at the bottom of the barrel opened my eyes to the mutilation from the hands of time. In each of them, they drank until the need to go home was greater.

Destined by past generations of learned behaviors, I stood at the edge of oblivion with no fear of falling. From love to loneliness, a fearless child walked across the high wire of life. My prayers were empty words which led me to rebel. Starved for affection, I was terrified of abandonment. From my barroom corner table, I saw the religion of men who drank their dinner. From my mind, a delightful unholy purpose rose never to honor my father.

Surrounded by drunks, I knew nothing was possible in this common man's place. I cultivated my imagination, for my eyes lost focus in the sold-out reality all around me. I wanted no part of the people who liquefied themselves into apathy. An undercover kid with an old soul. I couldn't sit in perpetual sadness and be immobilized. I unleashed my monster to search-and-destroy missions.

♥

Observing my classmates, they were swaddled in lullabies and this only fostered thoughts of mischief. I wanted them to wake up from their sheltered lives and feel vulnerable. I particularly disliked one of my classmates. He was brilliant, and his clothes were pristine and unwrinkled. He was well-liked, and everything about him seemed perfect. I wanted to rip his world from him and shred his security blanket. I plotted and schemed a plan to embarrass him. While everyone was at lunch, I stole everyone's writing instruments and placed every one of them inside his three-ring notebook. The binder has been put inside his desk's cubicle.

After lunch, all my classmates started to complain to the teacher that someone stole all their pens and pencils. A few minutes later, he decided to pull out his notebook. Everyone's writing instruments fell out all over the floor. Inside, I grinned and watched the frenzy occur. Like bees swarming,

Out of the FIELD

my classmates pushed him aside like he was nothing. The look on his face was priceless. I welcomed him to my heartbreak. Beads of perspiration crept across his forehead. I released my mischievous smile at the world.

♥

As for my fourth-grade formal education, I staggered back and forth between poetic musings and dysfunctional reality. My home life was too toxic for traditional learning. I couldn't study when I had to worry about my mother in the hospital, detested my father's existence, and wondered what I would eat next. Most days, I sat in the classroom and stared out the window imagining. I looked out from my soul of blue into a field of green, and I watched the yellow leaves of my thoughts fall from the trees and blow away in the wind.

The teacher always dragged me back by saying, "Mr. Lee, you cannot learn anything looking out the window. What are you staring at?"

"I am not looking at anything. I am searching for something."

"What you are searching for is in front of you, so please get focused."

I let my thoughts drift away from both God and school. In the blur of my mind, I found comfort in my observations. I saw beyond the dispersed boundaries of language the teacher taught and began to write. Misfortune opened my eyes, and my soul poured out through blue ink on a white page. I unfastened my eyeballs so they could look up, down, over, and under everything. I embraced what was ugly. In the blurred gray of words, I became a smoldering red sunset when I wrote. Life began to pass me by, and at the age of nine, I was disconnected by the insanities I observed. A lawless scribe was made.

♥

The need to be needed drove me to seek attention. I would take it from anyone that would give it to me. One day, a couple of sixth graders found me pushing a kid who cut in front of me in the lunch line. They ran a racket called "Gladiator Wars." These sixth graders would match up students to fight during recess. They let kids wager their lunch money on the fighters. I remember a couple of sixth graders asked me, "Hey little man do you know how to fight?"

"Yeah, why?"

"My name is Jeff, and my friend here will give you a dollar if you fight another kid at recess tomorrow."

"A whole dollar to fight someone. Sure!"

The next day came, and I was alone in my thoughts. My memories went back to the brawls with my father. By now, my monster obeyed my every command, and it gave me a monstrous will to survive. It puffed me up and snarled at anyone who stood in my way.

After we had finished eating, Jeff ushered me to the back corner of the school's playground. A circle of kids gathered around. Guided through the spectators, I stepped into the middle of the chaos. My opponent was a fifth-grader, and he was a few inches taller and heavier than I was. As I stood there, time slowed down. I felt at peace in anarchy. After all, I had been beaten by my father before and lived. I looked at him and knew he had no chance. I grew up and lived in a place where bad things turned uglier.

I was a rebel with a cause, so planned disorder was as simple as breathing. As I scanned my opponent, the movement of his eyes revealed his thoughts. Switching back and forth from the anxiety of doubt, he didn't realize he had passed a thin line. As a child, I jumped rope on the border between illusion and reality daily. As I looked down, I found the nothingness in my soul. As I lifted my head to look at him, his eyes wished for another choice.

My coiled angry thoughts sprung outwardly. BAM! After all, I had been beaten to the point I learned to hit back. BAM! As all my emotions and energy encircled me like a funnel cloud waiting to touch down, a terrible surge of silence raged in me. In the middle of chaos and fear, I opened up my hurt and became invincible. With a cruel smile, unshackled fury, I looked at him and roared, "You're a son of a bitch!"

His pupils enlarged and stared back at me. He froze. I hit him several more times before he went down. In his hesitation, I welcomed him to my Saturday night beating. He sat there on the ground, dazed, and did nothing. All the kids cheered. I won all six fights that year. After all, I had been fighting my father over the past two years. Scrappy, I learned to never back down from anyone.

In the lawlessness of the universe, I prayed to God to rescue me. God was too busy turning water into wine somewhere else. As cold and dreary as a rainy November morning, the dullness of the days of apathy wore me down. God did nothing for me, so I took my life into my own hands. Unanswered prayers and my family's abandonment made me think outside the sandbox.

♥

In 1969, it was made very clear to me I was on my own. My Grandmother Holiday came to live at our house. My mother had an extended stay in the hospital. My grandmother wanted to care for us while my father worked out of town. One day, she left and never came back, for she noticed my dad drinking whiskey for breakfast. Day by day, she watched him, and with my curious eyes, I watched her slowly turn her back on Robert and me. Abandoned by my family, I felt firsthand the impact of the depreciation of human life. The stresses of being alone in the world opened the door to emotional poverty, violence, and hunger.

As a child, I pondered how grownups can turn their heads in the sight of evil. My family pretended not to see and mainly cooperated with my father. I never had the luxury of feeling secure and rebelled against everyone's denial. Chaos frequently struck after midnight. I quit asking God for help and only trusted in myself.

One day, in front of my uncles and aunts, my father tossed Robert against the wall. No one did anything, for they didn't want to make it worse. Their inability to reason and investigate gave my father the power he craved. It was Darwinism in a Christian home. It was a mockery of the words love and family. This was my life, and I compressed, internalized, and hardened my heart to survive. With an ironclad grin, I sneered back at both God and everyone.

As I drifted further and further from any meaningful relationship, abandonment enabled me to piss on those who pissed me off. I declared war against the family detention camp and the ancestry of whimpering slaves. Sitting in the dark, the thought "an eye for an eye," gave me a woodie.

♥

With my mother in the hospital for months at a time, we only visited her on the weekends or not at all. No one was there to help me navigate my life. I watched the passing shadows of adults disappear into the sunset. I felt the need to talk with someone, but no one was ever there. The loss of love radicalized me. My senses grew numb, and I gazed out the window thinking of my next costume.

The vast internal conflict between life with my mother and life without her made me an actor. I performed every day, for the pieces of my life didn't fit the puzzle. Thrown aside, every fiber of my being loathed adults. I saw the truth twisted and turned into something else by family members. They made it something bearable that didn't remind them of what they didn't have. Surviving in silence, I trusted my observations, and the monster inside me continued to feed off the neglect of others. I walked the streets looking for a home. A small-town hoodlum was born by the loss of all hope in his family and neighbors.

I took full advantage of my family's two-faced actions and found the wildness in my heart that couldn't be tamed. I served no master, for my night school's graduate degree opened my mind to the visualization of the hypocrisies of society. The art of survival depended on knowing when it was time to act or to react aggressively. Fear didn't know me. Fear caused hesitation. I grew up in a dog-eat-dog existence. When my father was not home, I made myself a pack leader. Being almost two years older than my brother, I terrorized him into submission when I yelled, "Robert, I'll teach you not to pick a side."

The sound of a door opened, and he ran toward the tree line. A lion chased a gazelle. When I jumped on him, I took him down and used him to hone my fighting skills.

Back at home, I ate what little food we had in front of him. I threw him my scraps like you throw a dog a bone. I was bigger, stronger, and meaner than he was. With little to no food at times, I filled my hunger pains with dry rice and breadcrumbs. A luxury was peanut butter without bread or bread without peanut butter. My actions toward Robert were both godless and loveless. Survival hardened my heart into hatred.

♥

A bohemian redneck, my father's carefree attitude opposed family values. He went to work every day and sometimes I didn't see him for a whole week. After work, he went to the bar to drink with his buddies, and he crashed at some barfly's crib. Starved most days, I called around ten p.m.

Out of the FIELD

to the different bars in town to find him.

I asked the bartender, "Is Ronnie Lee there?"

"Wait a second."

"This is Ronnie."

"Hey Dad, we haven't eaten all day. Can you bring home a pizza?"

"You interrupted my drinking for pizza! If I have time. We'll see. Did you clean the house?"

We had a fifty-fifty chance we might eat that day. Everything depended on how drunk he was. He would arrive home after the bar closed, around midnight or one a.m. on a school night.

Several times, I called my grandmother, for we had not eaten for days. She and one of my uncles would bring up groceries that would last for a short time. Even then, no one ever challenged my father's conduct. All he would do was complain, "They eat it faster than I can buy it."

♥

As my father's life endlessly swirled out of control from alcoholism, I refused to beg anymore. I expanded the limits of my mind every day to rebel against my hand-me-down hardship forced on me.

My campaign against the world around me was fueled by my determination not to conform to the reality of others. My instincts were an internal sense to feel what I couldn't see. Fearless, I began to think beyond my suffering and searched for a solution. Adversity made my mind's eye open the layers of the universe and find a way to live. I was smart enough to know I couldn't play by society's rules and win. Freelance thoughts allowed me to grow bolder, stronger, and wiser. Abandonment had no sense of loyalty or good faith. With the feelings of disgust and envy, I stormed the castle walls of the ignorant and overconfident because I could. At the age of ten, my life of crime started by stealing food to feed myself.

As I saw my father's life decay before my eyes, my hatred festered into full-scale contempt for him. Anyone near us became collateral damage in our war. I attacked his ego and stripped him of all his possessions from his glory days. He had a box of no-hit, one-hit, and two-hit souvenir baseballs. Scrapbooks filled full of newspaper clippings and box scores went into the fireplace. I used all his game balls to play games with the neighbors or catch.

Several times, Robert noticed the faded blue ink on the ball and said,

"Dad is going to kill you if he finds out."

"You keep your mouth shut or else," I barked at him.

The ink on those balls disappeared like the days of my childhood. One by one, my father's precious baseballs ended up in the yard, weathering in the elements, like the disuse and stagnation of our brittle and rusted relationship. He also had a coin collection comprised of silver dollars, buffalo nickels, and other rare coins. I stole them to buy baseball cards for my collection. There were no rules in our war. I didn't see him as my father. He was an opponent I had to beat or die trying.

Without guidance, love, or affection, I wandered through the equation of life with no ground zero. I had no conversations to make me feel part of the human race. The world slammed the door in my face. An orphan, I was allowed to roam free. There were no Norman Rockwell moments in my life. I waited in silence for calloused knuckles to hit my face. I lived in a dark place, but the sparks of wisdom wouldn't let the hero in my soul perish. I existed by wit, creativity, and by scribbling my thoughts anywhere I could. Deep inside, I wanted to die and restart my life. With no past and no future, I lived in the moment of the rapture of the chaos I created. I rebelled against the world of apathy. A bomb inside my body, I exploded every day.

♥

In each of my fistfights, I stood my ground and asked no quarter. I didn't ask for forgiveness from my father or my classmates. I didn't trust anyone and slept with one eye open. I trained my ears to hear his automobile driving up the driveway. Once the car door shut, I stared at the ceiling and listened to each dragging footstep up the sidewalk. Anxiety shifted me into a survival mode the second I heard the screen door open. I hoped he would just go to bed.

Forgotten by all, even God, my father interjected his unsympathetic madness into our lives. His internal demons manifested themselves in different ways. He would kick open our bedroom door. He shouted out orders like we were being attacked, "Get your fucking little asses out of bed! This house has failed my inspection!"

Staring at the ceiling, I always wondered what God did in these moments? Was He on His fifteen-minute break? It really didn't matter

Out of the **FIELD**

anyway, for my father's actions bullied God out of our house. Smack! Smack! The sound of him hitting the door echoed throughout my room. "Get your asses moving! Clean the garage! Clean the kitchen! Clean! Clean! Clean!" he drunkenly shouted.

We had to get up and scrub down whatever he wanted so we could get some sleep on a school night. I tried to survive his exploding verbal blasts. His naval inspection flashbacks let me see his inner demon's eyes. From the right angle, I saw the demons nibbling away at what was left of his soul. They were like ants on a dead mouse scavenging to survive.

In the bombardment of his words, Robert's head spun in confusion. We had no toys, television, or any earthly possessions to clutter up the house. We didn't eat much, so there were no dirty dishes. He just owned a sofa, a stereo, a dining room table, and chairs. He was crazy-mad drunk. Robert acted like a puppy dog, obeying his master. I picked my battles. Sometimes, I would say, "Fuck you, old man! Clean it your fucking self."

A cat-and-mouse game occurred after a comment like that, and I never went back to my room. I had to wait until the drunk passed out to get some sleep. Some evenings, I couldn't take it anymore, so I unchained my monster. Fury strolled around in my head, festering and growing each second. As my thoughts grew stronger, my actions became bolder. I played with rage until it supplied me with the armor I needed.

I erased the lines between humanity and insanity and marched forward in our war. I defended my soul at whatever the cost. I didn't worry about the future, for I lived in chaos's hell. My eyes lit up bright like a Bengal tiger stalking his prey. I snuck up behind him, and sucker punched him. Once again, I was too small to inflict much damage.

He shouted, "You fucking little bastard!" as he backhanded me in the face.

He laughed as I fell down to the floor, and shouted, "Stay down, boy! You have too much of your mother in you."

"FUCK YOU!"

My heart couldn't stay down. I got back up and engaged my dad again. After all, my mother did. Bruised and battered, I entered the abyss of reckless anger and lived at the edge of scorn. Born into hatred, I existed in violence and learned scars make you tough. I privately continued to sow my own destruction. Attack, attack there was an enemy in my fort, and he must die.

3

The Promise

These Midnight Inspections continued every time he finished his drinking. One night, I will never forget. On Wednesday, January 6, 1971, he came home in his usual drunken rage. He barked out orders like we were on a flight deck under attack from North Korea's airplanes, "Wake the fuck up, boys! Daddy's home to play with you!"

We stumbled out of bed. We walked around in a sleepy stupor. Listening to country music on the stereo, I pushed a broom. We wiped down the furniture in an already-clean house. My father's madness roamed freely that night, so I chose not to fight him. As I meandered about placating his drunken confusion, I gazed upon my loveless father in his boxer shorts. Suddenly, the phone rang at about one a.m.

Crying, he came into our room and got on one knee with a drink in hand, and slurred, "Boys, that phone call was from Hartford Hospital's chaplain. He told me your mother had just passed."

He cried like a baby who lost his favorite toy. He hadn't even taken the time to visit her that day. He was drinking at the bar with his buddies. She died in her hospital bed all alone.

As my body was being surrounded by the loss of life, I was caught in a riptide of emotions. Morose gray waves crashed and pounded into my soul. All I could do was cry as the surge of waves kept endlessly coming and coming. Sinking, tumbling, and will-less, the sweet memory of my mother drowned in sorrow as I recalled her love. Battered, shattered, and trembling, my soul curdled and sank. Moored to her love, I dropped into a dark place unknown to me. In my mind's eye, I saw her as I faded with her in death. She was my all and everything. She helped me to read and see the truth. She gave me the love and confidence to be me. She made every wrong right. She was my mother and teacher. She was my best friend and instilled a passion for life, love, and laughter in me. She was no more than a memory as I neared self-pity. At that moment, her undying love cut the tether between heaven and earth, and I floated back to my life.

As I gasped for air between teardrops, it was my hatred for my father that grounded me when he said, "I love you, boys."

I pushed him away from me. Both he and his drink spilled out on the floor.

♥

In the days after my mother passed, I climbed my favorite tree. My heart and mind retreated into the fondness of my memories of her. Moving pictures played in my mind. Her tender love comforted my soul. I envisioned her tucking me in at night. We said our prayers together. I remembered the messages she wrote and placed in my lunch box. We went for a walk into town to get ice cream. She let me cuddle under a blanket next to her. I'd always fall asleep in her arms. I sat in her lap while she read me a story. In the inflections, she made the characters come alive just for me. One day, we were searching for four-leaf clovers in the grass, and I found one! She made me feel loved and cherished every day. I needed her. Lost inside, my memories clung to her love and found courage. Yet I feared life without her. I couldn't stop crying. I knew my life would never be the same.

Flickering in my mind was the promise I made her a few weeks before she passed. I looked into her sunken eyes as she lay in her hospital bed and saw only the beauty of her soul. Her skin was yellow, and she had many brown bruises on her arms from where the nurses tried to find a usable vein. Her liver was shutting down.

She called me over to her, and I lay in the bed next to her. She said, "Larry, I want you to promise me you'll grow up to be a good man. Please look after your brother, too."

I smiled and replied, "Yes, Mama. I love you."

I didn't know what death was, for no one ever talked to me. I just knew the warm smile of love from my mother. Being her son, I found comfort by her side. I found joy in being with her. I found the treasure in her smile. We had a connection between our two hearts like sunbeams warming the earth and needed each other. In her tender love, I was a child of this world. She put the goodness, truth, and honor in my heart.

I did not know she was dying when I promised her. She must have felt so helpless to ask that of me as a ten-year-old.

As my journey to fulfill the pledge I made to my mother began, the two years she spent in the hospital toughened me up. I adjusted to the miserable bane of the adults in my life. Galled by both my father and my extended family's lack of action, I looked up at them, only to look down at them in disgust. They didn't believe in communication, nor did they ever have that skill set in their lives. No one ever talked to me about my mother passing or her illness.

My relatives rubbed me on my head and told me in liquored voices, "It's a shame your mother passed so early." She was only thirty years old.

Everywhere I went, everyone had a drink in their hand. Anesthetized from reality, people laughed wildly and talked loud enough to be heard at the end of the street. Drunks bumped into walls, people, and things. They acted stupidly, without regret. I saw them asleep at the wheel with their eyes wide open. I could see and feel the lashed scars of misery all around me. I was a little boy who felt abandoned entirely by his family and the world.

My innocence was taken from me several years back, and the fog of war illuminated my bright blue eyes in the sunlight of truth. I began to poke at the complacency of the world. I stood in the ruins of my soul at ten years old, and it made me a beautifully brave boy. I grew up quickly in the roughness and spirit of defiance. I had many good, old-fashioned fistfights with my father. The freedom I deserved drove me to kick, hit, and spit on him. He backhanded, slapped, and threw me down. He shouted for the world to hear while I was sprawled out on the floor, "Shut your mouth, boy! You little bastard!"

4

Little Bastard

I wasn't afraid of my father and the army of ghosts that stood behind him. I knew my life wouldn't be cultivated in love. An evil man cannot become a good man. Nothing can fill the abyss in an evil heart. With lots of time alone, I had endless hours to analyze my father's behaviors and found the cracks in his rusted armor. I didn't have to eat to grow, for anger fed me. I pushed my mind beyond the obstacle of fear. My ability to think and use my imagination reaped a whirlwind of thoughts inside of me. In the midst of my struggle, I found thought made me invincible.

Madness opened my mind's eye to see my relatives marching onward like penguins falling into the sea. I questioned the unspoken inheritance bestowed from past generations. The broken pieces of my life revealed a reason for my existence. The light of my mother's love remained in my heart. Born in the eye of the storm, I found shelter in the battered ramparts of my soul, and my cannons remained undaunted. The deep roaring of my moral essence began to send volleys of fire downfield to all who witnessed the crimes against me. I didn't care what the future held and walked alone at war with the world.

A child terrorist, my organized hatred arose from a voice I couldn't share. My actions screamed the words I didn't know how to say. Rising up against complacency, I had two souls, two thoughts and served two masters. My pain nurtured the dogged strength within me to tear the world asunder. I thought about my enemies twenty-four seven and saw every one of their weaknesses. I wouldn't sit still long enough for the melancholy hometown vines to get a foothold. My mind scrutinized every uncomfortable thought. I dared to see life from a million different angles and found a billion ways to attack. I challenged everything and everyone. The hero inside pushed back the mean drunks, lustful sluts, and blind-eyed relatives.

♥

With little remorse from my mother's passing, my father didn't waste any time beginning his new sexual exploits. Each night, from the back of the bar, a perfumed paradise, I watched the clearance sale of dressed-up bar-flies in the eyes of dirty old men. I read erotica without knowing the words. I watched inexhaustible vice, and uncontrolled pleasures consume people's lives. One drunk old man shouted, "The good life is a warm body, cold whiskey, and good music."

Everyone in the bar cheered.

My father's sexual instinct was powerful, yet it lacked taste, decency, and manners. From my observation, he preferred a good-hearted servant. As a child, I heard the mandolin playing in the background. I saw, first-hand, the dark side of oblivion mirrored through my father's eyes. Anger, impulse, perversion, and insanity were things I witnessed as a child. In the moment of each day's disaster, my lungs burned. My temples roared! My rage swarmed! I glared javelins at anyone who dared to come close.

Each night, I watched my father stagger through the torturous events of the life he had chosen. The poison he drank decayed his mind, and his actions made me ponder reality. Every once in a while, he looked over to where Robert and I sat. His false smile disappeared back into his stupor of drunkenness. We were the baggage he didn't want to carry around, so he left us home.

With no regard for us, my father brought back a smorgasbord of fresh meat to our house. The monster in my heart grew stronger from my lack of sleep. Completely drunk and self-absorbed, he had no inhibitions to hold him back. He was pure unconquerable desire. At first, I couldn't imme-diately size up the moment of scattering perfume, smoke, and whiskey. I knew these women were unlike my mother.

Once they got into the house, they both stumbled around in the kitchen. I heard my father ask her, "Pat, would you like a drink?"

"Ronnie, I want more than a drink, darling. I didn't come here to drink."

"What you want is over here, so why don't you come and get it."

I heard their incoherent words and giddy laughter. Glasses clinked together. The sounds of passion moaned for more, "Oooh, Ronnie baby."

My father stumbled across the floor and turned on the country music radio station. My sentinel soul watched his little drunken festival. I listened to their whispered confessions from a crack in the door. The night was full of nothingness as the shadows moved across the living room walls. While a monstrous grappling frenzy ran its course, little by little, they removed all their clothes. I saw their posturing and positioning as all their self-consciousness melted away. A wild man, with a wild heart, he took what he wanted from everyone. My drunken father never tried to conceal his sex acts.

I sat like an angel listening to the sounds around me. Across the infinite expanse of night, the impalpable veils of cigar smoke could not conceal the nakedness of their bodies or stifle their sounds. I kept complaining to God about the atrocious events of my childhood. Images trapped movement in a still frame, my father showcased his X-rated life.

After he was done drinking and copulating, I pondered and planned my next mission. Always angelic, even in wickedness, I poked at his weaknesses. An invisible warrior, an apparition, I came out after midnight to attack his delusions of grandeur. I played with him like a cat plays with a ball of yarn. I tiptoed out of my room and through the kitchen to the other entrance into the living room. There I got on the floor and slithered like a snake toward the backside of the couch. I listened to their endless melodies of sound, ohs, ahs, and Ronnie babys.

Inching closer, I low-crawled on my belly toward the couch and pushed and guided my body around the corner of the sofa. There I seized my trophy from the floor, shoes, a bra, panties, or a blouse. Then I slithered back the way I came.

I placed her clothing item in an awkward place in the kitchen before returning to my room. I put her shoes on the kitchen table, hung her bra from the chandelier in the dining room, or threw her blouse into a corner like a rag. The next morning, before he drove her home, I heard her say, "Ronnie, I don't remember putting my bra on there."

"Well, we both were pretty stoned last night. I am sure you must have thrown it up there," he said.

"Are your kids still sleeping?"

I heard his footsteps get louder as he came to our door. I always shut the door when my mission was done. He cracked open the door and then closed it.

"Yeah, those little bastards can sleep all day."

"Ronnie, those are your boys."

They couldn't remember anything, so I mocked their existence. It was a small victory. I wouldn't let anyone spoon-feed me apathy. Women came, and women went. I witnessed a life where everything was free and had no commitments. Who could remember all their names, for he changed them out every few weeks like a cheap pair of socks. His drunken vigil showed me the delights of damnation, and how it became more profound over time. His faith was in the medicine he drank to forget yesterday. I, on the other hand, relived the utter boorishness of my father's sex acts in my nightmares.

♥

The purity of my heart radically rebelled against the limits of human indecency. My life began with my mother, and at eleven years old, I had seen many sultry breasts and saggy asses. In the midst of spiritual combat, the brutal battles made me an angry adolescent. As my childhood was stripped away from me, I saw myself surrounded by meandering, mouth-breathing cadavers. I didn't hold back my urge to fight back and made a superhuman promise to torture those who overlooked me. My heart and soul were intact, nor was my mind rented by others. The thought of me was a bad experience, and my father blessed his mistake by calling me "Little Bastard."

♥

As the year unfolded, I discovered my dad was a sex addict. He had swinging magazines with sex ads under the front seat of his car. Being no more than tagalongs in his sexual adventures, my father had no regard for our well-being. From time to time, he would take us with him to various parts of Connecticut. Robert and I sat in the car in a strange town looking out the window of his automobile. We sat there for about three to four hours. Using the streetlight, I read the book I lifted from the library. He was in the house drinking and engaging in his latest fleshly fantasy.

One time, my father brought us into a stranger's house. I remembered her. She had more clothes this time. And she introduced us to her kids, "Valerie, Linda, and Carl, these are Ronnie's sons, Larry and Robert. Boys, why don't you go over and take a seat and watch the movie with my kids.

Out of the FIELD

Your father and I are going upstairs for an adult conversation."

Her kids didn't even look at us. That made me wonder what number my dad was.

My father turned to me and said, "Behave yourself."

I looked at him and smiled, "Me?"

After the introductions, she and my father disappeared upstairs for several hours. The five of us looked at each other every fifteen minutes as we watched the movie *Chitty Chitty Bang Bang*. As we glanced at each other, we looked for the castle in the cobwebs of our parentless lives. We looked for something sane in the insanity of our crippling childhood. As for me, I found all I needed in my thoughts. As the circumstances veered beyond my control, I loitered around in my mind and opened my imagination. A playground of words and images passed in the unwanted hours. I sat there on the merry-go-round of emptiness spinning, regressing through time. I never could throw logic to the wind, nor could I be a farm boy plowing his lane. I walked the low, rocky road barefoot and passed many loathing faces. My heart kept reminding me I was another.

From the chasm of bright colors and poetic images of the words in my mind, I had to bounce back into survival mode once I saw my father stagger down the stairs.

The sultry lady asked, "Ronnie, are you okay to drive?"

"Yeah! Yeah, I am fine. I drive drunk all the time."

As the veil of smoke followed him out the door. I had watched him closely to see how much trouble he had putting the key into the ignition. My past experiences told me I would have to either be the co-pilot or drive us home. His mind resided in oblivion, and robotic muscle memory can only take you so far, as long as nothing unexpected gets in your way. While everyone pretended not to see us, I refused to die with him. He could barely walk, let alone read the road signs to know where he was going. I had to step up and make sure we got home. Once I drove us back home safely, I had to help him get out of the car.

"Come on get out of the car, you drunk bastard!" I yelled.

"Watch your mouth, boy," he said, "I'm still your father."

"Please stop reminding me!"

I pretended to lose my grip and let his ass fall to the ground, "Oh, did that hurt?"

Then, I accidentally kicked him while helping him stand up. "Come on, you fucking drunk, and get your ass up."

"I told you to watch your mouth, boy."

"What you going to do about it, old man?" I responded. "You won't even remember this in the morning, so shut the fuck up, old man."

Robert always watched me help our dad to his bedroom. Once in the room, I let him pass out in his clothes on the bed. After it was done and over with, I went outside and stared at the stars, and a tear trickled down my cheek. God had vanished into a childhood myth. In my state of naught, my actions were my life preserver. I expected nothing from anyone, and miracles were an expression of love. Disenchanted and disenfranchised, my only duty in life was to steal another breath and continue to fight.

♥

At the age of twelve, I understood the deception my father had used on his family. Thoughts, only thoughts, entered my mind, and I couldn't share them and trusted no one. A refugee looking out the window of a rudderless boat drifting endlessly at sea. My father drank whiskey every moment of the day. He floated away, unconcerned about life. He stopped off at the bar for two to three hours before any event. At a family gathering, he only drank beer to keep his buzz going. We were the first to leave. We went back to the bar until about midnight. Our home was nothing more than a flophouse. A pit stop between whiskey troughs and loose women. To ensure the perfection of his ruse, he never let anyone close enough to see him. Fight or submit were my life choices.

My father's ignorance continued to amaze me. The level of his crudeness had no boundaries. I tried to remember my mother Christmas 1972. I put up the fake tree my mom purchased a few years back. My father came home drunk while I was decorating the tree. Once in the house, he let out a roaring laugh.

I asked him, "What so funny?"

"You will get no presents from Santa or me this year."

"I didn't put the tree up to get presents. I put it up to remember my mother. She loved Christmas, and she loved me."

In a contemptuously stern tone, he blurted out, "Boy, your mama is dead, and she is not coming back to you. You better get used to it, and you better get out of my sight now."

Out of the FIELD

I grabbed my jacket and walked past him. Slamming the front door, I went outside and sat on the snow-covered front steps. I plotted and planned. I fired rockets at the moon. Full of broken thoughts, I toiled without relief in my resentment. Suppressed feelings brought back the old, familiar sensation of cold-steel hatred and armed my insecurity.

Growing up in no-man's-land, I couldn't help but think of my mother and choose to emulate her compassion. I remembered she always talked about forgiveness and how it brought her peace. Memories of her singing Christmas songs while decorating the tree brought a smile. Reflection released the hand of the stranger who tried to steal my life. I went back inside my house and walked by my father without saying a word.

♥

A white ghost in a colorless world, I stood in front of the mirror, invisible, and felt no obligation to join the human race. Anger powered my engine. I stood only five feet three inches tall, but I had an enormous heart filled with both love and hate. I saw adults who free-grazed and never gave back. Abandonment made me internalize shame. Never part of the village or tribe, I made all the ugly faces I wanted to.

Robert craved affection and acceptance. I heard the generations of dependency ushered in with his words, "May I please, Dad?"

Robert's loyalty fastened the chains of false hope around his neck. The intangible events transformed him into the servant of a bygone era. I observed how my relatives and teachers clothed deception. They dressed it up in a shiny, bright, eternal nothingness so they couldn't distinguish a lie from the truth. Robert's need to belong sealed his fate. He forgot the six years of abuse and neglect. His decision sterilized him. My intuition jettisoned any thoughts of this fucking loser family.

Passively, Robert interacted with our father, and it repulsed and angered me. A collaborator, Robert didn't know monsters and ghosts were real, and they lived inside people. I never hesitated to battle, claw, and fight my dad, for it was the right thing to do. Many times, in the heat of combat, he would yell, "Take that, you little bastard!" as I got slammed onto the ground.

Cheek against the floor, I looked over at Robert and yelled, "Get your ass in here and help me!"

His indecision spoke the words he couldn't say. His submissive eyes blankly stared into nothing. Jaded, I beat him without mercy. I learned to fight anyone at any time and couldn't turn off the wrath in me. Full of fury, I tackled him into the sheetrock. Body-sized holes were all through the house. I made him stay against the wall while I practiced sticking knives into it. He had nowhere to run and no one to protect him. He was trapped in the combat zone between my anger and his devotion to my father.

With nothing at home to entertain me, I went to school to amuse myself by playing with all the complacent adults. Their hands were tied by the rules they made. My education came from experimenting. They told me to go left, and I wandered right. I saw beyond the boundaries others tried to place on me. Observing conformity, the teachers' rules of language enclosed one's thoughts.

I thirsted for more than they could teach. The light in my eyes let me see the ghosts in the background of everyone's lives. I couldn't be a con-script of good will. The agony of being overlooked made me march in a different direction toward the sun. Cynical and cruel, I had the soul of a clown, the heart of a lion, and the mind of an actor. I mocked the world around me. With no place to call home, I advanced into the unmeasured to see what I could learn.

♥

Trouble always found me. One day, I was bullying the class nerd in the back of the library. I pushed him against the bookcase. When he bounced off it, I pushed him back against it and barked at him, "Are you going to tell your mother on me?"

"No, but I am going to thank her for my clean clothes."

His comment about the cleanest dirty clothes I wore to school that day pierced my ego. For a second, I sputtered down to the ground like an airless balloon. Clashing and exploding inside of me were thoughts of my vanity. The lines of my illusion got speared by the truth, by my situational awareness, and I knew no one was around. I launched a punch into his stomach and said, "Take this, smart-ass."

He never saw it coming and collapsed, breathless. He gasped for air like a guppy out of the water. I bent down and whispered in his ear, "If you tell anyone, I will make sure you get a beatdown every day."

By the fifth grade, I really untethered my monstrous soul. In the sixth

Out of the FIELD

grade, I wanted the world to feel my pain. I didn't care if I got in trouble. Punishment made me well-known. The teachers sounded like a broken record, "Mr. Lee, please report to the principal's office."

A badass kid, I opened my heart and waved the banner of my freedom. Even when standing in the corner, I thought of new ways to rebel against intellectual conformity. The school district refused to see me. The teachers often overlooked me for the children who had more potential in their eyes. You can't force someone to read my sign language. I would never underestimate the power of their ignorance again.

I couldn't ignore my heart and muddled in what couldn't be expressed. The teachers spoke about the magnificent promise of our lives. They talked about how our society played by the same set of rules. I knew the fairytale wasn't real. The words they spoke were utterly out of tune, and I couldn't understand the lyrics the classroom sang.

I was hidden and wasn't. I only existed by using my wit. Bad was terrible, misguided, muddy, and ugly, but it lived inside of me. I couldn't swallow the placebo pill of optimism the public school handed me. All around me, love and happiness blessed my classmates' lives. As I jumped out of my mind, I scraped some skin on my way to the principal's office. It was the only quality one-on-one time in my life.

♥

As I stared into the distance, my mind did cartwheels and rhymed words in my head. I knew miracles didn't exist. I lived in a house filled with burned-out light bulbs, and it was only a place to catch a few winks between ball games. Sports brought the worst out in us. I played Little League baseball and organized football. I excelled in sports, for I trained my mind to overcome any obstacle at an early age. Athletic and scrappy, games emulated the struggle of life, and my monster made sure I came out on top. While other kids were playing a game, my competitive relationship with my father prepared me to compete against myself. I played with the commitment to succeed, second to no one. The will to win was beaten into me by my dad, so everyone became my opponent.

One baseball game, each time I came up to the plate to hit, everything fell perfectly into place. I could see the ball turn ever so slowly. Locked in, I smacked it! The ball rolled past the outfielders and to the fence. I went four for five with three doubles and five runs batted in, and my defense was stellar, too. My team had beaten the first-place team. On an emotional high, the manager started to praise me in front of my father. "Larry had a great game today, Ronnie."

"He struck out once, so he failed."

My father's words picked at our wounded relationship and kept it bleeding. Verbal abuse is the gift that keeps on giving. At our football games, my father, who loved to be the center of attention, yelled at the top of his lungs, "If you don't win, you won't eat."

Most parents loved the shock value of his comment. What most parents didn't know was he meant every word he spoke. In our first football season, we lost every game, so we stayed out in the car without dinner while he got drunk in the bar. The mindset "evolve or die" helped me expand my criminal career. Hunger pains and dehydration were an obstacle I had to overcome as a youth.

I went to the bar and asked him, "Hey Dad, can I get a dollar from you?"

"What for?"

"So Robert and I can get a couple of sodas."

"Here ya go. Now get lost."

I had a plot to score dinner. I waited until several customers entered the store. Once I felt comfortable, Robert and I walked into the convenience store in our football uniforms. I told Robert, "Just shut your mouth and do as you're told."

He passively nodded.

I untucked my jersey. Once in the store, a heightened sense of awareness came over me. Assessing the store and its customers, I waited for the clerk to get busy and went to the meat locker. In the backlog of patrons, the clerk couldn't watch the mirrors mounted on the walls. Robert followed me around, naively. I opened the cooler with the lunch meat in it and stuffed two packages down my pants. I grabbed a few fruit pies too.

Robert's eyes blew out of his sockets.

I instructed him, "Here's the dollar. Let's go get some sodas, and you pay for them."

He looked confused, and said, "Larry—"

I did not let him get the second word out when I whispered in his ear, "Just fucking do it."

Out of the FIELD

As he stood in line, I stood behind him to conceal our dinner.

Back in the car, I provided dinner for us. He couldn't help himself as he said, "Larry, you know stealing is wrong."

I shook my head and snapped back, "You dumb fuck! The way we live is wrong, too. We would be starving if I didn't steal. Shut up and eat!"

My ability to read situations and people developed sharply over time. Brazenly bold, I became devious, cunning, and addicted to the rush of stealing. Shoplifting was a circumstance of desperation, and no one ever suspected me. Being a ghost had its advantages.

♥

I accepted being unwanted and unloved, I couldn't take being hungry. Hunger slowly twisted and wrenched my insides tight, and it became a cruel master. Starvation felt like a thousand sharp pins thrusting inside of me. It poked my conscience numb. I didn't have to justify staying alive. I openly mocked God's imaginary sin that would leave me famished. I stole food to allow me to fight another day. The saint inside of me dismissed all the ramifications I allowed God to have in my life.

The poorest of the poor, I found no joy in keeping God's great commandments. I couldn't afford to be religious. Somewhere between the forgotten and obscure, I found a place in me void of any God, man, or reason. I woke up every morning unafraid to find a new way to survive. Each day my hands stole everything they could grab, for tomorrow never promised one damn thing.

No more than a young man, I honed my craft daily. My hands became the instruments of my survival. A hunter and gather stood outside the circle of life, and enlightenment let me see the flaws in life. The truth was smothered with a justification. Without a noise, my eyes reached inside of my victims and removed their pride, lies, and all the games they played. I never learned to fight fair. Equality was a concept for someone who had something to lose. Thievery kept me alive. Catastrophic moments opened my eyes to clarity. I exploded inside, and I smashed my hand through a windowpane. Morality wasn't going to kill me.

5

Lawless

A child of vision, common sense aided me in my survival. Suffering allowed me the freedom to think beyond contemporary knowledge. I believed in nothing and no one. Emboldened by the blindness, errors, and betrayal, I studied and learned the color and emotions in words. Injustice, ignorance, and oppression conditioned my mind to see the denial in others. Morality was merely a personal choice, and equal opportunity existed only for a select few. I would not let being poor restrict the evolution of my mind. Discrimination nurtured the educated ignorant and defined modern morality. I saw the strings attached to a choice. My innocence was repaid with scorn. What horrible memories I have from the heartless authority figures who loathed my life in poverty and my silent cry to be loved.

I thought of myself as an artist or an angel trying to escape from man's moral constraint. I always put myself in the gnarled arms of reality to see if I could fight my way out. An underprivileged kid, I challenged the world around me. In the seventh and eighth grades, I attended Har-Bur Middle School in Burlington, Connecticut. My life was a series of awaiting conflicts and poetic thoughts. My imagination allowed me to immerse myself in words. I spun around, like in a washing machine, until a crystal-clear image appeared. My monstrous mind scrawled words with fangs. My spirit grew and strengthened in the reflection of my suffering.

A social terrorist in a perpetual state of fight, the whimpering middle-class slaves stood no chance against me. Each small victory or defeat created yet another problem, and it was then I discovered the power of a lie. I mastered words to color images and lead others astray. Born a drunkard's son, my actions smashed through the steely façade of the world. From a single footstep, I created the crackling red sparks to light up the night. My blazing blue eyes could stare a hole in a wall. I used profanity to express my displeasure of selfish humanity. I ransacked the luxuries of human decency

Out of the FIELD

by vandalizing, breaking and entering, and stealing what my eyes adored.

I used sarcasm to smash words into someone's face. A night prowler, goodness upset me, so I dragged my fingernails down the chalkboard. The teachers didn't like me rebelling against their shepherd thoughts. The wolf in my heart wouldn't let them domesticate my thoughts. Through my elective indifference, my art echoed the unimportance of human life. As all eyes were lost on the blackboard, I designed a dark calligraphic poster declaring it "Open Season to Kill the Class Nerd."

Everyone in my world was like travelers in an airport. I pushed them aside while moving forward. No one would bully me into silence. The struggle to survive defined me, and I lived to cheat and betray those who betrayed me. Words like admiration or friendship didn't exist. I posted my contempt for the world to see on the bulletin board. By the end of the day, the poster was full of signatures calling for the execution of the class nerd. The next day, I was summoned to the principal's office yet again.

As I sat in my favorite chair in the reception area, Principal Bruce motioned with his hand for me to come to his office. Once near the doorway, he said, "Please come in and take a seat, Mr. Lee."

Silent, I scanned the principal's office upon entering. An outlaw's smile revealed my private vengeance. I feared nothing and saw the lies behind his eyes. His morality tossed bombs into the fortitude of my stubbornness. I didn't lose my wits or stagger backward. Dressed for success, his pompous prattle went on about his position in the school, "Mr. Lee, as principal I am here to make sure each student has a safe environment in which to learn and interact with other students. It was brought to my attention that you posted a poster yesterday."

I scanned his office and noticed his walls were covered with academic diplomas from various universities. It was like he had to remind himself he was someone every day, and a piece of paper did that for him.

A devious smile encompassed my face before I snickered, "Golly shucks! You got me! It was only a joke."

"I appreciate your honesty, and I can see that you didn't understand the impact of your decision. After all, young man, don't you want to make your parents proud of you by working hard in school and doing the right thing?"

A stranger in a strange land, I glared at the idiot in front of me. Education has convinced people the uneducated are invisible and can be easily swayed. My mind untethered my monster. It strolled around. It festered a kindling in my eye. I looked at his smug face and thought, "How many more times will they overlook me?"

Happy with his conclusion, he envisioned his sandcastle virtues would never be swept away.

My march to safety counterattacked anyone in my way. "Well let's see. My father is the son of a drunk who pees on himself at night. My mom is dead, so I don't think either of them really cares. Is there anything else you want to know about me?"

I scored a technical knockout as he crawled into the vacuum of a stare. A few seconds later he uttered, "You can go back to class now, Mr. Lee."

In the rage of my destruction, I stayed after school and blew out all the electrical outlets in the science lab. The hell of my youth strolled the halls with laughter and thought, "No one cares. No one fucking cares what happens to me."

One hundred thousand miles separated me from the decency every child deserves. Every adult in my life had failed me. Every action in my life was part of the silent war I had to fight to survive. My heart wanted to compose words to make the world stand still. My heart knew I was someone else inside. Each day, I struggled to become another in my eyes.

♥

The God which Christians loved seemed to banish me even further from the circle of life. A slave to misfortune, life's discomfort pressed me to always find ways to improvise. A voice no one hears. A broken heart bleeds, and it cannot clot. My pain attacked the community around me with felony mischief. Bored, I remembered a stack of porno magazines at a friend of a friend's house. Being a bastard of pure impulse, the thought of looking at naked ladies drove my actions. Idle hands and the dullness of each summer day opened my mind. Embitterment seasoned my scorn. I stopped looking for that prize in a Cracker Jack box long ago. I borrowed sin from the devil to survive and paid it back by reaping havoc in others' lives.

A terrorist to society was formed by those good-natured people who always looked the other way. Stout in vengeance, every impulse I had was to survive. Something sinister drove my legs a mile and a half to their house. I fed my feelings bad thoughts. There was no wrong, nor was there right, just criminal disruption. I broke into a house, ransacked, and vandal-

Out of the FIELD

ized their home when I couldn't find the porno magazines.

An underachiever never thinks about the consequences. I refused to waste my time on others' thoughts or their rules. I never thought they would catch me. About one week later, a Connecticut State Trooper stopped by my house. Robert and I were hitting a tennis ball in the living room to pass the time. Robert was the first one to see the police driving up the driveway. He turned, looked, and shouted at me, "Larry, what have you done now?"

"Nothing, man. It's cool. I got this."

I waited until he knocked on the door. After opening the door, I asked, "What can I do for you, officer?"

"Is your father home?"

"Naahhh, he is not. I do not expect him until late tonight."

"Very well, I'll stop again tomorrow."

I nodded and smiled. "Fuck you!"

My father never came home before midnight or at all. Regardless, the officer stopped by every day he worked for two weeks. Each time, I told him my father wasn't home. Then, on the Fourth of July, my dad arrived home from work around one o'clock. Within an hour, the trooper showed up.

After the trooper and my father had spent some time outside talking, they came back into the house. My old man barked at me, "Larry, sit down at the table."

I moved slowly with a massive smile on my face. After taking a seat, the officer didn't waste any time when he asked, "Son, do you know about the burglary and vandalism of the house up the road?"

"Nope."

Frustrated, he came back with, "Where were you on June thirteenth?"

I didn't hesitate. "Here. Ask Robert."

Robert knew I would beat his ass, so he looked over at me and said, "Yeah, he was here all day I guess."

I kept denying the officer's questions. Frustration was setting in on both my father and the trooper as I continued to deny everything. They had nothing on me. However, out of the blue, the officer said, "We have a witness who saw you walk up Vineyard Road that morning. Come on, son. I know it was you."

As I scanned the room, I slowly stopped at my father's face. His masculine exhalations grew louder every second, like a bull in heat. I paused for an instant, for I wanted to see the blade of my words penetrate his ego. I looked at him, smiled and interjected, "Yeah, I did it to piss off my old man. He's a real bastard. Aren't you, Dad?"

WHAM! He slammed his fist on the table. He jumped out of his chair and came at me. "YOU LITTLE BASTARD!"

The trooper must have been a Vietnam veteran, for he jumped between us, his hand on his weapon, and shouted, "Everyone quiet down, now!"

I laughed at them and said, "Need a drink, Dad?"

They both went outside to have a conversation. It seemed to calm my father down. He came back inside and finished getting dressed. He got in his car and went out for the evening and left us hungry.

♥

Within a few weeks, my father and I had to report to the Juvenile Court judge. As my dad and I were escorted to the judge's office, Judge O'Sullivan saw us standing in the hallway and said, "Come in. Please take a seat."

The moment I entered his room, I looked for his weakness. His office was full of books and New York Yankee banners.

He introduced himself to my father and me. "Hello, Mr. Lee. I am Judge O'Sullivan, and this must be your son, Larry."

My father responded, "Nice to meet you, your Honor."

The judge began by asking me, "Son, you know why you're here. So why did you do it?"

I looked away and smiled and spoke to the window, "I was bored and angry at the world."

"Why were you upset?"

"First of all, I hate those damn Yankees."

"Sox fan, I can see," he laughed.

A long paused filled the room. I looked for the crack in this man's armor. Books, diplomas, and papers were undeniably what this man enjoyed. I felt his eyes sizing me up, as mine were doing the same. My father was right next to me, intoxicated. I wondered how smart this judge was. He did not even want to speak to me alone.

My father made his play and seized the moment, the minds of others. He maneuvered the conversation back to him. He recognized the name O'Sullivan, and he thought of one of his high school teammates. "Your

Out of the FIELD

Honor, do you know Sean O'Sullivan?"

"Yes, he's my brother."

My father smiled, for he knew. My father's words controlled the judge's thoughts, "I played high school ball with your brother. He was a good athlete. I am sorry he passed a few years back."

The judge was lost in the memories of his brother for several seconds.

At this point, my father knew he could say anything. He told the judge, "I got my sex education by hanging out on the schoolyard of Union School. Do you remember your brother's friends Lawler, Hogan, and Reardon? I see them now and then at a tavern."

The judge kept stepping back in time. Right before my eyes, a serious matter was being whisked under the rug. The judge confirmed my observation when he said, "Yes, I remember you had a good ball team your senior year. You guys almost took the state title."

Amazingly, my father orchestrated the conversation. The judge was his captive audience, and he was reminiscing about his brother in Unionville. They were comparing stories of old friends and sporting events. By the end of the session, they were laughing like friends having a beer in a pub. I watched my father work him to perfection.

As the two of them wrapped things up, the judge told my dad, "Ronnie, I suggest that you have a conversation with your son about sex, crime, and making the right choices. I see so many desperate kids come through here every day. I know you are a single father, and your son seems to be a good boy."

The judge turned and looked at me and said, "Nice to meet you, Larry. I want you to be a good kid from now on and listen to your father. He is a good man and knows what is best for you and your brother."

A juvenile delinquent stood between walking amnesiacs. My father performed a lobotomy on a living judge. Alone in my head, there was nothing I could do to bring this man down. The Good Old Boy Club was his galvanized armor.

I thought, "Wow, this asshole knows everyone in the world."

As I crawled deeper into myself to gather more strength, my father used a simple disguise that made others believe in him. He was a craftsman with his words, and he shaped the vision of others with a trouble-free laugh, quick wit, and swift smile. The cup from his glory days spilled over into my world. There was no urgency for them to do anything. They were content with their lives. An angry child, I didn't know how to speak up for myself.

As the judge and my father wrapped things up, I saw them shake hands and smile at each other. On the way out to the car, my dad turned, and he said to me, "You got lucky, you little bastard. I played ball with his brother. He takes care of his hometown friends. He is giving you probation, and your record will be expunged when you turn sixteen years old. You can thank me later."

I thought to myself, "Hell, I'm living in hell with you. The judge just gave me a life sentence without parole. If I knew where he lived, I would have broken into his house."

Each day, I had to keep quiet about my abuse. I disciplined myself. I withdrew even more, rarely talking to anyone. I trusted no adult. I viewed each of them as a silent killer. I couldn't run from someone I didn't fear. All my actions allowed me to deceive, lie, and steal. I baited them to come out from behind their walls and fight me like a man. Cowards! Cowards! My world was full of cowards.

As soon as we left the judge's office, my father stopped talking to me. We stopped off at the Old Town Bar and Grill, and my dad closed down the place. I had to steal my dinner from the grocery store and drive us home.

As for the conversation he was supposed to have, he never did. Our relationship was like two opposing magnets. We pushed away from each other. The saint inside of me grew wilder in my discontent. The more I tried to free myself from my father; the better he looked in others' eyes. He knew I could not be trusted, so he left one of his barfly lovers to watch us while he worked out of town. As she got out of the car, I remembered taking her bra and hanging it on the chandelier.

"Game on, bitch!"

Ester was her name, and she would cook and keep an eye on us. He had to buy food now, and we ate dinner every night. Most evenings, her daughter and boyfriend stopped over to keep her company. They chatted about the pornographic movies they had recently watched. They whispered about the sex acts they just tried, and they looked at those swinging sex magazines.

I escaped by scribbling graffiti words that defied the zombie adults in my life. My imagination climbed into the great luster of words, emotions, and colors. My sensitivity was black cloth, and it was covered in cheap, colored paints. I paused for a moment to wonder what the judge would

Out of the FIELD

have thought about my life now. The world might have forgotten me, but I recognized the wisdom that comes from defeat. Onward, I walked on my own, fighting all comers.

♥

As I tried to circumvent the smooth and polished spirits in my life, my resistance dropped its guard. I came upon a fork in my journey and easily foreseeable consequences. The fine line between delusion and reality erased the moment I crossed. Life's pain willingly disappeared completely once I got high.

Every day was lost. With no vision of self, I became a dope fiend. From father to son, the illusion of the drugs made me think I wasn't like him. To hell with reality. I hardly ever spoke and died each day in words. Numbing paralysis, every cell in my body craved it. A medicated life was neither good nor bad in itself. Invisible, insatiable, and indestructible drugs fed the silent monster inside of me. Many years without a home, I quickly explored other drugs with other lost boys.

Self-love is something one can't live without. I looked to find peace in something else and found my lover—alcohol and illegal drugs—at thirteen years old. I slow-danced with the energy of the dark shadow world. A family tradition, addiction became my obsession and checked me out of this world. A natural slave to my lover. My actions shouted every day, "Baby, I love you, please take me higher."

Life wasn't worth the fucking effort. Hooked on that wandering dim haze of enchantment, I wander aimlessly, borrowed, and returned nothing. I got high every day and stole from the drunks at the men's club we often visited. Everyone was plastered, so I helped myself. I gave the bartender a hand, helping clean the ongoing mess for a few bucks while lifting money off the tables. I hustled, lied, cheated, and learned to change my façade to fit the situation. Shame didn't know me. I freely helped myself to bottled beer in the cooler and enjoyed the biting kiss of whiskey. Without hope, I was free to act out in the cold, dark, slate-gray that encompassed me. Life stood still, and it was the same as it ever was. The cycle remained unbroken.

My ancestry couldn't be understood unless I enlisted in its army of ghosts, and the mirrors in my mind let me see they already lived inside of me. Christened as a toddler, I acquired a taste for liquor and beer from my father. He would give a sip or two when my mother wasn't looking. The temple of my family's ancient world pulled me into their prophecy.

The meek shall inherit each other, and they whispered their subconscious thoughts, "We're going to watch you from afar. You'll find we live in despair and grow stronger in isolation. You will never leave us, for we're the only comfort you'll ever know. Only the proud can defeat us. We have been around since the beginning of time. We're the enemy you can't see. Here's your medication. Go ahead and take it, all the pain will disappear."

♥

The story of most dope fiends begins when they believe the worthless lies they've been fed by others. A stimulating buzz let me kiss the sky, and all I ever wanted was another hit. If I didn't like my state of mind, excess changed everything. I wasn't sick or well. A few more shots of whiskey would let me forget hell. In the tyranny of self, I was a slave to anything that suspended time and awakened my inner eye. In my dying blueness, paradise looked unattainable. I lived behind a false smile, shattered by never belonging to a tribe.

The power of addiction oppressed and comforted my damaged self-esteem. Misery became my bride. Stripped of all my pride, ignorance made me cease to exist. There were now two of me. The conceited freedom fighter formed by injustice, and a half-corpse rotting in the sun. Outsourced convictions, I couldn't see beyond my immediate gratification.

♥

The only time I felt free was when belonging to a team. In 1973, the Babe Ruth Baseball League was formed in Burlington. My father was named coach of the Reds, and I was his assistant coach by default. Throughout the entire season, I managed the team in the background because he was never sober. Humiliated by my father's constant inebriated state, I always made sure to never let my teammates down. Arranging practices, setting lineups, and managing the players were my job duties. I kept the team together, never knowing if my father would show up. He was the most irresponsible person on the planet.

One ballgame, he showed up in a drunken stupor. As we were taking

Out of the FIELD

infield practice, he was leaning against a bat. Suddenly without notice, he fell like a tree. At my shortstop position, the second baseman said, "Hey Larry, it looks like your father just passed out."

I laughed and said, "He's a wuss! He can't handle his liquor anymore."

The second baseman said, "Is anyone going to help him up?"

I responded, "It doesn't look like he's moving. Oh well, someone will move him when it's time to play the game."

While my dad was passed out on his back, my teammates and their parents did nothing, until one of his drinking buddies dragged him behind the team bench and let him sleep it off. As for the ballgame, the same friend sat on the bench as impromptu manager. After our team had won, his buddy woke my dad up, and we went to the men's club to celebrate. I even relaxed by drinking a few beers I stole from the cooler.

When my father did show up for practice, it was common for him to yell obscenities at us while hitting infield practice, "Here it comes, you little pricks. Get your fucking little asses moving, now!"

This was the PG version of Ronnie Lee. No one in Burlington ever stood up for what was right. With bloodshot eyes, I saw the obvious. Neighbors overlooked me. Silence denied my existence. Everyone knew how the story was going to end, so they stayed away. There was no brotherhood of man in Burlington, Connecticut. There was no sense of community or village, for they treated me like an outsider in my hometown.

Compassion didn't exist. I saw the fallibilities in people, and no one ever extended their hand. No one ever drove my father home when he was too drunk to drive. They used their legs to walk around us, and their cold eyes made me invisible. Outside the fishbowl of humanity, an undeveloped addict looked through the glass and saw movement without emotion. Beneath my weed-smoked skin, I shook my head at everyone, and I spit on the ground in contempt.

Made up of piss and vinegar, I made the Regional Babe Ruth All-Stars. Each region put a team together, and they played each other for the state championship. Practices were in Canton, Connecticut, at four p.m. each day. I hitchhiked the ten miles to practice. After practice was over, all the parents came to pick up their sons. I waited for my father to show. The coach saw me sitting by a tree and asked, "Is your dad coming to pick you up?"

"Yes, Coach. My dad said he would be late."

I waited for him, but my intuition knew he wouldn't show up. After everyone had left, I got up off my ass and hitchhiked home. In the twilight, each passing second, each negative emotion flashed the headlights of change. With each moving automobile that whisked by my thumb, I fought the feelings of unworthiness in the innermost regions of my soul. By the light of the moon or stars, I walked home and mocked damnation.

♥

To minimize my suffering, I maximized my anarchy. From time to time, my father would come home early and pass out in his bedroom. I would take his car out for a joyride. After all, I had been driving him home from the bars for over a year now. I ventured out on the open roads, a free spirit with the radio blaring. One escapade, I was focused on changing the radio station while backing down the driveway. I didn't anticipate the curve while backing and slammed into a tree. The front left quarter panel had a huge C-shaped dent in it.

The next morning, I heard my father get up for work, and I waited. As I listened to the front door close, I peeped out the window. He looked at the dent and scratched his head. Dumbfounded, he just got in his car and went to work. General anesthesia allowed him to live his life in a permanent blackout.

♥

From time to time, I listened to my father's conversations with Detective Jerry about making his driving under the influence tickets go away. He worked for the city police department and helped those DUI tickets disappear. He was my uncle Burney's brother-in-law. They drank together at the Veteran's Club after work (a good old boys club). All the policemen, firemen, and veterans drank there, and they took care of each other in their everyday lives. Over the years, my father received as many as twelve DUIs, and Detective Jerry enabled my dad and kept him drinking. They drank together and suppressed all their natural instincts. Complacency breeds conformity.

A few weeks later, Detective Jerry called my father and told him, "Hey Ronnie, we found your automobile in the Connecticut River."

"Jerry, I don't even remember how I got home. Was there a lady in the car?"

"No, was there supposed to be?"

"No, I was with a lady last night, but I don't remember her name. I remembered we walked out to my car. I was going to spend the night at her house, but we couldn't find my sedan. Thus, we went back to the bar and drank some more. I don't remember anything after that."

"Ronnie, the keys were in the car's ignition. It looks like someone stole it and took it for a joyride. When they were done, they let it roll into the river."

♥

As my father continued to plummet into apathy, I grew up without the usual things my classmates had in their lives. They had good parents who made them work for an allowance or gave them money. They talked to them about making the right choices. In contrast, my life was about finding a way to survive. I stole everything and had become one hell of an actor by this time. The part I played depended on what needed to be achieved. Lying was role-play. I stretched out my imagination to modify my looks and attitude. I lied to myself all the time. It was the only way I'd make it. My thoughts were not confined by society's carbon-copy logic, and that made it easy to find the marks.

Morality was invented by those who ate four-course meals every night. Some people might have called me a thief, but an unending hunger powered my liberation. I knew there was no God, and no one was going to save me. Like a burglar in the night, I targeted victims who were all too trusting of the world.

A warrior does not give up in a fight. He always finds a way to attack. I became a snake and slithered across the floor to my father's pants, while he slept. Once there I reached into his pocket and pulled out his wad of cash. Taking my time, I counted his wad of money and made a judgment call on how much to keep. I'd only take what I needed to keep this cash cow grazing safely at home. The money stolen bought food and drugs. To me, it wasn't stealing. After all, he received five hundred dollars in Social Security money each month for our care. He never spent a dime on Robert or me. We always went without the spiritual, emotional, and physical needs a child deserves.

I couldn't leave this place or change my situation. The only way I could exist was to steal from others. A real thief creates a visual image to make himself credible. I learned how to fashion a ruse from seeing my father interact with others. Studious, my instincts whispered to me, and the answer would always appear. My dad underestimated me, for I found every place he tried to hide his money. One day, I took every red cent except for one US dollar. My score was over $100.

That day, I awoke before he did and headed toward the tree line. His voice echoed throughout the valley. "You little bastard! I am going to kill you! You better not come home tonight, boy!"

Fuming and foaming, he cursed at me for several minutes until he left to go to work. Up in my favorite tree, I roared, "Fuck you!"

A guerrilla fighter, I took it when it was offered, for my mind lived in each minute and never trusted tomorrow to come. There were no limits on the battlefield. His credit cards worked for a while. Once he caught wind of that gig, I forged his signature on his checks. I hitchhiked to several different banks and cashed his checks. He would never turn me in, for he was just a dumb drunk. He would expose his child neglect. I might have been a Little Bastard, but I outplayed him.

♥

As for the Lee family, they only got involved when Robert and I were utterly starving. Our hunger pains led me to call my grandmother a few times. We hadn't eaten in days, nor had I seen my father for weeks. I drank water to have something in my belly. We lay around the house like dogs on a hot and humid day. My eyes were vacant, but I remembered each of the distorted faces of my betrayal. My grandmother and Uncle Jimmy brought us some groceries. I watched them while I devoured my food. I noticed their lobotomy eyes. They were unwilling to face their feelings or endure any type of pain. They had no shame or guilt in their actions. We just existed in a closed-eyed township too. Our only crime was we were born. I wouldn't adhere to any of society's rules. The crimes of infinite cruelty made my will strong.

After all, I had received a graduate degree from night school, and I grew up in the dark without culture. Robert and I were like tomatoes left on the vine to rot in the sun. Everyone continued to fail us. Unwanted, my hurt festered, and decay danced in the long hours of solitude. I stood alone with all my senses in the duality of being both human and an animal. I couldn't stop seeing the circling lies. I assimilated all my pain into hatred.

I'd stayed watchful and stayed alive. My father's behavior was totally unpredictable, so I had to read the situation before it happened. On the other hand, Robert only knew blind loyalty. He was a follower and wanted a love that didn't exist. He couldn't see the chaos's jagged teeth coming up to bite, so he put himself in a place to be hurt.

One day, my grandmother and my Uncle Richard were visiting. My dad was drinking whiskey all day, and he decided he wanted to cut firewood for the upcoming winter. My father and Robert went out back. The movement of my dad's chainsaw was down, then up, after the cut had been made. In the upward motion, my father lost his footing and slipped further backward. I saw the chainsaw cutting through the air. Until, the saw blade stopped on the top of Robert's skull, cutting through his hair and scalp, and scraping his head.

Always in control and never wrong, my father stepped up and saved the day. He made an executive decision to drive Robert to the hospital drunk. My grandmother and my Uncle Richard were passive to my father's demands. While the three of us silently waited for them to return, I couldn't help but wonder if my dad knew someone at the hospital. I mused on the extent of the Good Old Boy Clubs he belonged too.

After about eight hours, Robert and my father returned from the hospital. The first thing my father did when he got home was he poured himself a glass of whiskey. Then, he proceeded to tell us, "Yeah, the doctor picked woodchips out of Robert's head. The saw blades just scraped his skull. He'll be okay in a few days."

My grandmother responded, "Thank God, it turned out okay."

I thought to myself, "Thank God for what? This fucking family!"

Then my father mocked the doctor. "Mr. Lee, please make sure that everyone is in front of or to the side of you while you are cutting wood."

Outwardly angry, my father replied, "Who does that college boy think he is? He probably never used a chainsaw in his life."

I looked into my family members' eyes while he was telling that story. They were open, but they couldn't see. Robert's heart yearned for their love. As I pondered on how my father almost killed Robert, my family did nothing. Their silence wasn't golden; it turned me into an inferior creation of God.

God could keep all His golden rules. I pushed Him out of my life. No more than a childhood memory, He remained in the deepest darkest part of my soul. Abandoned by everyone, God was dead to me!

6
Radical Bastard

My family's worn-out ideas and old-fashioned values were nothing but a cult tradition. A dysfunctional family is awful and ugly to grow up in, for the invincible and stupid smiles on their faces revealed they just didn't know. All their lies pushed me to the edge of life and death. Passionate and idealistic, I lit backfires to see them run. Their neglect and lies enabled me to find my inner strength. I couldn't surrender to sleepy mediocrity. In each one of my defeats, I stood back up and dusted myself off, for no one expected me to endure. The privilege of owning myself came from the sacredness of my tears.

Condescending eyes empowered me. Cast out of humanity, I never bought into the illusion of a clan, the neighborhood school system, or even a small town's values. Strong beliefs germinated snobbery. In my canned silence, I may have been powerless to prevent injustice, but I never failed to protest the ethics of inequity.

It amazed me how long people propped my father up. Even after he failed to pay his mortgage, no one saw that he lived in a permanent black-out. Hell! He was an electrician and made an excellent living. The kicker, he received an extra five hundred bills from Social Security for us. He literally pissed money into the urinal every day.

We lost the house on Spielman Highway. The way I found out—he came home and gave us five minutes to pack all our possessions. We didn't have much to gather, just some old worn-out clothes and the baseball cards I stole. He told us we were going to stay at my grandmother's house. It was a tiny two-bedroom house in Unionville. My bed was on the empty side of the attic, and Robert shared a room.

The move had some advantages. We had a cooked meal every day for the first time since I was eight years old. There were no more Midnight Inspections or fist fights. I wouldn't have to drive him home from the bars. We didn't have to switch schools either. My grandmother became the recipient of the Social Security checks. She provided the essential items for us to exist. She kept what was left over for herself.

Raised by thieves, I stole from those who took from me. When justice and love were denied me, I degraded the property of others. I kicked open the door and invaded their lives with a vengeance. I stole my grandmother's coin collection and cash.

One day, she asked me, "Larry, did you take the silver dollars from my closet?"

I smiled and said, "I sure did."

"Why, may I ask?"

"Well, let's see, you are pulling in over five hundred bills a month while we stay here, and I don't believe that your spending that much on us,"

Anger boiled. I upset her, but she took a second and said, "Okay, I see your point. I will give you a two-dollar-a-week allowance."

I looked at her and said, "Wow, a whole two dollars." My neighborhood crime spree continued.

♥

As I wandered through town, I stumbled onto a teenage wasteland behind an old shopping center. I partied with other misplaced kids. A master thief by now, I tossed my leftovers on the street like candy bar wrappers. Fearlessly walking through this world, heaven or hell didn't exist. My actions were the golden sparks that lit the darkness beneath my feet. The lure of sweet sin consumed me, and I recklessly embraced the beauty and purity of its illusion. I ran with freedom in its madness so I wouldn't be entwined and pinned against sweating walls of apathy. The fear of darkness helped me to discover the know-how to free myself. I analyzed and criticized, but I never hesitated or thought chance was a mistake. The envy in my eye made me feel beyond temperance and self-control.

Extreme individualism let my opponents know I had no weaknesses.

♥

One day, I hitchhiked and walked fifteen miles to my father's apartment. He always left his place unlocked. Like every other time, I raided his home.

Out of the FIELD

There were swinging magazines, an 8mm projector, and stacks of porno films on his dresser. Condom wrappers and emptied whiskey bottles were scattered on the floor. The smell of cheap perfume lingered and money were scattered throughout.

Cash was king, but his credit cards would also do. I went there to make him feel my pain. I wanted to sit back with a bag of weed, a pack of Zig-Zags and forget life. I didn't know him. I didn't owe him any fucking respect. The decorations of adulthood didn't intimidate me. Abandonment made me a career criminal and gave me an assortment of deceitful masks. My survival depended on the performances of optimism. I was what my mind thought, so I was a soldier at fourteen years old, who lived to shatter the illusions of false integrity.

A loser would sit back and hope things would get better. I always took things into my own hands, literally. By Thanksgiving, he eventually figured out I was up to my old thieving tricks. He showed up at his mother's house drunk. As soon as he stepped through the door, he started sending volleys of angry words toward me.

"You little thieving bastard. I know you were at my house."

In the progression of the moment, I smiled at the decrepit spectacle of his drunken anger. He stumbled around. Bang! Boom! He smashed into the tables and chairs. He slurred incoherent words and acted like I abandoned him. Then he started to walk toward me. Sharply, all the pain and sorrow inside of me rose up against him. My sarcasm attacked. "Isn't it time for a drink, old man?"

"You're a disgrace as a son."

"I'm a disgrace," I laughed while tossing Molotov cocktails toward at him. "You are nothing but a fucking loser. You're just a drunk who watches pornos. I bet you cheated on Mom, didn't you?"

"I am going to beat the shit out of you, boy!"

"Fuck you! You fucking fuck!"

His pulse throbbed through the air like a bass drum, and the smell of the alcohol sweated out his pores. My words breached insanity, and I advanced behind every street-sweeping expletive. My bombs burst in midair, and everyone took cover from the sharp metal of my rage.

The intensity of my verbal grenades left everyone in shock and awe. My grandmother, Uncle Richard, and Robert did nothing. It was all they knew how to do. It was not until I said, "Aren't you thirsty yet?"

My father woke up out of his blackout then lunged at me, knocking over glasses on the table. At that point, I removed myself from the situation and shouted, "Fuck you!" several times.

My grandmother yelled at him for showing up to her house drunk. Devoid of any human need, he stumbled back to the bar he had come from, and he drank some more. As for me, I sat in the attic staring at the walls. I was consumed by the red, smoky black, flashing and sparkling the tricolors of anger Thanksgiving Day, 1974.

♥

The invisible force of hatred pulled my strings, and it was so powerful it transformed me into a Radical Bastard. My actions screamed the truth I saw. Unfortunately, I spoke a language neither God nor mankind could understand. Helpless, ashamed, and damaged I couldn't see the thin line between recreational drug use and dependency. The trademark of addiction begins with a mood-altering dosage to hide from the unbearable. The swollen horror of my existence made me feel utterly alone in a world of four billion people.

I imprisoned myself, and in the isolation of my cell, I sang the songs of my ancestors. I stood alone. I saw everyone's improvised costumes, the secondhand thoughts of God and religion. People sang the same old Irish Catholic love song passed down from generation to generation. I traced my lineage back to the beginning where man became bored with God. I plunged headfirst into oblivion and darkness encompassed me.

A shadow without feelings, my desperate attempt to escape my torturing memories let me fall in love with drugs. A traveler through time and space, I passed the point of no return. It was a place of unbearable loneliness, and I flirted with impending doom daily. The heartless devaluing of self-commenced when the adults in my life never invested in me. Everything I did was merely to survive. I got high and listened to the noise of a dull world.

I said yes to drugs and experimented with harder drugs. The irony of my journey was no one could really blame me. I checked out and didn't feel. I'd spend the entire day overdosing in my uncensored thoughts. Fantasy became my reality.

Lost in space, I walked the school halls singing, "Teacher! Teacher!

Out of the FIELD

There's more to life than what meets the eye."

♥

As for my father, he was spinning in a vortex of whiskey with a life preserver. His employer, HELCO, forced him to go to an alcohol treatment center. I found out the day we were going to visit him. My grandmother, Uncle Jimmy, Robert, and I went to see the Crown Prince of the Lees.

As we walked through the door, the patients reminded me of the clientele at bars my father took us to as kids. Each patient acted like they were hopping from barstool to barstool trying to relive moments in their past. They were enslaved by something, or anything, that made them forget their pain. I saw no comfort in that place, only misery and loss. As my father showed us around the facility, he acted like he was a bigshot. A fool's pride told us, "I'm not like these folks. I can hold down a job and handle responsibility."

Listening to him, he mumbled one stupid comment after another, "Once I leave here, I will be able to control my drinking and will only be a social drinker. I am only going to drink beer now."

My grandmother replied, "I am so proud of you, Ronnie, for I'm glad you can admit that you have a problem. I love you."

He looked his family in the eye and fed them the hope they all lacked inside. He was cunning and crafty in the words he used. I saw no courage in this man. He preyed on the weakness of others. I slipped back into survival instincts obtained as a child. Every one of my father's betraying actions was re-experienced. Transitioning back into reality, he told my grandmother, "I am only here to keep my job."

As soon as he finished his last word in his sentence, I looked over at his half-witted family and saw them rallying around him. They were like soldiers saluting Old Glory at morning reveille. I smiled. I saw not one fiber of moral virtue inside any of them. The sight of the sightless gave my excuse to be a Lawless Larry. I got up and shoved my chair against the table. "Bullshit!" I screamed. "I see each of you for who you really are."

As I walked outside, I could feel Jesus creeping around my soul. I pushed back against Him with the dark energy of my anger. I yelled, "Leave me the fuck alone!"

♥

The foundation of my life was built on the art of deception. Being a master thief, the fortress I built was made from the bricks from my incurable broken heart. I kicked at the dirt and smoked a cigarette. I didn't want to experience any form of enlightenment and was comfortable being ignorant and numb. I envied what I saw and what my heart lusted after. My actions exhibited no values, and my destiny was to be a character in an epic tragedy.

In 1975, my father got a second chance at life and bought another home in Burlington. It was a smaller home, two bedrooms, one bath. My room was right across from my father's bedroom. Robert slept downstairs in the family room. Outside, it had a deck and an enormous backyard. It was a quaint little home. Once again, Robert and I didn't have to switch schools.

My idea of a good time was running wild and creating havoc, but my real talent was seeing the unnoticed. My Grandmother Lee was still the benefactor of our Social Security checks, and she stole every red cent from the day we moved out of her house.

We moved in August, right before school started. As I adjusted to being a freshman at Lewis S. Mills High School, Sweet Lou, a basketball star, asked me to join the school cross-country team. We played hoops now and then, and he knew my engine never quit. A gifted runner, in both a foot race and in life, I beat most of the varsity team in cheap Converse high tops. After the team had finished the run, I looked at my teammate's feet and felt out of place and ashamed. I didn't own a pair of running shoes, and I couldn't ask anyone to buy them for me.

Wanting to belong to a tribe, I hitchhiked to West Farm Mall on the weekend. The ability to scheme was all I had. Nothing was virtuous or true. It was all my responsibility to survive. I always accepted my burden and never grew tired of a challenge. I laid and waited for the influx of patrons to overwhelm the store. I blended in. The innocence on my face hid my intent. I saw the pair of shoes I wanted to steal. The clerk came over and asked, "May I help you?"

"A size nine in these please."

He came back a minute later.

I put both shoes on my feet and walked around. Out of the corner of my eye, I noticed the clerk with another customer, and I merely walked gracefully out of the store. I was a ghost no ever saw.

Out of the FIELD

I loved to run and became the team's fifth overall runner. (The top five runners score points for the team as they place in the race.) We went 13 and 2 that year. At one point, I ran the eighth fastest time ever by a freshman in school history. I felt a part of something and was on my best behavior and only partied after practice. I didn't want to let my team down, so I attended every class and did my homework. The team was the family. For two months, I put everything into my running and never thought about what I didn't have. The sun warmed my face as I ran across the field and it freed me.

♥

After the cross-country season was over, I went out for basketball and didn't make the team. I slipped back into a forgotten corner of the universe. I became a fiery meteor waiting to burn out. The exploration of drugs created a sense of euphoria. I found a band of brothers and sisters who would try any substance. Stoned free, I drank alcohol, smoked pot laced with dust and popped pills. A quick cigarette in the lavatory between classes was my sign of defiance. I only went to school to get high and to laugh at authority. I shouted, "Stand the fuck back!"

In a fool's dream, anger, resentment, and distrust changed my heart. I wanted inspiration, but I settled for dried pot smoke on my face. The truth wasn't worth the fucking effort. Practice made perfect, and I always drank one more beer, took a hit of acid, or popped another pill. I wanted to find the edge of life and hang on by my fingertips. A drug enthusiast, I was incorruptible and had no thoughts beyond using. Numb, I couldn't feel a damn thing. In each dying second, I engineered a sinister resolve to tell myself I was a hero as I stole my dinner. A faceless kid looked in a mirror one day and saw nothing. A seasoned soldier at sixteen, I was as bad as the worst the world has ever seen.

Sorrow squashed all my tomorrows. Teachers and I clashed all hours of the day. I couldn't bear the way they mocked me. Their actions told me, "Your life is your sentence."

My mind couldn't tolerate the codependent reason the teachers taught. An abused kid, drugs filled the void of never being hugged. Biology wouldn't feed me or keep me high. My science teacher, Mr. Binder, was the worst. Rigid in his thought, he only observed facts and found conclusions.

One day in his classroom, his judgment of my life was thrown out for the whole class to hear. I failed my third quiz in a row. He blurted out, "Mr. Lee you better start getting your act together and take some time to study."

High as a kite under the summer sun, I smiled at him. Who the fuck are you? I took my time to answer and said, "I studied all day and all night. Smoking dope has given me a retention problem, or it might be the way you instruct the class."

"Worthless! You are just useless! You will never amount to anything in this world, Mr. Lee," he blurted out in front of the whole class.

"You're a dick."

"Go to the principal's office, Mr. Lee."

The difference between respect and disrespect was the family I was born into, and my primal reactions drove my conduct. A junkie, I just wanted to get high. I didn't have a deep sense of belonging to anything or anyone. Emotionless, I stole Coke and Twinkies to ease my hunger. When God created me, He gave me a washable soul and millions of interchangeable parts. I plucked a mask from my imagination to attack the self-righteous and arrogant. Interactions seemed so artificial, with everyone hiding who they really are. A professional façade adapts to each moment to steal another breath or more.

The distance in their eyes revealed their thoughts of me, and that made it easy to leave me behind. In my school, the brightest boys and girls got all the attention. I wanted to write essays and do algebra too, but just like my family, the teachers sent the message, "You're no one."

I walked among them like a ghost. The voices of moral authority demanded punctuality and proper grammar on an uneven playing field. Starvation and abuse weren't an excuse in their eyes. Bad days never actually ended. My world was so cold. I had to do more drugs to keep my brain from listening to society's bullshit. Survival made me a hooligan, and I defied every rule and regulation the school had. I was suspended ten times my freshman year (a school record) for smoking, cussing out a teacher, fighting, and skipping class to get high. I couldn't just kick the dirt anymore. A monster doesn't become a monster overnight. The whips of neglect are held by the sterile complicit middle-class minds.

♥

Out of the FIELD

A Radical Bastard gave no quarter. "Good" literally sucked, in my eyes. I released my battle cry in the school hallways, setting off the fire alarm on occasions. I wouldn't retreat a single inch, and it made me redshirted the ninth grade. I failed my art class. The teacher told me not to come to her classroom, but I thought she would give me a C.

Stoning myself, life among the stars existed when I smoked angel dust. My mind grew wings, and I tried to find the angels living among us. Self-control didn't exist. "Fuck you. Fuck you! No, you just didn't!"

I drank anything I could get before school. Decimated by shame, seconds seemed like hours until I got high or drunk. Flashing lights filled my head with barroom signs, and the dependency on chemicals slowly consumed and altered my thoughts and actions. I hit the wall with my knuckles just to watch myself bleed. Trapped, I couldn't stop my silent self-destructive screams. Some might have cared, just not enough.

My tragedy was met with no resistance, for I preferred a room filled with pot smoke. It cleansed my mind of conformity's filth. Fuck your morality. You're the worst kind of killer, one who turns his back in cowardice.

♥

One day, my father came home drunk at about four o'clock and passed out on the floor in his room. He was in the late stage of alcoholism. I sneaked into his room and took the keys to his Ford Galaxie 500. I went for a joyride to Burlington and Harwinton to find some drugs. While driving, I recognized two stoners hitchhiking. I stopped and picked them up.

Jackpot! They had weed, so we drove around smoking bowl after bowl. I passed some old guy doing close to a hundred miles per hour on Woodchuck Lane. A few miles down the road, I turned around in my friend's driveway. After beeping the horn, we headed back down the road.

The man I passed recognized my car, and he stopped in the middle of the street. Twilight had fallen, and I never had driven in the dark before. His automobile blocked most of the road. I tried to get by him but scraped the side of his car. I panicked and punched the gas, fishtailing, and smacked his car one more time. I dropped my friends off at their homes and limped back home.

A few hours later, my old friends the Connecticut State Police knocked on my door around midnight. I opened it.

The trooper asked. "Is your father home?"

"No, he didn't make it home tonight."

"I think you should rethink your answer, son, for you might dig yourself a bigger hole to get out of this evening."

I smiled and replied, "Whatever."

In a staredown, I mustered all the contempt I could muster. The trooper calmly said, "Either you get him, or I'll bring a few cruisers down here and surround the place. It's your choice."

"Well, since you put it that way, I'll see if I can wake the drunk bastard."

As I observed the conversation between my father and the trooper, my dad looked like a bobblehead doll, fading in and out of consciousness. The officer seemed disgusted at both of us.

I blurted out, "I'm a minor. You can't do shit to me."

The officer told my father, "You better get him under control."

My dad stared into space.

As the saga unfolded in the weeks ahead, I had to appear in court in Torrington. The judge handed down probation and told me, "Son, you will not get a driver's license until you're eighteen years old."

♥

Eighteen years old seemed unattainable. I was hooked on the excitement of the disasters I created. My mind wasn't a prisoner to a goal or domestic happiness. Sarcasm was my offense. Sarcasm was my defense. I punched the encroaching world with an arsenal of smart-ass comments.

I had no sense of worth. My life was death without sorrow. Fear never let me feel safe, so I'd down a shot of whiskey and chase it with beer. I smoked blunt after blunt, popped pill after pill and wanted more. I created the illusion of being fearless. It was lonesome in outer space, and I wasn't equipped with landing gear.

Born without a chance, I made a family from those kids who left their clipboards and textbooks home. I rarely saw my father now, and my relatives were completely nonexistent at this point. The school district ignored me.

♥

Creativity was my only weapon to combat poverty. A thinker, I had the

Out of the **FIELD**

awareness to harness inspiration. I opened a party house, and it was a safe house where drug dealers could cut their drugs. Each Saturday night, I held a keg party. Investors would fund the kegs of beer. I handled both the operations and the logistics of the event. A cover charge of two dollars for gents and a dollar for ladies. My cut allowed me to buy pizza, beer, and drugs.

In my redshirt freshman year, I had seventy-eight kegs of beer at my house. I lived violently, drank enormous amounts of liquor, and explored the drug culture. The reckless part of me was lured to the edge and wanted to see how far I could get before falling.

Drugs eclipsed my life, and the consequences of overdose or alcohol poisoning punished me. I saw life through a yellow-tinted haze. Numbed, I enjoyed escaping my suffering. The root of my bastard wisdom became my fated happiness. Refusing to live in this world, madness bewitched me, and I never chose to recognize my own limitations. I kept walking toward the edge to wave my finger at God and ask Him why.

Yesterday's hangover kickstarted a new day's buzz. I hated the holiday spirit, so on Christmas Eve, I had a party with seven kegs of beer. Every stoner looking to get high came to my house. They even called my Grandmother Lee asking for directions. Out of control, gonzo-crazy, the party got so big I stopped collecting money. I estimated two to three hundred kids came that night. I pushed drugs at the door and made fat stacks of cash. I led a choir of drunks who sang Christmas songs on my back patio. I slept the whole day on Christmas. Mission accomplished.

♥

With a crowd partying at my house, I felt exhilarated and rebelled against what the world saw as normal. I managed these events with a firm hand and a crowbar. With the reputation of a scrapper, I didn't mind a good old-fashioned throw down. Some fool from Canton thought I would back down when he pointed his gun at me in my front yard. The moment was neither frightening nor agonizing to me. I looked him straight in the eye and told him, "Either pull the trigger or get the hell off my property."

My superman's eyes saw inside his soul, and it was etched with fear and twisted by his pride. At sixteen years, I was an actual suicide waiting for natural events to occur. As we stood face to face, he discovered the value of his life. All in, he folded. My stoner friends started to cheer and called me,

"Crazy Larry! Crazy Larry!"

I laughed and was the most dangerous man alive. I had nothing, and nothing made me bold.

♥

High school battered and beat me with rules and expectations. Genius couldn't be achieved by being a sheep. An emotional cripple, I crawled on my knees through time and space and discovered the de-arrangement of logic. I wandered in silence, by the moon's light, and I struggled with the things that made us human. A seer, I saw school was the auditorium for the living dead.

The walls I built to survive were so high and looked down on the tree-tops blowing in the wind. My life was one extended party. Robert moved next door into Catherine Zoef's house for his own safety. After all, he lived in a home without parental supervision where drug dealers cut up their drugs into smaller quantities. I had to feed my head and keep my soul dead. Chasing dragons no one could see, I was as thirsty as a dying man, and nothing could quench my desire to explore.

As it stood, my drug abuse led me to play many parts each day. I became aggressive to scare others away. A martyr recruited someone on my side. An innovator obtained what I wanted. The grand illusion exiled from the standard way of living. Outside the circle of life, I was the man with a plan.

♥

Without a morsel of love inside of me, I grew even harder toward my brother. Robert moved into the Zoefs' house. He was part of their extended family. They had so little to give, but they shared what they had. Catherine fed him most of the time, and Desi, Alexandra, and Charlie helped him heal his broken heart. We had been entirely forgotten by every relative at this point. Our lives were forever damaged by the amnesia of our family. They were fundamentally unaccountable, and they denied us our basic human rights. No one wanted to inherit a problem they overlooked. Our lives were easily ignored by those who were supposed to love and protect us.

♥

I stood aloof from life until grace found me. Looking back, this was the first letter God ever sent to my heart. Janet and Jim Mack, who had a straightforward, ordinary, and happy life, let me into their family circle. The openness of this family influenced me in a way that made me dream beyond the misery. A warm smile embraced my face every time I went to their house, and they made me feel wanted.

I was a dreamer who wished God was a liar. My instincts were to regress into a blue-eyed devil. I felt too cheated to worship or behave in society. I stood frozen in time and in front of the Mack family. Their love simply broke me down. My mind withdrew from its experiences, and the Macks extended their hand and made me new. The virtues in their hearts reset me. Around them, I found what my soul needed, the need to be loved. Happily, I sat down and ate at their dinner table, and my many pains and sorrows vanished. I so longed to be a part of a family, and their kindness was the element that empowered my heart to live beyond the moment. Their love made me feel unique, perfect, and even handsome.

I never wanted to lose my place at their table, so I mastered a double life. Every lie I told renounced my existence in this world. Continually condemning myself, my lies were the blanket of my self-destruction. A slave to my master's secret, my pride kept me hungry and cold. God would have to find me another way.

I couldn't relate to anyone. It seemed every path I took led me to nowhere. I'd always had to draw forth some extraordinary effort to overcome something. The Macks' love awakened my desire. So pure and infinite, it gave me superpowers. The winter of 1976 was one blizzard after another. I never told them my father didn't pay the oil bill. The mile-and-a-half walk home fueled my heart.

By the time I made it back to my house with the thought of the Macks' love in my heart, every heartbeat had allowed my muscles to twitch to remain alive. I never knew hell could be so fucking cold. To pass the time, I watched each breath freeze, fall, and break apart on the floor. Sick and tired of living, I couldn't feel my fingers and toes. When I got out of my bed, I sometimes slipped on the ice on the wood floor. I always staggered back to my feet and angrily smiled back at my destiny. My frozen lips cracked when I mumbled, "Is that all you got?"

I didn't see my father for over a month until the sun began to melt the snow away. I had to take my showers at school to stay clean. Robert slept next door at the Zoefs' house.

♥

As winter slowly turned into spring, I didn't know to love myself, nor could I accept my father. A warrior demigod, I never backed down from my dad or anyone else. Real life is nasty and cruel. Fights are won. Battles are lost. I always gave more than I got. A soldier who never prayed for peace. I picked at my scars each day in order not to forget who gave them to me. The madness of my morality let me lose sight of the end game.

The moment I only believed in myself, I'd lose the curiosity, wonder, and spontaneous thoughts that embraced the human spirit. My intolerance toward my father turned into hostility. Hatred defeats all. Monsters wage war on the innocent, and war creates more monsters to save themselves from a predator.

Instincts isolated and internalized my views. Ugly thoughts were evil things and lived inside of me. The extreme viciousness of child abuse and domestic warfare consumed my thinking, killing him. I'd lost every fight to my father, and the thought of "one day," gave me the strength to get back up off the floor.

Often, he greeted me with, "Son, what did you steal today?"

"You're a stupid fuck! I only steal because you're a fucking loser, Dad!"

My scar-ridden body deflected his words, but their meaning cut my heart open. We shared the same bloodline, but he was colder. I never forget the first lesson in fighting, "Don't hesitate!"

After one of my keg parties, I stopped off at a store and bought a can of Del Monte Beef Stew to eat for dinner. Dining at the table, my father walked through the door and flippantly mumbled, "Umm dinner."

"Umm, none for you."

He glared at me like he was about to punch me and shouted, "Fuck off!"

I accepted his invitation to dance. The radical bastard in me fearlessly walked toward his room, pot in hand, and asked him, "Would you like some?"

He looked at me with his cold, dark fish eyes and replied, "No, you probably stole it."

I laughed and left the bait out in front of me, "Are you sure?"

He took a long look at me. The hatred in his eyes sizzled. He grinned and said, "No thanks," as he flicked his cigar ash head into the pot.

The supernova inside me burst. I pushed him. He stumbled backward against the wall and slid down. Eye to eye, I raised the pot over his bed and poured it all over his sheets. I threw the pan at him and shouted, "You just bought it, bitch!"

A child amidst a two-thousand-year war that had been passed down from generation to generation, I was mean. I wasn't evil yet. I couldn't handle reality without a mood-altering substance running through my veins. My sweet face camouflaged the unconditional surrender of a guerrilla warrior. My explosion released hundreds of bomblets. I destroyed whatever stood in my way. I took a hammer to my father's metal footlocker to pillage what little he had left.

Uncomfortable in my own skin, the darkness of my life opened the purity of my misery. I walked among monstrous creatures with educated egos. At odds with the day, I set backfires just see the world burn. The ignorance of my actions was formed from not being loved. Alone, the world seemed closed and very strange to me. I didn't see anything worth visiting. I emotionally surrendered to the evil in my thoughts. I kicked the shit out of sorrow and knew repentance would mean I had to be in God.

♥

One afternoon, Robert and I were together when my father came home from the bar. The moment my dad saw me, the verbal abuse began. Judgments on both sides were locked and loaded. Rockets fired. Sharp metal pieces exploded. Words ripped through our defenseless skin. Our hearts bled.

Born with my mother's heart, I looked like her. It must have angered him every time he saw me. I imitated the only goodness I ever witnessed. My actions shouted, "I HAVEN'T SEEN ENOUGH!"

Anger made me seven feet tall with bulging biceps, and I remembered every time he slapped my mother. He continued bashing me, "You're a thief. You are nothing, and you'll be nothing your whole life."

Slowly, I walked up to him, for I wasn't going to back down. Standing within two feet of him, I reminded him, "I'm a reflection of your lousy fucking parenting. At least I have an excuse, you drunk bastard!"

Words cut deep. I found the only nerve not traumatized by an under-civilized life. False pride reacted. A right roundhouse SWISHED over my head. I used my downward momentum to spring upward with an uppercut. SMACK!

The Crown Prince of the Lees went down.

I saw the moment I've survived to see. Scorned, the hell of my fury filled my fist with rage. Fueled by adrenaline, blinded by my memories, silent rage hammered his face like a nail. I bore my knuckles deep into his flesh. As I stopped to breathe, I saw a steak knife on the floor. I reached over and picked it up.

When I looked into his dazed eyes, time ceased. My indifference had turned into inhumanity. Without thought, I only acted upon the abuse I'd suffered. Inches away from patricide, I only lived for the moment of his death.

Looking down on him, his eyes slowly opened and I shouted, "I should kill you, old man, for what you have done to my life."

"You can't do it, boy. You have your mother's heart."

He smiled a contemptuous, provoking smile. Darkness shrouded me, and the abyss urged me closer. As each millisecond flashed, my mind remembered every battle I had with him. I thought he must die, so I acted upon my thought. I lifted the knife to penetrate his chest.

Robert stepped out of the shadows for the first time ever, and yelled, "LARRY NOOOOOO!"

Somewhere between the seconds that seemed to linger for days, a thousand images flashed of what could be and what would never be. In those pictures, I reached the core of cruelty and found the paradoxical truth. I was the greatest obstacle to my freedom.

Tumbling back into reality, I fell from madness, passed through forgiveness and back into self-hatred. The force of evil inside my heart surrendered to a more formidable force.

Nobody can protect you from yourself. I drank from the cup of evil and spit it out. I might have lost my soul if I won the war. I got up and kicked him serval times. I said, "I'll let you continue to kill yourself." I walked out of the door to find some drugs.

♥

After our final battle, I rarely saw my father. When I did, he wouldn't look

Out of the FIELD

at me and kept his mouth shut. Little did I know, our lives together were almost over. A few weeks later, two men in suits showed up at our house. They were from his former employer. I answered the door with a beer in my hand and a cigarette in my mouth. "What can I do for you, gentlemen?"

"We are from your father's union and here to see your dad. Is he around?"

I laughed and said, "Yeah, the useless bastard is passed out on the floor in his bedroom. I have to go to a friend's house. Just shut the door when you're done with him."

His company fired him after twenty-five years. They paid for him to go to alcohol treatment twice. He loved his drinking more than his own life, and it consumed every aspect of him. I sat on the sidelines and saw firsthand the destruction of a single choice.

A silent victim, drugs eased the pain of living in hell. My altered consciousness focused on the party house. Being an addict, I found it easier to pick others apart than look at myself. Addicted to the chaos, I demoralized pompous authority for sport. Like a drop of rain, I belonged to no one.

♥

The school board obviously had me in their crosshairs when they changed the suspension policy. The maximum time suspended has been modified from ten to three times. The fourth offense would mean expulsion, and I hit the limit in March. I was also leading the school with one hundred and eight detentions on the books. One day, the intercom blasted, "Larry Lee, please report to the principal's office."

I finished smoking a joint with a friend and walked down to the office. Once I opened the door, Super Bruce was waiting for me and escorted me into his office. The superintendent, anal Joe MacDonald, and vice principal, Lemon Head Schmidt were sitting at the table in front of me. My old middle school's principal was now the superintendent. Super Bruce asked me, "Mr. Lee would you please take a seat in the chair in front of you."

A long, glowing smile covered my face before I replied, "Sure thing, Bruce."

Super Bruce proceeded, "Mr. Lee, we have brought you here because you have been suspended three times this year. Under the new school policy, your fourth suspension will be an automatic expulsion from school. We have also noticed that you have one hundred and eight detentions on record. You must immediately start the after-school detention program. You must not miss one session, or you will be expelled.

"Furthermore, we want you to understand if you get one more detention, miss one class or miss one more day of school without a doctor's note, you will be expelled. Do you understand what is expected of you? Do you have any questions for us?"

As I listened to Super Bruce's words jab me into a corner, I thought what cowards these men were, for I was only sixteen years old. Their eyes covered me in prejudice, and equality meant the entire world fit nicely into the small regions of their brains. My snarky pride rose up, and I couldn't betray my instincts. A wretched soul backed into a corner, I responded, "You boys got me good! Right where you want me!"

Free-spirited, I stared at them with a smile on my face, and as each second passed, it made them feel uncomfortable. My courage wouldn't let me run. As a child, I learned to fight for what was inside of me. Nerdy men were oddly excited about words like can't, won't, will, better, and understood. My superman's eyes saw no beauty, no love, and no compassion inside of them. I stood up, still with a smile on my face, and said, "Is that all you boys got?"

I walked out of Super Bruce's office and lit a joint my friend gave me. Pot smoke roamed the halls with me while everyone was in class.

The line was drawn in the sand, and I always played the game to win. I went to every class and got high before each detention session. I even got an A in business math, which amazed the teacher. I played their game and reconnected with boldness, creativity, and independence buried in my soul. The last day of school, I walked by the principal's office window waving my middle finger at him.

♥

Shortly after school ended, my uncle Jimmy's orange station wagon pulled up in the driveway. I was smoking a joint in the backyard and proceeded to put it out when he got out of his automobile. Without any notice, he instructed me, "Larry, you need to pack your things up, for you're coming to live at my house."

"Why?"

"Just get your things, Larry. The bank is foreclosing on the house this week."

While gathering my stuff, I asked, "Where is Robert going to live?"

"Mrs. Stoppani, the middle school nurse, took him. He's going to live in Harwinton with her family."

I never asked him about my father, and he never volunteered any information.

High as a kite, I smiled while retrieving my dope from my hidden stash. On the ride to my uncle's house in Bristol, Connecticut, I wondered what happened to my old man.

7
Homeless at Eighteen

Lack of self-esteem let me live in excess. A drug fiend, temptation had its wonders, and exploration allowed me to escape ordinary life. Reality never really impressed me much. Words! Simple words! I lived in their shades, vivid tones, and cruel variations. The silence of others let me discover my insatiable desire to fly. Hash oil inflated my lungs and opened my mind to the onrush of the scenery of the world around me. Contemptuous, every kind of drug let me expand my mind's eyes. I wouldn't be a cow standing in the fucking rain. So many never live. The end is just the beginning. What seems real is just an illusion, so it's onward and onward. I could never turn back. I was a martyred slave to drugs and words. Simple words! Let me describe my fucked-up life.

Yesterday didn't matter anymore, for I changed my face every day to fit the situation. I moved in with a Catholic family. The capacity for friendship with God was appalling. A malcontent, I existed outside the sandbox, and my heart was hidden from God. A gypsy sense of adventure lived inside of me. I tried not to sleep in the same bed every night. A wild dog, I kept moving, kept getting high, and roaming the streets. Home life with Ward and June Cleaver and their two children made me sick. The city of Bristol provided me with a playground to escape the fake happiness of my new family.

♥

In the summer of 1977, my uncle and his family dragged me on a vacation to upstate New York, to Lake George. We were one big happy family. Drugs allowed me to tolerate Ward and June Cleaver. A hallucinogenic dose eased my sorrow and sought a better tomorrow. Chainless and free, I had to escape what my father did to me. Every toke, every hit, and every pill put down the memories in my mind. Living, dying, I was naïve and such a fool to think I could control addiction. You only know what you'd learned and no more.

One night while we ate dinner, my aunt noticed all the teenagers walking by our camper site waving at me. She said, "Larry, it's nice that you can make friends so quickly. It's a blessing you know."

"You're so right! It's a blessing being high-spirited and full of nonsense."

My aunt and uncle didn't know I brought over three ounces of Columbian Gold with me on the trip. Wasted! Smashed! Fried! Bashed! High! There were the words I loved and lived by. Trapped in the darkness, my nocturnal eyes let me see just fine. I wanted to hold on to this feeling delusional on drugs.

♥

As fall whisked its way into my life, I attended Bristol Eastern High School with a student population of around fifteen hundred students. It didn't take me long to get in my first fight. The main smoking area was filled with reefer-madness kings and queens. As I walked into their courtyard, I felt the sharpness from their eyes scratch my skin. One by one, I passed each of them on my way to the back wall. I lit up a smoke and perused their kingdom. In my weird and cruel sense of humor, I smiled back at the stupid and misinformed who stared at me.

I mumbled to myself, "Fuck you, this is America. Leave me the fuck alone!"

One of the stoners decided to walk over to me, and he said, "This courtyard is a closed community. You have to be invited in by a member."

I lifted my eyes up from the ground and stared at him like he was stupid. I told him, "The sign says, 'school smoking area.' Hey, dude, I don't want any trouble. I just want to finish my smoke."

He grew, and he began to put on his armor. He was bigger, louder, and uglier than me. He shouted, "It is a closed community!"

"Okay! Okay! I got it, man."

I took one last drag off my smoke. While exhaling, I walked toward him, and without warning, I flicked my cigarette into his face. His hands went up to protect himself. I attacked. BAM! BAM! He hit the ground. I savagely kicked him in the ribs twice before someone yelled, "Teacher!"

The teacher walked into the courtyard and asked, "Mr. Wilson, are you picking fights again?"

"No, sir!"

"What is your name, son?" the teacher asked me.

"Larry."

"Well, I hope you're not starting trouble in my courtyard."

"I'm just finishing my smoke before class."

Wilson didn't rat me out, nor did he understand the number one rule in juvenile delinquency—don't fuck with someone unless you're stronger or wiser than they are.

♥

With a massive chip on my shoulder, I never looked to get my picture in the high school yearbook. While cutting class, smoking a cigarette outside, Jake asked, "Can I bum a cigarette off you?"

"Sure man," I said. "Where you from?"

"I just transferred here from Oklahoma City. This school seems to be full of punk-ass losers. You're the only one to talk with me so far."

"I know what you mean. I haven't met anyone cool here either. Hey, do you smoke weed?"

"Yeah, why?"

"After school, you meet me here, and we'll do a few bowls before I have to go to work."

As fate would have it, we became friends. We got high every day at his house. He would take me into West Hartford to buy some more exotic drugs. As our circle started to grow, other kids wondered why we always had weed. The Bristol underground market was as dry and barren as the Mojave Desert. One day after everyone left, Jake came up with the idea and said, "Hey man how much cash do you have?"

"About six bills."

"I know a dealer who only sells a pound or more. We should get these fools here to pay for us to get high. We'll use the profit to go to rock concerts and buy other drugs."

With a handshake, I instantly became a high school drug dealer. I pulled out five hundred dollars, and we drove and picked up one of Jake's friends, Chris. We went to the dealer's home. Jake said, "Larry, you'll have

Out of the FIELD

to wait in the car, for he doesn't know you."

Chris said, "Jake, you'll have to wait here, too. You have been gone too long. You know the drill."

With Jake's friend in the car, without hesitation, I turned Jake and asked him, "Do you trust this guy?" I looked for any inconsistencies.

Jake immediately said, "Yeah, he is cool."

"Okay, let's do this."

I gave his friend my $440.00. About five minutes later, I bought my first pound of pot. I started selling quarters, halves, and ounce-bags at school. Jake and I cornered the market at school. We sold a pound or more a week. Business was buzzing. I fed my head every exotic drug I could—angel dust, hashish, hash oil, uppers, downers, acid, and cocaine.

I quit smoking pot for it was dry and nasty. A connoisseur of hashish and hash oil, I liked a finer and smoother buzz and smoked it all day. One day, I pulled out my hash pipe in business law class. While the teacher was writing on the blackboard, I lit it up. I got stoned in class.

A rocket sled on rails, I blasted off on the roller coaster ride of my life. I streamed a fiery trail through space. I raged war on myself, for my enemy was gone. A warrior without a war, I took refuge in peddling dope, going to rock concerts, and committing crime. I crawled into the poverty of abandonment of self.

Hatred inspired my actions. I never pondered more than my next high and became insane looking at sanity. I shut my eyes when I snorted dust, and the universe got smaller. At the top of the world, the fires of hell looked like warming coals. I couldn't remember the last day I was sober. My life made perfect sense, more rocket fuel! I was headed to the moon, so get the hell out of my way.

As I numbed myself with pleasures, fate got in my way one day. Some fool I sold an ounce of weed to was waving the bag around in Jake's driveway. The whole world could see, even Jake's parents. They fucking lost it big time! I had to take my dope home with me. It was the worst hangover I ever had.

Once I had made my decision to sell dope from my uncle's house, fate conspired against me. Within a month, I noticed my stash bag had been opened. Nothing was missing. A few days after that incident, my uncle Jimmy told me, "Larry, you're now eighteen, and things aren't working out here. I want you out of here tonight or by tomorrow morning."

I looked at him and said nothing.

♥

February 1979, I stepped out of his home, spit on the ground, and hoisted my burning flag for the universe to see. Eighteen years old, I was officially on my own, with two knapsacks and over a thousand dollars in cash I had saved from dealing. I left my key on the nightstand and walked three miles toward the nearest motel. I got myself a room and set up for business the next day.

The only time I went to school was to sell drugs. In 1979, the minimum wage was $2.90 per hour, $116 for a forty-hour work week. I was making over $200 by selling a pound a week. Cash was king, and like any other kingdom, it fell on hard times. It happened a lot quicker than I wanted it to. A hustling dope fiend can move lots of product, but I couldn't keep my hand out of the cookie jar.

I hitchhiked back from West Hartford with two pounds in my backpack. A street kid, I never thought to add in the expenses of paying for a room, food, beer, and cigarettes. My cash flow was walloped in the flux of the market. The pipeline cracked, and my business went belly up after five weeks.

I drifted away from Jake and couldn't always find a ride into West Hartford. Reality's fingers held me by the throat, and it began to squeeze. Six weeks after I was thrown out of my uncle's house, my accounts receivable plummeted. I called a Catholic Church for help, and they told me, "Son, you are eighteen years old, and you are on your own. May God bless your life, and I will say a prayer for you."

"Wow, you Catholics amazed me. You can't make a decision unless it comes down from the pope. Maybe you should pray for yourself to grow a pair."

♥

As I stood in front of the motel mirror before I checked out, I combed my hair different ways hoping things would change. I had two hundred dollars to my name and had nowhere to go. I wouldn't let life bring me back to my family.

Out of the FIELD

My heart was strong, battled-tested, and it wouldn't let me be extinguished. I walked out into March's cold and cruel world. I passed the time of the day by smoking cigarettes, joints and scribbling broken poems in a notebook. In each unforgiving minute, I looked for a safe place to lay my head. At the end of my first day, I found a place not far from the motel and slept behind a department store loading dock, under a semi-trailer. I put some cardboard boxes down to insulate me from the frozen ground and used the tire to brace my knapsack to use as a pillow. I slept fully clothed and passed out as I exhaled and woke up each time I inhaled. I shivered between breaths and listened to the poor partying in Section 8 housing across the street.

Every night on the street, I heard the city alive and breathing. With each unexpected sound, I felt the city strip me down to my mortal guilt, and in the confines of being homeless, I was no longer immortal. Each night, the clusters of echoes savagely danced around me throughout the evening. As my slumbering eyes clung on to the moon's light for security, I slept with one eye open. My mind constantly deciphered every sound my ears heard. I interpreted the silent language of life evolving from the unknown. The murmurs of the breeze whistled the thoughts and discoveries never seen through my watchful eye. The enormous uncertainty made me dream of life's invisible splendors. In the lull of my sleep, snuggled in the undergrowth of the city, the unnatural light was the edge of where I lived. Until the city's morning traffic whispered into my ear, it was time for me to vanish into the monstrous waking morning.

The supermarkets provided me with lunch and dinner. A vagrant at eighteen, I was lost somewhere between the minutes and hours of each day. Invisible and ignored, no one ever cared what happened to me. I kept walking Main Street, and no one could see the little boy waving his arms for help. As I watched the social brotherhood on the streets each day, I pondered my suffering in silence, and in every breath, the torturous air reminded me I was alive. I was forgotten by all who knew my name. My ambitions were continually crushed, but my restitution came from the freedom of the words I played with and describe what I saw. Since I couldn't seize up eternity, my mind's eye saw the boorishness in both good and evil. God has been glorified for ages. Now at eighteen, I waited for His Assassin to come, for I was without hope in God. There was no God or love, for there were only the trampling feet of humanity in pursuit of one's selfish dream. There was just me trying to survive being homeless.

I had no time to be hard on myself and had to keep my wits about me. Just like any other game, you use what your opponent gives you to your advantage. I had to adapt to each situation and never let my ego expose my vulnerability. I looked back at my childhood and saw how each moment in my life readied me to survive to live on the streets. Lying, cheating, and stealing were weapons I used to fight back creeping death. A week and a half passed, I could even smell my own stench by now.

Walking out of a liquor store, Jake saw me while he was driving home from school, and he pulled into the parking lot. He said, "What the fuck happened to you? You stink, dude."

"Yeah, I know. I can even smell myself. I hit a bad run when my pipeline broke."

"Get in, and I'll take you to my house so you can get cleaned up."

After a long hot shower, we got high. Jake decided to let me sleep in his parents' unattached garage. The nights still hovered around freezing, but I was safe from the crazy street people. His parents found out a week later. They invited me to stay at their house. After a few days, they thought it would be a good idea to call my uncle Burney, my godfather, and ask him for help.

♥

After several days, a lot of phone calls and numerous long pauses, my uncle told me he would stop by and pick me up the next day. I put all my earthly possessions and three ounces of seedless weed into my two knapsacks. He took me to his home in Greenwich, Connecticut. He lived there with his wife, Alice, and their three children, Emma, Landon, and Burney, Jr. My uncle's three children were fortunate as he sent them to private schools. I hadn't heard from my uncle and his family in over four years. As I walked through the door, a vagabond street kid with my suitcase on my back, I looked at his children in their private school attire. My first thought of them was, "Weakness in conformity."

I always verbally engaged Emma, for she was daddy's little princess. She acted like a primadonna rich bitch. She said, "Long time no see, Larry. How's life been treating you?"

"Out of sight, out of mind, I guess. I had a few classic adventures.

Out of the FIELD

Something someone with your status couldn't understand."

A street kid, I sized up the moment. Blessed, I read linguistics through moments, for the crude rhythms of their voices let me really know, "We forgot all about you."

The Holiday children's lives were blessed with many beautiful things. The splendors of a community, teachers, family, and friends adorned their lives. A poet's eyes saw possession kill the sense of wonder and mystery of life. Unarmed by poverty, my mind was my only weapon. My instincts shielded me from danger. Relatives are eternally muddied creatures of habit. Their serial thoughts and actions maimed my core being. I'd never let myself fall or stumble helplessly into their ludicrous love.

There was a fight going on inside of me. I was torn apart by anger, yet my heart held on to my mother's promise. My family might as well have spoken Japanese, for they were foreigners to me. In the sweet spot of life's torturous moments, I opened my eternal eye and found a soul waiting to be known. My mind held on to the thought, "I am another."

Beneath the surface, my underground thoughts and reality clashed daily. I daydreamed about discovering the truth of my existence, the evolution of morals, and a movement of love and compassion. In my uncle's house, boredom fancied thought. I wouldn't be charmed by things. Each of their thoughts was scattered between enchantments and the insatiable need for more. My reflection bought to light the corrosiveness of his family foundation. Money was more important than his sister's children's well-being.

Idleness let my thoughts sail like red balloons toward the sun, and they disappeared among the clouds. I stood in front of them, beat to shit by the world. I was something they could analyze or even criticize. Their lack of action let me know there was no place at their table.

Was it me? Was it me? Was I diluting the bloodline? Was I making a mistake not to honor my grandfathers? Their apathy terrified me and motivated me beyond self-doubt. I envisioned the future without having to live it. DELETE! DELETE! DELETE!

♥

An independent documentary broke free from a mainstream theater idea. I got a chance to say goodbye to both my uncle and aunt when they took me to see a psychiatrist. In my first and only session, I walked into the shrink's office. It looked like a library. It was too tidy for my taste. There wasn't a speck of dust anywhere. It was an illusion of impermanence.

Everything had its place. I thought to myself, this man must be hiding some huge secrets. A noise from the corner of the office found my ears. I turned my head and looked his way. He said, "Welcome. Welcome, Larry. Please have a seat in the chair near the window and relax."

Silent, I followed his instructions.

"Let me tell you why you're here. Your uncle and aunt want me to talk with you about what is going on in your life."

The moment of truth came when the strength and prowess of my eyes took a stand. Two psychics stared each other down. The obese man with a double chin and droopy eyes spoke first, "Please make yourself comfortable, Larry. Is there anything you care to share with me?"

I hung an "Out of Order" sign in my eyes and said, "Nope."

He continued to shoot longbow arrowed questions over my castle walls. I hid behind the fortitude of my stubborn thoughts. Always gallant and gorgeous in battle, conflict defined me. As the minutes fell into dead silence, my soul rose from the ashes of birth into the thought I was another. I was free from the people that surround me.

The silence of my family let me know the price of the human soul.

Mumbo jumbo! Babble words! Strength found me when I muted the world around me.

Blithely I ignored every one of his questions and statements until one comment hit a nerve. The plight of being an orphan born into a family opened a cruel devilish smile when he told me, "Your family loves you."

My eyes glistened! My temple roared back! My mind unlocked and prepared to attack. I looked into the shrink's eyes and laughed. I told him, "They know not how to love anything but themselves."

The rest of the session I pushed him back into his chair. One by one, I maneuvered around his silly questions. I merely played for a stalemate. Every time he asked me a question, I looked out the window and told him, "Just look how beautiful those tiny little yellow flowers are."

Time was on my side. I continued to talk about those tiny little yellow flowers. On and on he assailed my walls with grappling-hook questions. I stood firm at the top of my castle walls. I severed the strings that bound me to my family. Enamored thoughts let me see the magnificence inside of me.

After the session had ended in a draw, my uncle and his wife entered the room. Mr. Double Chin proceeded to tell them, "Larry likes the tiny little yellow flowers outside of my window."

My uncle chirped in, "Chief, I know you had it bad, for your father wasn't a good man. You're eighteen years old now, and you have the rest of your life ahead of you. The good doctor was only trying to help you."

My aunt repeated my uncle's words. "Yes, Larry, you have your whole life ahead of you. You should listen to a real doctor."

In the company of complete strangers, I sat in a quiet place surround by endless chatter. In the clearance sale inside my mind, I threw out the family heirlooms one by one. Everything now would be up to me. My ears grew weary as I listened to the soulless talk of humanity. They were hypnotized by their alibis. I watched them nod to each other. I watched them shuffle back and forth between positions.

From out of nowhere, my aunt chimed in, "Larry, everyone in New York City has a therapist. It is now the in thing."

From a dead silence, I roared, "Have you ever been so hungry you drank water to have something in your belly. Have you ever stolen your dinner because you wouldn't get it anywhere else? Have you ever...? Fuck it, I am out of here!"

I felt like a book that sat on a shelf unread. I was the author of my fate. Courage let me believe in tomorrow.

My uncle was a good businessman, but he wasn't an honorable man. Being my godfather, he failed me, time and time again. The rich never lie. They protect and hoard what they have. I knew the Lee family rallied around their firstborn, and they stole all they could from Robert and me. I recognized their faces and forgot their names. I couldn't play with them anymore. We shared the same features, but the tiny little yellow flowers had awoken me from the insanity of my family. I called Jake once I got to my uncle's home and asked him, "Hey man, do you think your parents will let me stay there until I get a job?"

His parents picked me up the next day after work. I walked away from my family and never looked back.

♥

Each day, I walked up and down each street looking for work. At the end of the day, I ended up in a bar just like my father. Asking only for workman's wages, no one would hire me. Drinking and drugs allowed me to forget the day's failures. Each night, before I closed my eyes, I looked up into the star-filled sky and wondered what life had in store for me. I wanted someone to believe in me, but my disappointment was unavoidable. My heart was out of tune. The future was hard to know, but the energy from a rock concert attracted my mind. Jake told me about the Texas Music Festival at the Cotton Bowl in Dallas.

I called Jake's friend, Brad. I met him when he visited Jake for three months in 1977. After talking with his parents, I got the "Go" to stay at his parent's house until I found a job. The stage was set, and the stars were glistening. The decision to flee Connecticut came suddenly. I scrambled to get enough cash to buy a pound of weed. I paid a visit to my Grandmother Lee to get my Social Security check she had been stealing for years.

With a whopping $625.00 to my name, I bought a bus ticket for Oklahoma City, and I purchased a pound of weed to sell there. On the second of June 1979, I waited outside the bus station and smoked a cigarette. I observed the actions of others define them.

I stood and watched as life diminishes second by second. I separated what was nostalgic from the truth. I saw the sleepy shadows that followed all of us. In the ancient busy street, I wasn't sleeping. My weariness vanished, as I listened to the song inside my heart. I envisioned those tiny little yellow flowers, blossoming a love inside of me. Born a prisoner of shame, I hit the open road, a common criminal. I wasn't an ordinary young man, and I knew my life couldn't be undone. I could reinvent it, beyond the frightened ruins of my memories, until I got it right. I looked for a morsel of hope in my dumpster of thoughts. I was far more deserving than those who preceded me. My apprenticeship in life opened my mind to colossal concepts, and in my imagination, I found the road to be someone else.

Out of the FIELD

8
The Field

I noticed the long, lonesome road had an assortment of huge and brightly colored billboards along the roadside. I realized the only real mistake in life was to not believe in yourself. In each oncoming headlight, a long, silver-bright strand of beams brought me a galaxy of dreams. My liberating thoughts were gentle and without guile. I only had the memory of my mother's love to fuel my heart. I am here. I survived being born into a social vacuum.

I mused on the word "family," and it was a lovely word they never fully understood. They never dared to see their imperfections, for they lived in a code of silence passed down to them. I was the happiest person under the stars. My thoughts changed, fragmented, and separated along the sides of the highway. Mile after mile, the frenzy of insufficient reason drove me to define the word "love." As I mused internally, I stretched out the edge of darkness until I found the cresting sun's rays warming the discovery of a new day's thought.

Suffering inspired me. Struggle awoke my inner dreams. No one's plans ever included me. I saw the grace in each moment, but I wouldn't let my heart feel the presence of God's providence. The solution for everything was determination and a combative will. After all, I was medium in stature, dirty, unkempt, and not well-spoken, but I could steal inspiration from human cruelty. I pursued an ordinary life and made a superhuman promise to myself. I dared to aspire to live in the illuminating brightness of my mind's eye. My tattered boots were an instrument of my heart, and I plucked my rhyming thoughts from the rays of the sun. I anointed myself the "Prince of the Vagabonds." The desire to be someone else let me see I had a choice, or I could ricochet through this life.

♥

Every few hours, the bus stopped in a different city along its route. I had nothing but time on my hands. My mind pondered the faces and the lives I saw. In my captured assumptions, incomprehensible life became apparent. Emotional fabrication and attachment made the imagined real. As I thought, something inside of me changed. Ideas opened the joy of human diversity. My façade of invincibility was being stripped away. My first spiritual experience led me into a minute of pure love, ten seconds of grace, and a glimpse into gratitude. Into new horizons, between each mile marker, my thoughts must have sounded like prayers to God. The mirroring effects of self-reflection revealed the measurement of my morality. I listened to my heart speak. A prisoner unto myself, I held the key to my freedom. I sent two promises into the wind. I wouldn't die all alone like my mother did, and I wouldn't live my life in poverty.

Somewhere between all my thoughts and daydreams, I took the time to fall asleep every now and then. As I awoke from a nap, the bus pulled into Columbus, Ohio, at 4:40 p.m. As soon as the bus parked, the driver announced, "Everyone, please be back to the bus before 5:50 p.m. I will wait for no one."

Wound up like a ball of yarn in my seat, I awoke from my dreams and stumbled back into the slum of my existence. Life pushed me back into what it wanted me to be. My desire lived between the variance of my needs. As reality closed in on me, I climbed back down behind my walls and no longer lived in my dreams of one day. My gargoyle eyes ascended and were transformed by my mammoth fears. My preconceived ideas defaulted back to what kept me safe. My intuition was a sacred gift I used against servants of the world. An actor, primitive survival made up all my costumes.

Getting off the bus, I made sure my backpack was with me, for it had a pound of weed, a few hits of acid and a dozen Black beauties. Walking off the bus, two brothers noticed my pot leaf belt buckle which concealed a pipe. They began to pester me. "Hey man, I know you got some weed stashed on you. Let's go toke it up, bro."

My eyes met their eyes, and I looked away. As I got off the bus, they followed me into the station, and one of them said, "Come on man, we'll give you five dollars if you get us high."

I looked at them and through them, "Five bucks for two joints."

"Sure, that's a deal."

"Let's go."

As we walked a few city blocks away from the bus station, I looked down each alley away from the main thoroughfare. I walked a little behind them to read their body language. I made sure my buck knife case was unbuttoned, in case my knife was needed. I didn't know, yet I trusted my intuition. It never failed me before. I always sensed someone's intentions. A street kid, I survived by living in situational awareness, common sense, and true grit.

Locating an alley, I said, "Let's go down here."

"You're the boss man," one of them said.

The alley was opened at both ends, and it seemed to have little walking traffic. I stopped near a dumpster and said, "Where's my five bucks?"

One of them pulled Abe out of his front pocket and gave it to me. I pulled out my cigarette case and opened it up. I had several pre-rolled joints and lit one up. Taking a deep bellowing huff, I held in a long time, and then released a smoke signal of my defiance into the world. I passed the joint to my right. One of them said, "This is some primo weed."

Before we finished the first joint, I lit up the second one. A smooth buzz slowly lightened my eyes. I began to float on the river of being unconcerned. Red-eyed, I scudded along the frayed corridors in my mind. No man had ever had so much desire to escape reality as me. Suddenly without notice, reality strong-armed me back into sobriety. Columbus's finest showed up at the end of the alley. I could tell they didn't like me smoking dope in their city. A small whisking breeze blew my cover.

Five-O shouted, "Stop right there!"

Fear made me a gazelle. I ran in the opposite direction and passed the two brothers who took off before me. Shifting into overdrive, the echoes of the officer's cry for us to stop grew faint.

I thought to myself, Fuck me. I zigged and zagged throughout the downtown streets of Columbus. My fleeting feet increased their torque and traction in each step. Fear of prison completely overwhelmed me. My heart and lungs were motivated by the thoughts of a first-degree felony. As soon as I found a safe place, my denim jean jackets came off, for it had a Union Jack flag embroidered the back of it. My pot-leaf belt buckle pipe came off too. A small fish just escaped Jaws.

As my memory recalled a high-rise landmark near the bus station, I blended in with the other walking citizens on the street and moved toward the high-rise. I forged my way back to the station and made it back to the bus a few minutes before it took off. I never did see what happened to the other two brothers, and they must not have narced on me. The bus rolled out of the station on time without them.

♥

The rest of the trip I kept to myself. A day later, the bus arrived at Union Bus Station in Oklahoma City. I didn't see Brad anywhere. As I waited to get my second backpack from the storage under the bus, the change in temperature began to blitz my body. I saw clear white heat oozing off the asphalt and back toward the sun. With both my knapsacks, I walked away and scanned my surroundings. Everyone noticed me. My East Coast street-punk attire stuck out in this cowpoke town. In the middle of downtown Oklahoma City, every homeless person, drug addict, and criminal seemed to hang out around the bus station.

I had been in some rough places before, but this was a rustler paradise. Old men weakened without love. Hard-luck cowboys roamed the streets. Jehovah's Witnesses tried to save someone's soul. A Native American, who stood between six foot and six foot four, watched my every movement. The heat overwhelmed my senses, and my pores let everyone around me know I was new fish to the city's cesspool. I got lost in the surreal mixture of desperados and vagrants, and the withered hope in their sun-dried eyes. I saw their choices slowly strangling them into nothingness, the homeless of Oklahoma City.

Out of the blue, some fool decided to rob the corner store. Within minutes, four Oklahoma City police cruisers showed up outside the establishment with their red, yellow, and white lights and shrieking sirens full-bore. I pulled out a cigarette and lit it up. Against the bus station wall, the unexpected opportunity captured my mind, as the outlaw was in a standoff with the police. In his act of desperation, I saw a childlike man muffled into silence as they placed cuffs on him.

Oklahoma City's finest got their man. I was in the middle of the Wild, Wild West. My world was reduced to a single thought as multiple street people passed before me. My invincibility was lost somewhere on the highway between Hartford, Connecticut, and Oklahoma City. Unnaturally absent, my mind was infinite, equal, and pure. The clarity of my awakening revealed the youth of my eternal heart and my graying soul. I had no

Out of the FIELD

intention of ever going back to Connecticut.

Just as I finished my cigarette, Brad and his buddy drove up in a black Chevy pickup truck with mag wheels.

"Where the fuck have you been?"

"I had to wait for Craig. Larry, this is Craig, and he is always late for everything," Brad chuckled.

Craig said, "So you're Jake's friend from Connecticut. I hope you're not a partying lightweight like him."

"No, I'm a functional blackout."

Everyone laughed.

As I looked at the truck's bed, it was covered with beer cans. I threw my backpack without my dope in the back of the truck. We drove around Oklahoma City getting wasted and listening to heavy metal music. Brad dropped us off at his father's apartment.

As soon as Brad opened the door, a massive cloud of pot smoke escaped the apartment. It rushed by me and into the freedom of the invading light trying to breathe. Brad's father was home doing bong hits and watching Three Stooges reruns all day. My mind flashed back to my old man's house. Although they were entirely different human beings, they had to escape the boredom their lives. They both lacked art, culture, family pictures, and furniture.

Brad turned to his father, who was in the middle of kissing the bong and said, "Dad, this is Larry, my friend from Connecticut."

Brad's father turned his glazed red eyes in my direction, and he handed me the bong while blowing out a huge hit of smoke into the room.

I took the bong and sucked down a huge hit of Oklahoma Skunk Weed. It was dry and almost made my mouth bleed. As I wrestled the severity of its taste, my suffocating lungs fought off my desire to choke.

As the bowl played out, I reached into my backpack and pulled out my ounce bag of Columbian Gold. I filled the pipe with a choice bud and handed it to his father to take the first hit. He lit it up and passed it to Brad. As his father exhaled, he said, "Not bad! It's as good as some of the Mexican weed I can get from Dallas for twenty-five bucks."

"Okay, he's a dumb Okie," I thought to myself as I tossed him an ounce of weed. "Thanks for letting me stay here for a bit until I get settled."

He said nothing and took another bong hit. He stared at the idiot box. He never seemed quite real to me. A zombie high, he appeared to live in the haze of a moment suspended in time forever.

Brad and I went upstairs into his room. The next order of business was to sell about twelve small ounce-bags of weed. I needed some cash for the trip to Texas. Brad made a few phone calls, and by the end of the first day, we sold eight ounce-bags. Word got around fast, and the phone rang off the wall. Everyone wanted the dope I packed in from Connecticut. I made a tidy profit selling three finger bags for forty dollars. I bought myself PCP to celebrate my newfound freedom.

♥

After a few days in Oklahoma, I met Vern, who went to high school with both Brad and Jake. He was the one driving us to Dallas. The Texas Jam was a huge rock concert, and 80,000 rock-and-roll fans went there to party with seven bands: Blue Oyster Cult, Heart, Van Halen, Nazareth, Sammy Hagar, and TKO. I already was blitzed when our wheels headed south on I-35 to Dallas. I took a catnap in the middle of a three-day high. I drank massive amounts of alcohol and smoked enough dust-laced weed to make a rhino's knees wobble. I could never have just one drink. A social drinker never wants to find the edge. Each high was Magellan's voyage into the unknown. Explore, explore, I wanted more until I reached the sun! I didn't care if I died along the way. My life made perfect sense to me.

I woke up around Paul's Valley and dropped a hit of acid. I downed a few Little Kings and found myself lost drifting in the corridors of my mind. I reached belief mortally traveling among the stars in the Southern sky without wings.

Once we found the Cotton Bowl, a marine layer of pot smoke oozed around our automobile. It was the biggest damn party I've ever seen. I was coming back into focus as we tried to find a parking spot. Once Vern stopped the car, Brad opened the door, and the sounds, aromas, and feelings from the crowd overwhelmed my senses. I had surrounded myself with other misfits of society.

The Cotton Bowl parking lot was a drug addict's paradise. A child in a candy store, I looked out the car window and said, "Holy shit! Look at all those corn-fed Southerners."

Vern snapped back, "Watch yourself here! Some of these Texas motherfuckers don't play around and still think the Civil War isn't over with."

Out of the **FIELD**

"Hey Vern and Brad, I have to go pee." I paused and looked around and said, "I'll be back in twenty minutes."

Brad replied, "We won't wait forever, so don't you get lost."

I nodded solemnly and walked away looked for a place to pee. Drugs made me ADHD, and I always wandered off-task. I partied with every petty-crime schemer and day-tripper. I skipped along the fallen night sky with no remorse in my eyes. The world kept getting smaller and darker. I traveled through the black hole of time and space. I even tried to steal the tri-colored gold stars outside the gates of heaven. Nothing could satisfy my soul. Life's natural colors darkened, danced, drifted, and streamed within my mind's eye as I raced toward the sun to find God, and like Icarus, I fell back to earth too soon.

I refused to slow down. Rushing, a storm inside drove me. I awoke beside someone's car and found my senses scattered at various points in the parking lot. Staggering around picking up the pieces of myself, a stranger doing bong hits entered my eyesight. "Hey dude, I lost my buds. I have a violent hangover. I appreciate a hit or two if you can spare it."

As he handed me the bong, he said, "From your accent, you're not from here. Where you from?"

My mouth opened in protest and inhaled a huge hit, and I suddenly was lifted out of my hangover. It was my favorite—pot laced with PCP. Reeling inside of me, I couldn't stop and smiled at the darkness as it smiled back at me. I said, "Good shit! Connecticut."

He smiled, and I saw nothing mattered in his eyes.

He offered me another hit, and the "High Life" kept going. Spacing out in the parking lot, I saw both Vern and Brad a hundred yards, or miles, away. I took one more hit of rocket fuel and blasted off to get to my friends. I looked at the stranger and said, "Thanks, man!"

I walked up to them and said, "It's about time you Okies started partying. I got my second wind, so let's roll."

Brad asked, "Where the fuck have you been?"

I smiled as I responded, "Somewhere between Earth and Mars."

"Here's your ticket, smart-ass."

We headed toward the gates. Along the way, I bought a few beers from someone to christen my eyes with the birth of a new day. I resurrected myself from my crucifying hangover. Teenage wasteland, I was a drug enthusiast, and every day, my mind entered a flying machine. I wished to avail myself beyond all the theories of society and the shoddiness of the human heart. I achieved the impossible with no one ever watching.

In the subculture of self, I found 80,000 other misfits from society standing in line with me. We didn't care what anyone thought. We lived in the moment and wasted the day away. I was fugitive standing alone in both rage and boredom. Marvelously, my mind was out of this universe and danced from star to star at the Texas Jam 1979.

♥

The day after the Jam we headed off to Corpus Christi. Along the way, Vern wanted to stop by Waco to see a girl he once knew. As we drove around town looking for a motel, I noticed a truck following us. In a concerned voice, I said, "Holy shit! Those assholes are following us. What the fuck did you do, Vern?"

"I broke their little sister's heart."

Instead of cutting loose, Vern pulled over and got a room. I guess he didn't want to look soft. As we drove around that day, the pickup truck had multiplied by three. A quick count made it eight against three. Texas Justice, the long arm of its homemade bylaws made me feel vulnerable.

Being a Yankee in Texas, I told Vern, "Hey, let's roll out of here after they fall asleep in their truck. I don't have a good feeling about this town."

"You're probably right, Larry."

Brad responded, "I agree."

We never took anything out of the car, so we were already packed. Time seemed to creep by until those boys fell asleep. It was somewhere around three a.m. when we pushed the car out into the street and started it. We headed south on I-35 to Corpus Christi.

We skipped out of town in the blackness of the night. About two hours later, Vern fell asleep and drove into a cornfield alongside the highway. I awoke to my head hitting the ceiling and screamed, "What the fuck!"

Vern answered, "I am tired."

We decided to pull over at a rest stop and get some sleep before beginning our voyage. We spent a couple of days getting drunk and high in south Texas. I wasn't a slave to time and lived without virtue. I slept fine alongside the open road. My life pretended nothing, and I existed only to amuse myself. Each day, I became an entertainer, a vagrant, an artist, a

Out of the FIELD

thief, and an atheist.

♥

After we had arrived back in Oklahoma City, I started to look for work. I landed a job shoveling cement all day in hundred-degree heat. After working four days straight, I was aware this job was too simple for me. The weather was too hot, and the work too labor-intensive. I knew they would do fine without me, so I drank myself into a stupor to quit.

The day I met Mace, one of Brad's friends, I chose burglary as my new profession. In my present state of mind, I liked the excitement of high risk and high reward. Opportunity knocked one day. Mace and I studied our marks until we both felt comfortable. We broke into a few drug dealers' homes. We both noticed it had to be either Tuesday or Wednesday. The middle of the week was when they made themselves vulnerable. They ran their errands those days, and they couldn't take their dope with them.

Each time, Mace stole a car. He'd let me out, and I walked up to the dealer's house. I rang the doorbell to see if anyone was home, or to see if they had a dog. Once I knew no one was home, I lit a cigarette and became the lookout on the opposite side of the street. Mace walked toward the front door and hopped over the fence. He broke a window and ransacked the house until he found the stash.

Mace knew most of the dealers in the city, and we picked off the stupid ones. We scored weed, mescaline, amphetamines, and barbiturates, and he fenced it out of town so no one would suspect us. The lure of fast cash and an endless high was the only way I knew how to make a living.

♥

All good things must come to an end, and after six weeks of living off Brad's family, I finally managed to land a job as a janitor in a nursing home. It was about a mile from the apartment. I hadn't yet received my first paycheck when Brad pulled me aside one evening about eight o'clock, and he told me, "My parents would like you to find another place to stay tonight."

Brad tried to ignore me when I asked why.

"It's complicated."

"Yeah!" I added. "And where am I going to go?"

He stared down at the ground and knew I had nowhere to go. Orphaned into silence, I had been homeless once before, but this time, I was an outsider in a strange land and didn't know anyone here. In the frightful laugh of an idiot, I snickered to hide my emotions. I replied, "Sure man. Not a fucking problem."

As I placed all my earthly possessions into my two backpacks, I found something inside of me, and it undoubtedly was my miraculous heart. It beat faster to let me know I wasn't alone, and it began to comfort my mind with the memories of the sweet stupidities I had already overcome. I climbed down inside of myself and found a superhuman strength. As I walked out the door into my death sentence, the blackness of the world opened its hand and swallowed me whole. I pushed it back with my harsh, cutting smile. The hard road of my life led to this day, and I wouldn't bow down to it. I wouldn't let the world make me weep. I spat on the ground beneath my feet and walked toward Britton Road.

With each step, my thoughts changed and reformed. As I crashed head-on into the blackness of the night, I knew my survival was a jigsaw puzzle. By the moon's light, I saw all the pieces of the puzzle were black. Sequestered from humanity, I grasped for answers and solutions to make it to the next minute. Like everything predestined, the events began to manage themselves. I always found the will to survive when I rummaged around in the attic of my mind.

The tragedy of my life let me feel each dying second. The feelings that accompany loss gravitated toward me. My Night School Graduate Degree gave me faith in my own abilities. It offered me a unique view of the world. I kept things in perspective as they pissed me off and opened my mind to look for the answer.

I recalled a field across from the apartment complex near the corner of Britton Road and Rockwell. Its image inside my head was a respite on the eternal quest to suffocate the impending thoughts of hopelessness. The field was concealed from the road by a row of pine trees, and another row of pine trees slanted downward on both sides of the area toward the lake. I found a place to make my stand against the encroaching world. Steady with the sternness of a great warrior, I walked across the street and made my claim to the field. In the middle of the careless city's urban sprawl, I looked out upon the moon's light bouncing off the water. Society seemed so empty, bare, and cold. I was an orphan to the world and not a thought

Out of the FIELD

in anyone's mind.

I put my knapsacks under a tree and began to ponder on the things I needed to survive. My childhood gave me the ability to think straight and not let stress overcome me. My former life benefited me in the current situation, for the skills I acquired as a youth were lifesaving. Standing alone in my mind, I recalled the location of a threefold lawn chair and ran back across the street and stole it. I went back and took several towels for my bedding. My instincts whispered, "Trust me."

As I sat down and gazed at the starry night's sky, I didn't think of anything at all and listened to the stunning sounds of endless life moving around me. Throughout the evening, the echoes from automobiles, semitrucks, dogs, and people's voices were tumbling through the air. Extraordinary, my senses sharpened instantly, and I mused on crime, hunger, peace, and love. I respected the strangeness of my thoughts, and I drifted between the cold shadows martyred by time and the echoes resounding in the air. I floated in the undercurrent of the night in day one in the field.

I awoke to the sun's golden rays caressing my face, and the birds chirped a song for me. I checked my watch and had plenty of time to get to work. I walked about a mile to my job and went to the back door. I didn't want anyone to see my scruffy appearance. A ghostly presence overcame me, and I was invisible to the world once again. At the back of the facility, I cleaned myself up and wiped the homeless look off my face. Looking in the mirror, I got ready to play my part. Denial fed my desire and covered the vagrant.

I began to pillage everything needed to survive and commandeered sheets, blankets, a flashlight, and batteries. I stole an alarm clock from an elderly woman who just talked to the wall all day. I put everything in a trash bag and marked it with a looping "L." At the end of my shift, I took the trash out to the dumpster and put my bag on top.

Finding the bag in the dark would be easy. I passed the time by getting something to eat and drink. I walked over to the wall overlooking Lake Hefner and smoked a few bowls of weed. The mirroring effects of the sun fostered its reflection upwards to heaven. I thought and felt the silent answers inside of me. My life was a poem I hadn't yet written. I fed off the powerlessness of decadence, for I didn't mind stealing my daily bread. I watched the skyline gray into darkness. I dreamed, once again, of a revolution in morals without strings attached. I achieved the stillness of enlightenment for one brief second before reality kicked me in the teeth.

Night fell, and I fought hopelessness by planning the next day's mission. I walked by work to gather my loot and stumbled back to my field. Once there, I organized my camp like a child arranged his room. Sheets were placed across my folding lawn chair. A blanket was made into a pillow. After working all day, sitting in the sun for hours, I was hot and sticky and changed into my shorts and grabbed a bar of soap. I walked across the street under cover of darkness and jumped into the apartment complex's swimming pool.

I thought and found the actual meaning of misery, and against its invading force, I remained alive.

♥

Day after day, I defended my foothold against reality's smothering hand. I walked over the same old ground and kicked the same old can down the road. I looked for a lucky penny to change my fate. I never surrendered and did whatever it took to make it to the next day. I ate the meals left in patients' rooms, for I knew which patients the nurses believed were unstable.

I walked by a few times and heard the patient arguing with the nurse, "Nurse, I am hungry! I want to eat my dinner."

"Well, Ms. Cousins, you ate everything on your tray. In fact, I am very proud of you today, for you ate everything on your plate. I will get you some crackers to nibble on until morning."

"I don't want crackers! I want my fucking dinner, Missy," Ms. Cousins said.

I was remorseful for my action, but my hunger pains drove me to act. I hadn't eaten in a day in a half. A few times, I even ate the patients' leftovers off their trays. I wasn't a prisoner of someone else's reason or conscience. With no thoughts of God or morals, I lived like an animal and stole everything I needed to survive. Uninterrupted by day or night, time didn't matter anymore, for nothing ever changed. Today was tomorrow. Yesterday was today. The purity of my suffering made me shrewd and crafty. I reached the darkest region in a human soul and couldn't turn around.

Manufactured out of my family's treason, my survival wasn't a matter of chance. My life wasn't subdued by happiness or things. Sorrow opened my eyes to see humanity as cruel and self-serving. Life has no meaning

Out of the FIELD

without experiences. It was in the silence of the world I discovered my voice. Words not yet learned. Knowledge not yet understood. Prose not yet written. I was acutely aware of the odds stacked against me and marched onward as a thief with many faces. I had no obligation to be part of mankind and meandered on the open road of life. I saw everything everyone took for granted.

I took a bath in a pool every night. I washed and dried my clothes in the apartment complex's machines. Window shopping, someone else's dryer afforded me a new shirt or pair of jeans to wear. A hunter and gatherer, I prowled around the night like a coyote in the evening. A criminal lurked in the shadows waiting to commit a crime. The only downside to my camp was that it was in the center of a white middle-class neighborhood. A homeless drug fiend tended to get the middle class uptight and trigger a massive fear reaction. My life was a covert operation, and I viewed everyone in the world as traitors and liars. Earthly damnation stalked my every move. I lived in a densely populated urban environment and had evaded all human contact.

My instincts gave me eyes in the back of my head. The universe didn't play fair. My soul sensed what I couldn't see. I pushed my cart around the aisles of the grocery stores like any other shopper. Night School readied me to survive. I moved into position, avoiding the eye in the sky, the manager's office. I woofed down lunch meat, milk, and Fig Newton cookies. Once full, I would put my waste in the trashcan near the restroom and always covered my tracks. Then, I would purchase a small item or two and disappear back into the darkness of my field.

♥

The nursing home was a treasure trove of opportunities for me. I stole from Alzheimer's patients and took any cash sitting around. I handpicked my thievery and made sure it couldn't be traced back to me. I thought five moves beyond my desires and gave everyone a quality impression of myself. A smile and kind words dupe everyone with the illusion all is safe. An impure heart scammed every angle so I could continue to get high. Desperately wicked, I refused to look in a mirror. I didn't want to see what I had become.

♥

Every Saturday morning, I had to stand in the bank's drive-through line to cash my check. I felt the horror of my life through other people's eyes. My hair was long and scruffy. I just woke up from an alcohol-induced binge—short-term insanity to escape my mundane fate. I waited on foot behind several cars and saw people look at me and then look away. I remembered this feeling from my childhood. I read their thoughts before the utterance of the words expressed. People respected those who were beautiful, smart, and had added value to their lives. I was foul and rotten, and they pretended not to see me. I waited in line behind their classy automobiles. They sat in their air-conditioned vehicles without a care in the world. The temperature exceeded ninety-five degrees. As my body tried to cool itself, I climbed down into myself to escape social judgment.

An island in the sun, I was the only one in this world and crawled deeper into the anxiety of poverty. Paranoid and delusional, I heard their voices through car windows. It could be a flashback from the blotter acid I took a few days back. Hallucination or reality, I stood there in thought and smiled. As my island boiled under the sun, I read a bumper sticker on the back of one vehicle, and it proclaimed "Jesus is coming soon."

In the name of destiny, I could see the flames of hell rise off the asphalt, and I burned in my hell. Until the teller asked me, "How are you today?"

I nodded as my body resisted talking. I felt dizzy and needed alcohol. I managed to mumble, "I need to cash a check."

"Would you like to open an account?"

"No thanks, I am passing through this town."

♥

After every payday, I hitchhiked to Stars and Stripes Park to buy some drugs or party with complete strangers. On my days off, I sat beside my bathtub (the pool) scribbled poems and got high. I sat back and observed all the dandies and peacocks illustrating their vanity. Vanity talk about themselves. People loved to discuss their lives like they are living the dream. I traveled between and around every word they said to pass my time.

My thoughts weren't a slave to orthodox views. The unconditional love in my heart tried to fight the cruelty of silence, and the stillness of

Out of the FIELD

oppression slowly broke me down. I lived in a field and saw no way out. I roasted beneath the sun. The dust of the earth covered me while I slept. I pretended each hour someone was going to rescue me, and it kept hope flourishing. At eighteen years old, the silence of the world encircled me. Half agony and half hope, I thought.

Alive for some reason, I didn't have to believe in hell and lived in it every day. I saw the vision of justice and love was for honorable men who maintained their neutrality. For five-plus weeks, the field was my home. Sometimes, I closed my eyes to have a moment of peace. A homeless drug addict, the shutters of my eyes rose and fell at the mindless cruelties life handed me. The splendors of my magnificent soul had to fight for the nothingness of my life.

♥

One day, the weather moved in while I slept. Two fronts collided and the scent of clean air was the calm before the storm. Suddenly without warning, raindrops the size of dimes fell from the sky. My eyes opened quickly as the ocean fell from the heavens. My thoughts were pinned down for a moment.

Someone forgot to turn off the faucet. A flash flood raced down toward the lake. Chain lightning blasted! Rain pelted a thousand times a second, and a bolt of lightning hit near my camp. My feet ran first, and my mind had to catch up. Barefoot and half-naked, I remembered an uninhabited part of the apartment compound. I found a wood gate and kicked it open. I huddled my half-naked body next to the door under the overhang. I shivered to stay warm and began to crack inside. The energy of the storm lasted for an eternity, almost a day.

After the sky had become blue and the air was washed fresh, I walked back to my field. Everything was soaked and covered in red mud. I had suffered to the brink of madness and fell into the loneliest moment of my life. I stood alone on the moon and looked back at civilization. It was 238,857 miles away. I could do nothing but swallow the eternal damnation life gave me. I was no longer a hero in my eyes. Like a pig in the mud, I remitted my soul beyond this universe, and in my expression of humility, I resurrected the belief in a childhood God. In the act of pure desperation, I fell to my knees, bowed my head, and prayed to a God I shunned for mercy or death.

♥

On the merry-go-round ride in my mind, I rode a dark horse named Doubt to the point where pain ends, and faith begins. God opened the sky and released a thunderstorm to humble me. It opened my heart beyond my suffering and shame. No other force could have brought me to my knees, and the miracle began. My prayer allowed me to release my rage. With each word gracefully expressed, I gave God everything. Prayer was the only thing I hadn't tried yet. As I grappled in my hell, I began to tinker with the thoughts of God, and the seed planted as a child began to grow. With my barroom red eyes, I saw the incomprehensible universe of God's grace flow all around me. Each breath I stole released the contradiction within me, and it humbled me and caused me to open my hand. He brought comfort down to my side, and I began to cry.

Covered in red mud from head to toe, I focused on the task of cleaning up my camp. Everything was wet and started to dry from the heat of the sun. All my sheets and blankets were covered in muck. My encampment was basically ruined by the flash flood. I focused on rebuilding my home and not on the impossible. The next day, I stole some more sheets, blankets, and trash bags to keep my things dry. I went shopping in the apartment's dryers for some new clothes. As I walked back to my field, I couldn't help feeling the battle for my soul.

♥

There was no service manual for me to follow, so I walked blindly beyond my moral malaise. On the way home, I noticed for the first time the North MacArthur Church of Christ. It was across the street from my work. From my perspective, I understood the basics of both God and Jesus, but I always liked to tinker with mechanical parts of thought until there was nothing left to discover. The chamber inside my heart was unlocked, and my heart opened up to God. The next day, God determined my steps and moved me to go inside the church. I opened the door and met an extraordinary witness of a man named Jesus. The church's secretary introduced herself, "Hi, my name is Janice. How may I help you?"

I looked around at the modest setting of her office. She had a picture of her family on her desk and an assortment of papers. I glanced at her and said, "I would like to talk to someone about God."

She looked me in the eye and asked, "May I ask your name?"

For a millisecond our eyes met before I replied, "Larry, my name is Larry."

"Please wait for a second, Larry. I'll see if the minister has a few minutes for you."

Reading her gestures, she felt uneasy about my scruffy appearance, but she went into his office. She came out about a minute later to usher me into his office, and she said, "Larry, this is Minister Layton."

He reached his hand out for me to shake and said, "It's nice to meet you, Larry. Why don't you come to my office and let me know what is on your mind?"

I smirked and answered, "Nice to meet you, too."

As I walked into his office, his desk was at the back of the room with two chairs in front of it. The bookcase had many books and an assortment of his kid's pictures. Minister Layton said, "Please take a seat and tell me what I can do for you, young man."

"I've come on some rough times and have lived in a field close to six weeks now. I survived only by my wits and have no family or friends. I am from Connecticut. The monsoon the other day wiped out my camp. The only thing I could do was pray, and for some strange reason, I'm sitting here. I peruse life around me every day, so why does God let me live in a field?"

The pastor's eyes almost popped out of his head. He rummaged in his mind for words to say to me. After a long pause, he said, "The Bible is bestowed to us by God, and Jesus died for our salvation. Have you read your Bible and prayed with all your heart, son? The answer will come to you."

I looked in the eye and thought, I have seen your kind my whole life. You're the ones who can't see me.

"I do not have a Bible, sir."

He opened a drawer and handed me a twenty-dollar bill and a blue King James pocket Bible. He proclaimed, "I am late for a meeting, but I suggest you get a room and call your family back in Connecticut. It was a pleasure to meet you, and may God bless you, Larry."

"Yeah, I guess there's no other choice."

As I walked out of that church, my mind sank somewhere beyond the sinkhole, past the roots of the pinyon pine trees. A boy lost forever, I laughed at the Big Man in the sky. I thought, not yet. I've still got some fight left in me.

As I strolled out of the church, I hitched hiked down to 39th and May to a motel. No one picked me up, so I walked eight miles in the sun. Strange thoughts came and went through my mind. I had just won a consolation prize, a one-night stay in a cockroach motel. I didn't know God and didn't think much of Him either. I wondered if my life was mine to live.

I paid for a room and took a thirty-minute shower. After that, I walked over to the liquor store and bought two six-packs of beer. Sitting outside in a chair, I watched the sun set. My mind flashed a thought about a man named Jesus. I toasted Him. Forget about me, I couldn't help but think, look what the silly human race did to Him. I didn't stand a fucking chance.

My mind attached a string to every desire as I lived at the edge of madness. Compassion had lost its foothold in humanity. Among the dark shadows of mankind, I existed like an animal, and in the darkness of my sin, my only thoughts that night were under the influence of Jesus, who could free a man's soul. Strange ideas like this made me nervous. Maybe it meant something, perhaps it didn't. I was a dead man walking. In the long run, I just got high to forget things for a while.

♥

The next morning, I had a mild hangover, and the unkindness of the world led me right back to my field. I walked by houses, golf courses, and businesses, and I saw the great American dream. Life with sunglasses, flowers in front of the house, and a consciousness of the comfort only abundance can bring. From my vantage point, I viewed the world and everyone who lived in it as terrible liars. I shook my head, dumbfounded, and said, "What do you want from me?"

Back in my field, the temperature reached nearly a hundred degrees. The heat was my mortal enemy. It attacked me relentlessly from every angle. I sat in my chair overlooking the lake and listened to myself inhale and exhale. Aloof from my soul, I couldn't even recognize myself. A smile hid my pain, and I waited for the Assassin to come. At the edge of life, suicide became a reality. The thought was a means to an end, for I could see no way out of here. I played my part and took my chances. Life just didn't work out for me. I wrote these words in my notebook, "Born to live and born to die. Born to live for what reason why?"

Out of the FIELD

Abruptly, my thoughts were broken up by the sounds of children's laughter in the yard next door. I looked down the hill, through the trees and saw a family moving into their new home. I watched the mother chasing her children around their large yard. They rolled around in the grass, and their smiles were as bright as the sun. Their laughter seeped through the cracks of my sun-dried skin, and it brought loving memories of my mother.

My broken thoughts sailed away on the gentle breeze of change. I opened my mind and became restlessly bored. I reached into my backpack and pulled out my Bible. My beautiful eyes were enlightened, and I twisted the key with each word read. I opened the door with each page turned. The beauty of Christ's words touched my soul, and I stood in the breezeway between two worlds. The impossible seemed so small next to my beating heart.

Spontaneously, my spirit soared upward on the wings of grace. I could see no way out of my fate. Sacred to my senses, worthy of my trust, my heart felt something I couldn't describe. Time stood still as illusions dulled into the twilight. I had to sit and listen to my angelic instincts. I had no choice, for the light from a thousand stained-glass windows, radiated through my soul. I stood and looked for something to observe. Nothing was within view, so I closed my eyes and tried to hide within the barriers of self. I clung tightly to the banishment of the shame, for I had been its prisoner my whole life. Thrown away by both my family and society, I lived in a field and felt the presence of God silently examine my heart.

In a phenomenon, the clandestine was exposed. I was another in the eyes of God, and the scenery of this world was just an illusion, a moment in time. I began to awake, beyond no reasonable hope. I extended and strained every one of my senses. My poet's eye captured a realm of freedom beyond the control of this world. The liberty of God's loving grace made me feel noble and whole.

Detached from the bitter damnation of the war, I continue to fight. I experienced the light from the moon and stars. I got down on my knees and prayed. My heart opened to the distinction between the past, present, and future. I searched with my mind's eyes until I found my face, behind my many faces. No greater miracle could have taken place, for, in an instant, my soul was enlightened beyond this world, and my empty silhouette filled with hope. I cried and struggled to breathe. Tears rolled down my face. God showed me the beauty inside my heart. I cherished where the moon's light collided with the air, for it was there that reality put illusion to death. I could see the other world where I journeyed to.

As the evening passed, I fell asleep with the thought of God in my head. While my eyes were shut, I stretched a rope from star to star looking for Him throughout the night. My mind wandered in search of more. My inner soul brimmed with passion and excitement. In the ugliness of the world, my dreams let me see grace didn't discriminate. It was the light in a human heart. I awoke the next morning to sounds of birds chirping and the sun warming my face. I was so much more, and my dreams christened me into another.

I rubbed my eyes open and smiled at those thoughts deposited in my mind. As I immersed myself back into survival mode, my mind snapped back, and it believed I was under attack by God. I mumbled to myself, "Creeping Jesus snooped around my camp. O, MY GOD! He's going to evict me. I need some more drugs."

I fumbled around with my pipe and smoked a bowl to calm my nerves and talked to myself, "Why would I follow You? I'm hungry and need to eat! Let see, the dumb clerk in this store is working now, easy score."

My enlightenment didn't last long, and I fell back into my thieving ways. My moment with God was a passing aberration, and my physical and mental strength was exhausted.

Last night while I slept, I dreamed what a marvelous error! I broke out of my heart. By now, there were signs I was losing control of the situation. I had lived in my field for over six weeks. The yellow moon rose each night, and August's heat wave strangled me slowly. With no need, I sat in my field, and in its great design, my eyes became vacant and blind. Each evening, I walked around the strip malls and perused other people's lives. I lit a cigarette and let each manic notion pass into another. Reality looked at me and never blinked. I tricked my mind into believing I had a sliver of hope in my pocket. I hung on to something and dishonored my fatal incompetence by not surrendering.

Pain and suffering showed me who I was. Helplessly, I started to write my suicide note, but I had no one to leave it to.

I once read in a textbook on survival, instinct tells you to stay put and wait for help to come. I took life's best shot on the chin. The love in my heart gave me the courage to hang on to nothing. Silence opened my heart to hear the voice of God. Death stalked me, but I doubled back to hide

Out of the FIELD

my trail. I kept opening my mind to something greater than myself. It was unlike anything the human mind could imagine. It only existed if you owned your soul. It was powerful, yet it was meek. It drove scientists mad, for it couldn't be defined by them. It contrasted all earthly reason and fact. It couldn't be manufactured in a bottle or sold for a profit. I gave into the thought of God's loving mercy. I honestly wished I was lying when I did so. My heart reached out beyond the burden of proof and pulled faith's string. Ten thousand church bells in heaven rang. I must have been something for God to observe. Faith was all I had left in this world when I said, "God, please have mercy on my soul."

9
Love Rescued Me

God didn't hesitate and put His rescue plan into action. He didn't send a legion of angels to save me. He sent a legion of chiggers to feed and live off my body. One by one, those pesky little creatures bit and irritated my skin with a red rash. Day by day, the chigger siege stripped me on my invincibility. Dumbfounded, I had no earthly idea what they were. God's infectious mercy hit me like a plague.

Then, one day my supervisor asked me, "How did you get all those chigger bites on your face?"

Shame made me look down at the floor. I replied, "I have been living in a field for over seven weeks now. How do I get rid of these things?"

Shocked! Despite all the false faces, we all wear every day, she couldn't hide her humanity for another being. She said, "I think you should contact a church, for they might be able to help you."

After work, I hitchhiked a few miles to a supermarket to steal my dinner and walked back home. Sitting in my lawn chair, gazing out at the stars, I was drinking Big Gulp rum and coke and had a nice buzz. I blazed up my last joint. Around ten p.m., my friend Mace drove up and parked alongside Britton Road in a stolen black Trans Am. It had a Firebird on its hood. This happened to be my dream car.

The car door shut, and he yelled, "Larry."

I recognized his voice and yelled, "Over here, Mace."

Within a few seconds, he walked up the hill and into my camp. He looked around and asked, "Is this where you live?"

"Yep, this is my waterfront condo. Each evening, I get high and fall asleep under the stars. I have no place else to go."

He lit a joint and asked, "How long?"

"I have kind of lost track, but it is over seven weeks now."

A criminal's smile covered his face as he said, "This is your lucky day. I just stole this Trans Am, and I'm heading to Connecticut to see Jake. Brad told me you might still be living here. I want you to drive back with me. Do you want to go?"

I thought of my family. Bastards all of them!

Mace was pure evil, and I lied to him, "I am moving in with a friend from work in a few days. I already paid my money, so I'm going to pass."

"Come on man! Don't be a pansy. It is a long drive. You know Jake would love to see you! He will break out the premium gold when you get back home. You know, he is a big-time dealer, now!"

My mind walked backward without falling. Temptation let me see the future without having to live it. Solemn and majestic, I saw the splendors in wandering the earth alone without a home.

"It's not going to happen. I'm staying."

Mace fired back, "What the fuck, man? You live in a field."

"I am staying right here. Things are going to turn around for me soon. I am moving in with a friend in a few days."

Frustrated and committed, Mace continued to badger me to go back to Connecticut with him. "Come on man, I have some acid for the trip. You're living in a field, and you could be staying with friends when you get back there. You have a one-way ticket back home right in front of you."

I stood my ground, and Mace drove off into the darkness.

I pondered the word, home. I knew Connecticut wasn't my home anymore with no one there I could count on, my family didn't serve me well as a child. Standing between temptation and homelessness, I picked the one that had the least chance to fail me. A simple lie kept me from an error so grave.

The path was set, and I was the last one to know what destiny held for me. Neither a servant nor a slave, I obeyed my heart and knew my family would never change, so I chose to make my stand in a field.

♥

My heart traffics in feelings, not in deep thoughts. Common sense isn't life in the fast lane. My silent thoughts were overheard by God. I didn't belong to anyone, and that's a shame most people will never know. My past shadowed my actions. My current demeanor was "Finish me and be done with it."

The future days of my life were written without me knowing. I believed in miracles, and they were scathing comebacks. My footsteps weren't mine, and they marched over to North MacArthur Church of Christ again. The state of comparison with others ceased to exist in the eyes of God. I opened the door and walked into Janice's office. She was sitting at her desk and said, "Hi, Larry. What can I do for you?"

A voice spoke for me, for I had forgotten how to speak and the meaning of words, "I would like to give the pastor back his money."

I looked at Janice for only a millisecond. I was stunningly ugly, broken, and lost.

Her voice cracked nervously as she asked me, "Are you still living in the field?"

Young in years, weathered hard by the world, I ignored her, but the Spirit of life spoke for me, "Yes, over seven weeks now."

She didn't swear, but her eyes said, "Holy shit!"

There was neither happiness nor misery at that moment someone recognized me as a human being. I was no longer invisible, for God did what I couldn't do for myself. Conversing was even strange by now.

Janice looked at me from head to toe and said, "Please pardon me for a minute," as she stepped into the pastor's office.

In the background, I heard her talking on the phone. After about five minutes passed, she came back and asked me, "Larry, are you using any drugs?"

Of course, I lied to her and said, "No, I'm not doing any drugs."

After all, I just smoked my last joint last night, so I was clean and sober for eight hours by now. That was a lifetime to me.

Christianity is a blue-collar faith. The Deaton's workman-like approach made all men equal, and they knew in the eyes of God, a poor man was a mighty prince. Jesus stripped away my pride. I trusted my instincts and wasn't afraid to believe in the miracle at my feet. Jesus offered me love before I could love myself. Counted as nothing, I stood before both God and Janice a homeless teenager thrown away by the world. Living in my shame, I wondered why God spared my life.

In a Christ-like action, Janice's single act of kindness not only saved my life, but it helped me find my way back from the edge of humanity. My living hell miraculously disappeared right in front of my eyes. I sensed the surreal spiritual movements whisk all around me.

Out of the FIELD

Janice drove me back to my field, and I retrieved my things. As I stared out the window of the automobile, I remembered the lie I told Mace, and the fortunes the day brought a smile to my face. As we got close to the apartment complex, I told her, "Pull in here, and I'll get my things."

"Sure thing."

I got out of the car and ran up the hill to retrieve my garbage bags filled with mildewed clothes. I stopped for a second and stared out over the lake. The whispering wind brought my poet's eye to see the hand of God. I felt Him close to me. He who views all was watching from afar. Through the air so crisp and clear, I simply got lost in the miracle itself. Without a noise, I smiled and nodded at Him.

♥

After we had picked up all my earthly possessions, we drove back to her house. It was a four-bedroom ranch home located in a nice middle-class suburb. The yard was mowed, the bushes trimmed, and an assortment of brightly colored flowers was placed perfectly around the front of the house.

Once I walked through the front door, I saw everything was neat, orderly, and family-oriented. The decoration of this household was mid-west contemporary. The colors matched the friendliness of their souls. That evening, I met Janice's husband, Gene, and her two children, Jody and David.

Each family member scanned my face carefully with their eyes. They had never seen a human being as broken-down as me. I smiled and commented, "I am real."

As we sat down for dinner, Gene said grace.

I picked up a fork and inspected it for several seconds. Everyone looked at me and wondered.

Janice asked, "Larry, is something wrong?"

I laughed and responded, "I don't remember the last time I used silverware. I use my hands to eat everything. May I have another glass of water?"

"Yes, you may, young man," Gene replied.

I stood and listened to the water pour out the faucet and heard the rushing current of life. I filled two glasses and drank them before returning to the table. I think my actions made everyone uncomfortable.

After dinner, Janice asked me, "Larry, do you want to take a bath?"

"I'll take a shower if you don't mind. That's how I roll."

"Sure thing. I'll wash all your clothes for you. Here is a pair of gym shorts and a t-shirt you can wear after your shower."

"Thank you," I said in a weak whisper.

After my shower, the whole family was watching television in the living room. Small chatter about everyone's day whisked into my ears. Janice interrupted everyone and asked, "Why don't you come over here and take off your shirt."

Once over there, I took off my shirt, and my malnourished body looked like one colossal acne scar. It must have had ten million chigger bites on it. One by one, Janice put nail polish on each red dot to kill them.

Their kindness made me uncomfortable. The conservative optimism of the middle classes freaked me the fuck out. An animal who couldn't sob in sorrow, I didn't talk to anyone and waited for them to ask me to leave. Everyone always did, it was only a matter of time.

♥

Throughout the next week, the ironic habits associated with being human came back to me. I slowly connected to eating twice a day and used silverware with each meal. In my white, box-shaped room, I slept on a mattress and stared at the ceiling until my eye collapsed. I missed the stars and the sounds of life evolving. My ears couldn't trust silence. Uncomfortable in my own skin, no one ever wanted me. I needed to fight back the tears I couldn't cry.

I forgot a few things, like flushing the toilet. I had to force myself to look people in the eye. I missed being high, but Jody gave me a quarter bag of weed. She probably had a Come-to-Jesus moment in her life. When everyone left the house, I got high! I wasn't very devoted. Loyalty almost killed me many times.

As I slowly opened up, Janice wanted me to call my uncle Burney, so I did one day. My millionaire uncle Burney answered the phone, "Hello."

I replied, "Hello, Uncle Burney. Janice wanted me to call you and tell you I was all right. I told her you wouldn't care, but she wouldn't listen to me. She doesn't know you like I know you."

"Who is Janice?"

"She was the lady that took me into her home after I lived in a field for nearly two months. She thought you might be worried about me."

His silence always made me feel unwanted, and this conversation was no different than any other one we had.

"Well then, let me speak to Janice."

I handed Janice the phone and walked out of the room. The frustration on her face told me everything. She didn't understand my uncle didn't care. I wanted to run back to my field, but God's grace pressed hard against me.

An act of kindness changed my heart forever. I spoke not a word to God, for there was too much at risk to get Him involved. I often thought charity would be the death of me. I didn't know why God saved my life, for I showed no promise to reform.

♥

Sunday came! I began to regret my decision to go to church with them before I strolled through the doors. Okay, God, I thought. I'm not getting baptized, repenting, or becoming a missionary for this man named Christ. I committed too many sins in my life, and their wisdom is all I have.

As I followed the Deaton's like a puppy dog, I looked at the blanked-out faces of the members of the church. Born with x-ray vision, I could read people's thoughts, and their eyes let me see they prayed for me. I felt like an animal in a zoo everyone wanted to see. My mind had a panic attack, and it screamed, "Get me the hell out of this place. All these people are the same!"

That day, as I listened to the sermon, my great sorrow made me understand we don't get to choose our lives. I really, really wanted to know what would happen if I fully trusted my instincts about God. Would it lead me to beauty, beyond bonfires of my ruins, and beyond the things of this world?

I stared into the air and looked for Him throughout. In His temple, I feared neither God nor man. My greatest advantage was I detached from everything earthly. With no country, no family, and no friends, I realized the streets were full of wicked men and idiots. There was no dishonor in being here, and I felt forgiveness awaited me, only if I could ask for it.

♥

With no money in my pocket, Janice and Gene helped me get set up in an apartment on 7th and MacArthur Avenue. My apartment was located near all the bars and strip clubs. That same week, Janice took me to the Goodwill store and let me pick from everyone's leftovers clothes and furniture.

Janice had no excuses, only results. I pieced together my very first home with an old bed, a table with no chairs, and a brand-new wardrobe of used clothes. On the cusp of being human, amidst the waking moments of clarity, I continued to search for the face of God each time someone gave me something. Day by day, the Deaton's commitment made me feel loved. The simplicity of their compassion began to reconcile my life. I learned to walk between two worlds and two Masters without suspicion or a conscience.

The darkness of my childhood made me feel inadequate. In the hopelessness of its surrender, the sensation of fear kept me a thief. I would do anything to have something. One day, Mace showed up at my door. Bad habits are hard to break. We continued to break into houses and businesses. We stole things, just to take things. It was a rush!

One time, Mace took a truck. He knew where I could get some chairs from an apartment complex. Everything went fine in the beginning. We broke in and stole an end table and three chairs. I got greedy and wanted two more chairs, so I walked back behind the building while Mace waited in the truck.

As I rounded the corner with two chairs in my hands, security rolled around the curve. Mace saw them and started the engine. I walked calmly to the truck and threw the chairs in the back. I jumped into the truck, and Mace peeled out. Security turned on its flashing lights and gave chase. While driving down the road, I climbed out of the window and hopped into the bed of the truck.

As their car approached our vehicle, I yelled, "Come get some!"

All in, I threw a chair in front of their vehicle. The security vehicle swerved and missed it, and they didn't give up the chase. I threw another chair at them. This time, they stopped. Three chairs were better than none.

Once we got back to the apartment, we unloaded our loot and ditched the truck. Mace said, "You're a wild man."

"Whatever it takes not to get caught."

♥

Out of the FIELD

Church services were on Sunday. I still smoked pot out of a bong and had watery eyes during the week. My existence still depended on what opportunity offered me. What does the eternity of damnation matter to someone who has nothing or has no future?

God wouldn't let my life sit on the discounted rack. I was still alive! With dried marijuana smoke in my hair, I continued to poison my body with drugs and alcohol. I didn't know the battle for my soul would be so brutal. The gnarled arms of reality kept the thoughts of Jesus creeping around my mind.

Every now and then, guilt started closing in around me. Not even the Son of God wanted to watch me anymore. Monstrous chemicals pushed the limits a human body could endure. I was so full of myself, but my heart belonged to God. I staggered into the church for free meals and made Jesus my legal counsel on October 31, 1979.

♥

A week later, Mace and I walked to the Red Dog Saloon. There was a bold, yellow-striped line between reality and oblivion, I just never saw it. Before we left, I drank a pint of Bacardi 151 rum and smoked enough hashish to make my eyes dilated to the size of dimes. The world looked like a massive pinball machine. Bright lights, tilted, I howled at the moon, "Fuck yeah, one more hit, and I'll see Jesus soon."

Mace laughed and ripped open a beer. He said, "You shouldn't have smoked that hash. Can you hear me?"

I looked at him and said, "What?"

As we passed a car wash, I saw two Iranians washing their vehicle. A few days earlier fifty-two Americans were taken hostage by Islamic students. The path I was traveling in orbit slung me into another space. A zombie walking in a black abyss, and it lasted minutes, hours, and even days. Time forever disappears.

Mace shouted, "Americans don't take any shit from those Persian pussies."

I whipped out my buck knife and gave chase. I screamed, "Free our hostages or die," several times.

They left their car and ran down the street screaming for Allah.

"You're a wild man. Maybe next time you shouldn't smoke as much."

Two weeks later, I went out to a bar to celebrate my nineteenth birthday. I stumbled back and forth, blacking out into reality. In between, I kissed every girl in the bar that would let me, and one that liked it. Her boyfriend drew a gun on me. I was thrown out of the bar.

A few weeks later, I was arrested for public drunkenness and disorderly conduct. I hit a cop with my elbow while urinating alongside a building at closing time. While in the Oklahoma City jail, I sobered up just enough to think about God. He wouldn't leave me alone and wanted something from me. He acted like I owed Him something. My poor faith didn't comfort me from my crimes, and I deserved my present weakness. A junkie, I searched for my next high to escape living. I was lucky not to suffer more from my sweet stupidities.

As my mind fluxed between the duality of life, I was a walking contradiction and strolled past the fires of hell on the way to the liquor store. The sweltering heat from my sins made me continuously hydrate myself. I never learned to scream, cry, or share my feelings. The clandestine unseen world outside of me forced its weak and childish ways into my life. I personally resented being human, so I got wasted.

♥

One day, Nancy, one of the mothers from church, started up a conversation with me. She noticed I didn't fit in with either the adults or teenagers, so she asked me a question, "Larry, have you studied the Bible much?"

"I've read it every now and then."

"I have noticed the children of the church just love you. Would you like to help me teach my third-grade Sunday school class?"

"That will give me something to think about during the week. Sure."

Well, good God, I just backed over the devil at forty miles an hour, and he never saw it coming. Grace's manic notion quickly passed, for being blitzed brought out my own discord. Nothing else mattered for it was all I knew. So close, so far away, I never opened myself to trust what was inside of me.

Sunday came, and I put on my best disguises. Hardly a hero to anyone, I still believed in puppy dogs, ice cream sundaes, and rainbows. Kindness is the magical ingredient, and it began to make me whole. The secret parts of me were illumined by Christ's words, and it showed me my empty heart.

Darkness lit the light of humility in my mind's eye. I immersed myself in the Word and separated myself from the world. The prism of thought helped me avert self-damnation.

The whole design of love was given to me by complete strangers. In my curious subtlety, my memory flashed back to a conversation with God when I was seven years old. In the guise of the moment, I felt there was something inside of me. It was bigger than the life I had been given. Each day of my life, I had one foot in the grave, and the other stood in this world saying a prayer to live. So onward I marched toward the abyss of God.

10

Spaceman

Every day, I wrestled with the madness, and the ghosts of my past pinned me to the mat. I tapped out so I could crawl off into a bottle or my next high. My first instinct was to protect myself from feeling anything. I never felt worthy, for the foundation of my distrust traced back to my families' abandonment of me. An immigrant without a clan, I wandered in and out of consciousness. I never tried to change, for anything new frightened me. I didn't believe in tomorrow, for I did know the importance of today. The road to heaven was to experience life, but I had no idea how to free myself from the cobwebs that ensnared me.

Every Sunday morning, I visited a strange place and perceived every one to be genuine, smiling, and caring. I watched them stand and sing hymns like "Amazing Grace" and "Love Rescued Me." They spoke of heaven like they went there on vacation. They came from everywhere to make a stand for this man named Jesus, and they talked about His ways.

Their actions shouted, "I believe! I believe!" as they huddled next to the cross for His salvation. Behind my blue eyes, I existed in my pain, but I saw the unbounded love in the sacred name of Jesus. It harnessed the vast sky and rendered the divine to my poet's eye. As the wind called my name, I reached out to touch His robe so I could see the possibilities beyond the limitations the world gave me.

A con man sees only the opportunities to benefit himself, and I was conning everyone at that church. I stood back and looked at everyone. Happiness and contentment brimmed over in their lives. I couldn't help but covet their goodness, for the magical lore of His love revealed the secret to success. Life was no more than a journey of faith, and forgiveness allows us to see His grace. Sins are absolved. The human mind never can be wiped clean, and humility indirectly saves us from ourselves.

Terrified of this new place, my gnawing remorse began to wash the mud from my eyes. Honestly, my need for food and shelter kept me coming back. I learned what to say to conceal my defects so no one would ask me to leave the table. The world's greatest actor, I had been a common criminal since I was eight years old. I played all parts, and before God and the mothers of the church, I stood erect with my arms folded like a fortress. The only crack in my walls came from the seed of faith my mother planted. All-knowing God used the mothers of the church to seep His infinite love in my life. They wouldn't stop hugging me every time they saw me, and agape love made me feel welcome.

During the week, the ineffable winds blew and tossed me about like a rowboat lost at sea. My drug use opened my eyes to see the sun from the top of a waterspout, and it opened the bottomless night to swarming creatures poking me from beyond. I crawled into and out of oblivion, just like my forefathers.

At nineteen, I eternally spun in the blueness of mortality, and still aiding felons, I acquired several near-death experiences. I held onto the thought of "Jesus" like a life preserver. I looked at the world through a man's eyes, but the circling motions of the stars made me dream of being more. Higher, higher I wanted to fly to block gratitude from entering my heart. The world was an unsafe place, so I never stayed in one place too long in order not to be seen. I never completely trusted an adult.

My barricades were complete, and a sign was posted in my eyes, "Keep out."

Alone in my fearful conscience, pedestrians didn't venture too close, for my seemingly dead eyes, which throbbed with no human emotion, kept most people away. Despite all my defenses, I couldn't hide from God who had a thousand ideas every second. He freed the thoughts inside my head not exactly seen yet.

One day, after the church service, I was leaning against a wall waiting for the Dentonss to take me back home. I perused the social event from afar. I thought children were the moral law of the universe. They unleashed their imagination and the gaiety from their smiles. They lit up the room with love. Adults laughed. Jokes were told, and everyone got a congratulatory hug.

An internal warning signal was alerting me. A middle-aged gentleman was walking my way, and his eyes revealed I was his destination. As soon as he got close, I turned toward him and said, "Hello."

"Hi, I'm Steve. Why don't you come on and join the fun?"

"Hi, I'm Larry. No thanks. I'm fine right here."

I could see he wanted to ask me something. It took him a few seconds to gather his courage. He asked me, "So, I heard that you once lived in a field."

"Sure did."

"May I ask how long?"

"Somewhere around seven or eight weeks. I really thought it would never end."

A stunned look overcame his face, but then, he asked me, "Wow! How did you make it through each day?"

I looked down at the ground and saw the particles of dust floating in the air near my feet. I paused, and my mind's eye flashed through the thickets of my memories. I felt the scraping pain emerge from that branch of thought. While Steve blinked, I reached into the back of my pocket and pulled out one of my many false faces. I had to hide the sadness in my heart, for it was ashamed of being a failure and unattractive. My eyes went black and strolled back into the field. I looked away for a brief second and said, "I did whatever it took to get by each day."

"Good gosh, what field did you live in?"

I pointed my finger to the west and told him, "It was a field across from an apartment complex on Britton Road and Rockwell."

With a huge smile he said, "No way. My wife, Joanna, and I just bought a house across from that apartment complex."

"Do you have a boy, a girl, and a Doberman Pinscher?"

"Yes, why?"

A smooth, warming smile softly overcame my face. I replied, "I watched you guys move into your new house."

We both laughed and smiled, and he said, "No way!"

I let my guard down so he could get to know me. The genuineness of his heart made me safe, and it was his humility that let me feel like I belonged to the world for fifteen minutes. We laughed and smiled at the story of my survival.

He asked, "Larry, what are you doing for work?"

"I have a few more weeks left in a seasonal job. I help tune church organs across Oklahoma."

As we wrapped up our conversation, Steve told me, "I bet you write a book one day on how you survived living in a field."

Out of the FIELD

I smiled back at him and thought about my eighth-grade education. I walked away fading back into the nothingness, but my life was forever changed by that conversation and his friendship.

♥

As the months passed, I saw eternity in each sunrise. The strangers I met upon my journey opened my soul beyond my banal existence. I saw forgiveness was the gateway to other choices. My mind's eye saw the miracle meant for me, despite my hooliganism. True Christianity makes everyone feel like a friend. I saw something inside each of them. Optimism guided my thoughts to match what I saw. True religion only knows kindness, and it forgives and embraces imperfection to find its perfection. As my compassion expanded, I reflected on my past to determine my future. I couldn't understand love until I experienced it. The mothers of the church were the purest extension of God's hand.

I felt compelled to accept their hugs, for they made me feel like an angel despite my dirty clothes. They treated me like I was a member of the tribe of Jesus. One day, several mothers surprised me on my nineteenth birthday. Everyone was dressed in the latest designer fashions. My poet's eye took the time to notice each family had more than enough. Inside, I didn't feel deserving, and it was the abandonment cruise my family gave me. Trapped by fifty loving souls, I tried to find my way to the door, but each person grabbed a moment of my time. I was a stranger to them, even to myself. Gracious for their thoughts, I couldn't remember the last gift I'd opened.

There was nothing like a gift to make you forget your troubles. Each was wrapped in bright neon-colored paper, and on top, a card with "Larry" scrawled in ink. In their day-to-day actions, the evidence of their miraculous lives touched me. In the grand design of abandonment, the brutal, ugly, and vicious cycle of negative beliefs sequestered me from ever belonging to part of anything. I couldn't help but feel lonesome in a room filled with people. I never learned to trust anyone.

I wondered how I could see the wisdom beyond this world. I couldn't swallow the lie, smile without knowing why, or be crippled by tunnel vision anymore. God brought me here to do some thinking. They loved me as God loved them. I stared mutely at the world around me, and I didn't know how to speak of the invincible thoughts inside of me. I never dreamed of true happiness until that moment.

♥

Every one of my actions made me my father's son, and his memories morphed into my behaviors. My misguided reality drove me to use chemicals to find the newness of the same old dull day. Delusion had convinced me I wasn't like my dad. A child always covets a relationship with his dysfunctional parent, and by doing so, I gave up my rights to want for myself. I was a voiceless human being, worthy of all my tortures. The torturous days of my past never died. The world was illuminated endlessly black and narrow through my drug abuse.

A slave to my birthright, I surrendered to the humiliation of being thrown away. I went to church each Sunday because someone told me there was a heaven. The idea that something was eternal and invincible sparked my curiosity, for I lived once in a place where God and family didn't exist. Sitting in a back row, hungover, the warm smiles, kind words, and free meals kept me coming back.

One Sunday, I had an acid flashback. I never understood the mechanism of my own thinking. A twitch of a dark thought moved in and out of my head. It creeped out one ear and slinked all over my body. It slimed its dark nasty feelings all over me until it returned through the other ear. I told myself, "No more drugs for me."

With no oath of allegiance to my soul, my derealization disorder never allowed me to attach myself to reality or anyone. A one-eyed undertaking, I lived in a strange and complicated adventure between good and evil. I waited in the dark and dulled my strength into despair. Passed out on the floor, I awoke and felt worn-out at nineteen. A lifetime of minutes had passed since I was abandoned. The memorial of madness remembers only the abuses, rather than the blessing of the day. I could never leave my scars alone. In all the wickedness I have seen, I couldn't find anything beautiful or uplifting on earth, so I flew away to kiss the sky.

"Jesus!" I cried many times.

There was no escape from the violence of my ancestors. When I'd lost all hope, I lost everything. There wasn't a problem alcohol and drugs couldn't cure. To be put in the ruts of ordinary perception was to be apprehended by a small mind. My ever-present urge to discover my own self-transcendence opened the doors of insight. Out in space, I saw problems don't exist, for they were created out of our own desires. I lived a life in which nothing was gained, nothing was lost. I navigated from star to star and darkness never scared me at all. Suffering, pain, fear, and doubt let me see the simple thoughts the herd followed.

♥

In each act of kindness bestowed unto me, I felt the tenderness of His love and grace. Like a thief, I reached out to steal my own feelings, for they were new, unfamiliar, and exciting. I wanted to keep them in my pocket like a lucky coin. I fought the notion to believe in something that didn't make sense to me. I lived in one world and passed out in another. I doubled down in more ways than one.

There were countless acts of God's grace in my life every day. I could see most of them, but I never moved east, past the decimal point. I could see for miles and miles. Any small thing seemed intense when you really don't matter to anyone. Life gave me crumbs, and I never thought I was worthy of any more. From job to job, I hitchhiked through northeast Oklahoma City's ghetto to work at a hospital for a few weeks, cleaned pools for a week, and stole a newspaper each day. I looked for odd jobs that paid cash and searched for a lucky penny in the street. With no skills or education, fate showed up one day at church.

Steve asked me, "Hey, Larry how have things been going for you?"

Looking out into the distance, I answered, "I'm making ends meet."

"Well, let me talk with my father. We have an opening for a delivery driver. Do you have a driver's license?"

A sad smile came over my face as I said, "No."

"Have you ever driven a car before?"

"Yes, illegally."

He left and came back five minutes later, and I was offered a full-time job. He told me, "We'll have someone pick you up every morning at seven thirty. You'll be a laborer around the shop until you get your license."

"Really! Wow! Thanks!"

♥

For a survivor, the simple things are hard. As for learning how to drive, I passed the written test my first go-round, but I failed the hands-on driving test twice.

My first road test was taken when I only had a few hours of drive time under my belt. The instructor's face screamed for his life. He was as scared as a groom at a shotgun wedding. He scratched on his form like a mad scientist. Once we pulled back into the parking lot, he took a long, deep breath and asked me, "How long have you been driving, son?"

"A few hours, I think."

The muscles in his face went all directions. He took another deep inhale and said, "Let me give you a little advice. You shouldn't speed, speed in school zones and roll through stop signs next time you take the test."

The second test went a little better, but I still failed. Steve took me under his wing, and we went driving on the weekends. He let me drive his wife's compact car, and it was a better fit for me. I finally passed and got to keep my job.

They gave me a company truck to drive to and from work. Almost human now, I could drive to the store and buy groceries instead of pushing a grocery cart a mile and a half each way. A steady paycheck allowed me to purchase chemicals and booze to numb my conscience. Otherwise, it would whisper to me all day long.

♥

In my trashcan dream, I wanted to be an angel, a star or something magical in life, but I couldn't stay sober one day. I lived distinctly between the crystallized and the un-crystallized views in my mind. Black or scarlet, any gleaming thought's color faded into a deeper shade of black. I watched everyone's life evolve before my very eyes. Floating into outer space, high above it all, I saw life's ardent flow. Dying from oxygen deprivation in space, the possibility of my collapse was a cheap alternative to living. The shadow world of my ancestry's legacy continued to encroach on my life. The shame I felt from their abandonment opened my eyes to see the world as morally indifferent.

From day to day, hand to mouth, my faith was lukewarm. I only attended church when I was sober enough to look someone in the face. It was usually when I ran out of money and needed a free meal. I didn't know

Out of the FIELD

how to surrender my will. With no family, the neon bar lights occupied my mind with their flashing colors. Strangers often looked into my eyes, and they told me, "We have met somewhere before. I know you from some other place."

I toasted them and walked away into the shadowlands.

In the abstract of being unknown, I sometimes couldn't even remember my own name and voluntarily took up residence in oblivion. Shadows passed before my eyes, and a whisper came from the darkened doorway where I dared not go again. Sometimes, the clarity of my thoughts withered all human hope inside of me.

Self-destruction disguised itself in the illusion of blackout. The walls I built kept the wonder and enchantment of the sun out. I impaired myself to block out time and space and the hours of the day completely vanished. Driving while blind, impulsively out of control, my ancestors held me hostage, for they were lonely in limbo.

I undoubtedly would have continued into this unknown abyss without living one second in happiness, but God wouldn't stand for it.

Isaac Newton once said, "Every object continues in uniform motion in a straight line, unless compelled to change that state by an external force acted upon it."

I realized you can't force life. It's either there, or it isn't. Memories sometimes charted my course. I continued to fight God's serenity with a pill, drink, or a toke. The conquest for my soul began in a field, and the war could end in a simple choice. I refused to humble myself. My heart was empty and yearned for things of this world.

I amused myself and became an artist. Pretending to be what people wanted gave me the urge to feed my head. I stretched my soul out like it was Gumby to see if it would bounce back in place. I inspected it, tested it, and learned from each session. In the derangement of my thoughts, I looked long and intensely into the unknown parts of me, and I found the purpose of life was to fix my childhood over and over again. I wanted to be faultless but couldn't focus on day-to-day tasks. Frustrated, drugs made me feel nothing, and utopia was a blackout. I was happiest when I lived outside my head. It was always easier to give up than to work for something.

Immediate gratification was life on a Ferris wheel, and nothing is more terrifying than a ride you cannot get off. I specialized in the meaningless. I rented a bed in the bargain basement of worthlessness and felt incapable of doing anything useful. I mimicked what I mocked as a child and couldn't see the irony of what I become. My father's voice reverberated in my mind, "You'll never amount to anything."

♥

Birthdays and Christmas were terrible for me. My twentieth birthday proved to be more than just another loser day to me. I went to work and felt sorry for myself, so after work, I stopped by the liquor store and picked up a case of beer. I went home and drank my dinner and drowned myself into unconsciousness. Most days, my long, irrational suffering made me crawl into some stink hole and pass out. Spiritually, I knew nothing else, so what else could I be. I seemed to be destined to be an absolute failure, but Steve and Nancy wouldn't let me go down that road.

About eight o'clock, someone knocked on my door. I stumbled to my feet and looked out the peephole. "Shit, it's Steve," I slurred to myself.

Twelve beers drunk, two joints high, I didn't answer the door. About five minutes later, someone else knocked on my door again. "Shit, it's Nancy," I slurred to myself.

Just like a mother, she wouldn't stop knocking on the door until I answered it. Pound! Pound! Pound! She wasn't going away, so I opened the door.

Jumping in and out of a blackout, I was only half-listening to her as she looked down on me from her 5'2" frame. In a stern voice she said, "Larry, our third-grade class planned a birthday party for you. I want you to get in the car with me."

Just like my father, I could sober up in a split-second. Fear can desensitize the crippling effects of alcohol, but it couldn't stop me from slurring, "I can't go to church drunk. I can barely breathe or even hold a thought."

"Larry, God and I love you either drunk or sober. You have a dozen kids who want you to feel special today. I know you don't want to let them down."

She threw a five-star death punch at me.

It was all too ironic. I enjoyed my hatred so much. I never got to experience the love in front of me. Hatred cradled me like a baby, nurtured me into thinking I could never be more.

"All right. I'm going to come with you. This should be fun."

Out of the FIELD

"Good."

I thought to myself, I just started a really good buzz. No problem, I can pull this off. After all, these are Christians and trusting people. I sobered up like a champion. As soon as I walked into the multipurpose room of the church, I had one hundred people singing "Happy Birthday" to me.

God flanked me. Guilt set in, and it was all she wrote for me. I crumbled from the tenderness of love they had for me.

All the church mothers were on my left, and all the children were on my right. I walked over to the table and began to cry small baby tears. Overwhelmed by both the feelings of love and shame, I looked at the table piled high with gifts. After everyone had stopped singing, all the kids in the church flocked around me. They wanted to see my facial expression when I opened their presents. The mothers of the church stood back and frisked me with their eyes.

♥

I couldn't help being a drug fiend. It's was just the card I drew out of the deck. I continued to smoke my grass, pop my pills, and do anything that suspended time. I partied with Tuck, the other owner's son. We drank and smoked weed. We went to some redneck strip clubs. We talked about the rock concert we went to. We shared crazy stories about Mace. We drove around listening to music. One Saturday evening, Tuck and I were partying in my apartment. He went to use my bathroom, and he came out glazy-eyed and subdued like he had just seen Jesus. He floated euphorically away.

After a few more rum and Cokes, I went to my bathroom and saw the needle and the spoon. I hated needles, so I confronted him. He was high on heroin. We were both young and under the influence of something, and our blackened worlds clashed. Once I got on top of him, I pulled out my buck knife and pounded it into the door.

"You're not fucking going anywhere."

"Okay, killer, calm down. You're ruining my high."

I got him calmed down, but ever so slowly, an invisible force more formidable than any other power transformed me into a snitch. Before my eyes, my character was influenced more by what I couldn't see. For the first time in my life, I ratted on someone. I called Tuck's father to come and get him. Within a few days, Tuck was shipped off to some treatment center in Kansas.

♥

As for me, being a survivor meant anything short of dying was a victory. I lived with a weak sense of worth. Unlike any other person, I could talk to anyone about anything, but I couldn't trust anyone—even God. The constant fear of being homeless and abandoned again ran wild in my mind. I waited for the day to come, for someone to ask me to leave. I never felt so uncomfortable in my own skin. I numbed myself. My appetite was sickened in excess. I slept on the rocks at the edge of my grave, so I could just roll into it when I died.

I bought a one-way ticket to the moon and had no intention of living in this world. The explosion lights kept my mind occupied on the other side. I toiled and spun endlessly in outer space. I got so high everything was without form. I turned around and couldn't see myself. With no sense of danger, after three days of drinking and drugging, I stumbled back to life and lived in fear of being alone, yet I chose to be alone. I had drunken periods so destructive my spaceship landed in an unknown field.

♥

Every action I committed fulfilled nothing. I went to weekend rock concerts in the company truck. One show, I went down early and drank a quart of Bacardi rum. I smoked some laced dope with some strangers at a park. During the show, I stumbled into the restroom, and some frat kid bumped into me, probably by mistake. As I teetered and tottered between the painful places in my mind, I remembered cursing at the frat kid. I hoisted my burning red flag for the world to see.

They held me against the wall and took turns pounding my face completely black and blue with their fists. Conscious, I received each blow with a smile. I stared back at them through poisoned eyes and smiled.

I stumbled back and forth between blacking out. One day, I chased shots of whiskey over at Brad's friend's home. As Lady Luck would have it, she made me lose all the time. After eight shots, I staggered out to the balcony and passed a black man. As I let it fly, I thought he said,

"Lightweight" to me, so I called him a nigger.

The host, a Vietnam infantry vet, came outside with the fury of a funnel storm and landed his fists across my face. He repeatedly hit me, and then, he grabbed my hair and proceeded to bang my head against the metal hand railing. Still conscious, once he stopped, I swung and hit him square on the chin. It knocked him back into his home. I staggered toward the door as blood ran down my face. At the door, he hit me three times over my head with a crutch. Born of sturdy Irish stock, I never went down and turned around with a smile. I pulled my buck knife out and charged in after him.

The bystanders decided to stop it before someone got killed. I had crossed the point of no return, and the fatal attraction of the poison I took enamored me in its delusions. I want it! I wanted to die! I ended up in the hospital that night and didn't remember how I drove the company truck there.

From dusk to dawn each day, I wasted time incarcerated behind my bleary barroom eyes. I couldn't turn the page or erase all the pain and sorrow. Memories have power, and survivors have guilt. Inside and out, I danced with doom and the profound sense of being unlovable made me howl at the moon. Just like my father, and his father before him, I drowned my life in a sea of chemicals. I hurt and used drugs to ease the pain. I wanted to live and wanted to die. I didn't know which way to turn. I existed in the void created to be safe from others. I looked at life through a window pane of my spaceship.

Like a black hole in space, my soul spun endlessly shallow and small. Tumbling down below, the gravity from the dead pulled me closer to the edge. It was there I heard my ancestors saying, "We've been waiting for you."

I lived each day to tell a lie, for I had to protect what I loved most, using drugs and alcohol. I needed my medicine to sedate my mind. Glazed hollow, my eyes sought not the kingdom of heaven anymore. Stoned on some old magic potion, handed down from the beginning of time, I lived in a one-room, ungodly hell. I once came close to a conversation with God, only to wake with twenty-four empty beer bottles around me. I would die of thirst before I could call out the name Jesus. I listened to everyone preach about the Promised Land, and as I looked out into this world, I saw mothers, fathers, sons, daughters, friends, and girlfriends. I was so lonely in this place. I had to kill the pain of being born an orphan without a tribe.

♥

At twenty years old, I couldn't escape the war with my father's and families' abandonment. Scar tissue hardened my heart. I secretly and desperately held on to my baptism. I experienced every delight in self-damnation, and the creativity of being maladjusted became more profound over time. The closer I got to the edge, the more I lost my judgment. I deserted the human race and my feelings. My fall into nothingness made me an eyewitness to a crime against myself. Regret would make me a hypocrite, so I fell further into the abyss, stoned immaculate, tumbling endlessly in space.

In November 1981, I turned twenty-one years old and received the money my mother left me in a trust fund. I bought my first car, a brand-new Datsun 310 hatchback and put a killer sound system in it. In December, I took my first road trip back to Connecticut, and as each mile passed, I traveled across the bridge and back into my past. In my heart, I knew my family didn't care for me, but my DNA called me homeward to see them.

I had to look each of them in their eyes one more time and see the faces of those who betrayed me. I felt nothing for them, so I stayed at Jake's house most of the time. We partied like rock stars, for I bought a pound of marijuana and a quarter ounce of hashish with my Christmas bonus. Most of my old friends and clients stopped to see me.

The highlight of the trip, we went to New York City on New Year's Eve, and I strolled around the city from bar to bar in my Boston Red Sox hat.

Toward the end of my trip, I visited my father in West Hartford. I found his brown brick apartment building aged tan by the sun, and I pushed the button and buzzed his place about ten a.m.

His garbled voice asked, "Who is it?"

"Dad, it is me, Larry."

He said in a grumpy and confused voice, "What do you want?"

"I am leaving town tomorrow, so I just thought I would stop by to see you for a second."

After a long pause, the buzzer rang for the door to open, and he said, "Come on up."

As I walked up the stairs to the second floor, my heart and mind secretly yearned for a father figure every child needs, but with each step, another thought came. Suddenly without notice, the memory of almost killing my father appeared in my mind. Once I knocked on his door, my mind was emptied, and when the door opened, an entirely naked lady stood in front of me.

She said, "Hi, my name is Cheryl. Your father is a really nice man. Everyone in this apartment complex just loves him."

I thought to myself, "He still loves his whores."

About that time, my father staggered toward the door, and he gently gripped her by her arm and ushered her into his bedroom. Astonished, he walked toward his kitchen table without inviting me, so I followed him. I scanned around his dusty old apartment. I saw crushed beer cans, opened condoms wrappers, and a woman's undergarments scattered across the floor. On the coffee table, I saw a stack of pornographic magazines. His past was his present, and it was all he would ever be. He hung on to the trophies and medals he earned playing sports in high school. The salt and pepper shakers he collected from all the counties and cities he visited on his trip around the world were scattered about his living room. He needed a constant reminder that he was once someone.

As I followed him to the kitchen table, he kept mumbling something that made no sense. At the table, I looked out the window and viewed the parking lot. He went to his refrigerator and retrieved two beers. He handed me one and then he sat down. Like we were twins, we cracked open our beers at the same time. After we both had taken a swig, he asked me, "Have you seen Robert?"

"I saw him for fifteen minutes one day at Grandma's house."

"He's a Marine you know, a clean-cut American. Maybe you should get a haircut."

Just like the old days, he picked a fight with me.

It didn't take long to remember why I hated him. I finished my beer and helped myself to another. I needed something to dull his insanity.

He still was rambling on about Robert, "You know he made all-conference catcher in high school?"

"No, I didn't," as I grabbed another beer.

My resistance dropped, and I feared I might take his life. I said, "Hey, I have to go to meet a friend."

Suddenly, without warning, my father's bedroom door opened. Cheryl walked out still naked as the day she was born. She looked at my dad and asked him, "Honey, do you think it would be all right if your son takes me to the free clinic a couple miles down the road?"

My father looked at me and asked, "Do you have time?"

I wanted to leave. "Sure, whatever. I have to go now, though."

She went into his room and closed the door. My father told me "Do not mess around with her, Son, if you know what I mean."

I stood there, and I wanted to touch him to see if he was real or something my mind made up. His churning words turned on my mind's disorder. I was consumed and oppressed by fear. In a moment of sheer clarity, I looked into the eyes of a dead man walking through life. He was unnaturally absent, and he was as detached as a beggar pandering money in the street. My heart wanted to love him, but he wouldn't let me. I knew what love was from what others had been given in their lives, even though I couldn't get the basics from him. The eternal yearning to be loved by my father burned inside of me, and the child in me couldn't rise above his abandonment. As I looked into his eyes, I saw the reflection of myself in him, and I took my love and walked out the door to get stoned into another world just like him.

Off to my appointment, I bought a pound of pot, a quarter ounce of hashish and other premium drugs. I transported them back to Oklahoma with me. Back home, this spaceman blasted off every night after work, and I even got high while pumping nitrous oxide at work. Oblivion was my lover, and we nurtured each other in compassionate solitude under the desert night sky. On the weekends, I attended every rock concert that came into Oklahoma City and bought my exotic drugs there.

I never tried to date and was unlucky in love. Abandonment gave me strange innocence which exiled me into the slavery of addiction. I wanted to tranquilize my feelings and lived in the compromises I made up.

From blackout to blackout, I sometimes cried out to God, "Help me!"

♥

One Friday night, the local high school was playing football, and all the cowboys, hippies, and freaks lined the parking lots alongside N. W. 39th Expressway. I cruised up and down the strip once drinking a beer and lit up a bowl laced with dust. Instantly, my eyes went black. Rocketing through space, I crashed to earth when my tire hit the median's curb.

Out of the FIELD

Stumbling out of my car, I saw an enormous gash in my tire. Suddenly behind me, I heard several brakes squeal, tires grabbed the road, and metal met metal. I turned my head and looked.

"Shit!" A five-car pileup a hundred yards behind me. I had a cooler of beer and an ounce of PCP-laced weed in my car.

I sobered up in a second and could have worked for any pit crew that night. While I drove away, three police cars came driving up with their lights flashing. Sneaking off to a side street, I promised God and myself I would quit using.

Twelve hours passed before I got high again.

At twenty-two years old, the loop-the-loop of addiction made me powerless. My cup overflowed, and still, I was thirsty for more. My tolerance levels dropped, for my system soaked in alcohol and chemicals from the days before. Grasped in the teeth of entrapment, the horrible pangs of addiction drove my actions. I achieved in ten years what it took my father twenty-five years of using to do. Like my father before me, I hid it all too well from others, for after all, I was my father's son.

All alone and trapped in the past, I used and an arsenal of lies and costumes to disguise myself each day. Dependency made me an actor, and the parts played were formed on the go. My life was out of control, but I loved the high-wire act. I walked between angels and demons without a care in this world.

I never saw the Wanted poster God put out on me. Ghost Whisperers and Soul Hunters took action. God sent forth an expedition to save me from self-destruction.

11
I Am My Father's Son

Secrecy is the gatekeeper of self-oppression. To forget the accountability for my life, I drank and drugged in excess. Blackouts snared me, and they reeled me into the oblivion. It was when my secrecy failed, reality attacked the credibility of my life. It is hard to free myself from the past when I'd honored the values of my ancestors. Their abstract spirits squatted in my soul. I pitied the living while partying with the dead. A slave from birth, my slavery was confined by the narrow limits of one choice.

Born to live, born to die, I wondered what purpose my life had. The days of my life added up to nothing. Somewhere, where the old shadows hang, the new shadows are formed. I heard a voice from the other side say, "You're one of us, so don't you try to be more."

I froze and remembered the first commandment in being a drug fiend has two points: the trip begins, and your journey through virtual space finishes when you run out of rocket fuel.

Lost somewhere in the universe, I pretended to be what others wanted me to be for so long. The shame of being rejected forged a gorge that made the Grand Canyon look like a sinkhole in someone's backyard. One drink, one drug at a time, I tried to fill the enormous region of space and time with anything but God. The illusions that controlled me began to shatter the minutes of each day.

♥

In January 1983, Steve talked me into buying a brand-new home. I used the remaining balance from my trust fund for the down payment. The house wouldn't be finished until September. Under the fog of alcohol and drugs, my life continued its downward slide. I spied on the world and covertly dreamed I was in another.

Love is grace, and God pulled me down from a galaxy unknown to mankind. At the beginning of the work week, I showed up to work still buzzing from the weekend's space odyssey. A simple smile let everyone know, "I don't know you, and you don't know me."

Grateful for God's company, our relationship was a casual word among friends. I'd tell Him in confidence about my dream of "freedom." So, He waited, and He listened to my soul crying out for help. Then He kissed me on the forehead, and my incarnation began.

A human soul wasted cannot find his way back home to heaven. Honestly, I'd never accepted responsibility for my life, not one moment. One day, my past, present, and future intermingled. The future pressed so hard, my history moved aside, and the present became now. The mystery of choice rippled throughout eternity. I'd either shrivel to nothing, or I'd stretch out the universe to achieve the impossible.

The clanging sounds of metal gas cylinders let everyone know I was at work. Dan walked back to the shop and opened the back door. I smiled at him and said, "Morning."

He said, "Morning, Larry. I need to speak with you for a few seconds. Would you please follow me?"

As I looked at him, his face was different. I sensed an ambush. Something wasn't right. It was those angels poking in my gut. I didn't listen to them and responded, "Sure thing."

The office was unusually silent. I stopped and pondered. As I entered the room, twelve pairs of eyes took me by surprise. Ethel, Dan, Steve, Paul, and David sat around the sides of the table. One man stood, a stranger with a black beard and tiny, black, fish eyes, walked over to me. While shaking my hand, he introduced himself and said, "Hi Larry. My name is Bob, and we've gathered here today out of our love for you."

I whispered to myself, "Oh shit, I am screwed."

Bob continued his prearranged words, "Please have a seat, and I will let each person here talk about your behaviors and how they affected each them. It has been brought to my attention that you had used drugs at some point in your life, and you still might be using alcohol. Larry, this is an intervention, and I am here to assess whether you need to go to a treatment center for drug and alcohol abuse. With that, I will let Ethel start it off."

The drug fiend voice inside my head said, "You better be careful. They are gunning for you."

My mind told me, "You got this!"

Ethel started out, "Larry, you know I love you, but it is when you withdraw from everyone, I get concerned for you."

Genuine love filled me with weird, zealous remorse. It began to shatter my will, and I felt each crack form and move beneath my feet. Sentimental bullshit developed a tear in my eye. It was part of my act. After all, they would be amazed by what I lived through. The shrewdest hooligan ever to walk this planet was never out of the game. They had nothing on me, for I never partied with other employees. A street fighter, my heart beat slow and steady, and I looked for the opening to attack.

One by one, each of them talked about my behaviors. I sat and listened to them. Their words jack-hammered through my walls to find my heart. In each moment with my colleagues, I didn't hear the sirens or the alarms of "Fight or flight" going off.

I listened to each one of them say, "I believe in you."

The sweetest sounds my ears ever heard was the words of kindness they spoke out of dignity and respect. God's plan kept flanking my thoughts. He knew I would play for a draw. A warrior finds a way to fight another day, so I began to lie. Chaos was a smoke screen, and I fired a warning shot over their heads by stating, "I can't even remember the last time I used drugs or alcohol. I'm no drug addict." (My apartment was covered with beer bottles and roaches in the ashtray).

Bob chimed in, "I have nothing personal against you, but you exhibit the characteristics of a heavy user. Larry, when was the last time you actually used?"

I looked him straight in the eye (it always worked before) and replied, "Well, sir, I can't rightly remember. It's been a long time, though."

"Indeed, Larry. Well, I have heard enough, and I recommend that you be admitted and have our counselors evaluate you."

"What, you can't determine I'm an addict from a conversation. You're a joke, dude!"

Steve jumped in. "What do you think, Larry?"

I sat there trying to find a way out of this mess. As all the eyes of heaven were upon me, I had a choice to get up and walk out, but my heart kept telling me I was another. The sunlight of my mother's love radiated through my heart. Scared, I closed my eyes and saw an open door. There was only one way out and was afraid to leave what I knew.

Everyone looked at me and waited to see what was going to happen.

I retreated to regroup and attack another day by telling them, "I'm not an addict, but I'll go to treatment to prove it to you."

Steve said, "Larry, the company would pay the hospital bill and your salary while you're in treatment."

Dan said, "You'll have to complete the program to keep your job."

On March 31, I drank a quart of Bacardi rum. On April 1, 1983, I had the worst hangover I ever had. I entered the treatment center wearing street colors. My jean jacket was embroidered with the Union Jack flag and the name of my favorite rock band, The Who, on the back.

Steve walked me through the door of the center, and an assistant opened the door. He asked, "Are you ready?"

"No, I am not ready for this. This place reminds me of a jail. I will be out of here in a few days!"

"It can't be that bad. Take care of yourself."

As I walked down the halls, red warning lights went off in my head. Goodness me, this place looked like a church revival held at a crack house.

Somewhere in the corridors, someone shouted, "It's time for group therapy," and everyone scampered into the four doors like cockroaches avoiding Raid.

"Jesus," I thought, "What a terrible thing to endure sober. I need some drugs."

The assistant said, "Please follow me."

I followed him to the new patient room, and he asked me, "Please dump out your bag and let me go through it."

He grabbed my Listerine and confiscated it. I asked him "Why are you taking that?"

"People get so desperate in here they drink it to get a buzz."

I chuckled and replied, "If I need a drink that bad, I will just walk out the door."

He didn't laugh and searched everything.

"Lighten up, we have some time to spend together."

He looked at me and said, "Please take off your clothes and put on these blue scrubs in front of me."

"Dude, I go through life like a commando."

He shook his head at me. After he had checked all his boxes, he released me into the unit. Group had just ended, I walked down the hall. I strolled into the community room, and all eyes were on the new fish in scrubs.

I continuously scanned my surroundings. Miserable and wretched souls lingered about the room. This was a terrible thing to inflict on someone. The boring switch from being badass to the sudden dramatic thought, "Don't be a dumb fuck," and let me look for the crack.

Redneck drunks, heroin junkies, potheads, and cocaine eyes publicized the side effects of the products they used. Everyone looked for their next fix. I listened to the sober corporate buzzwords being flung around by recycled people: Detachment, Dignity, Expectations, Awareness, Acceptance, Action, Control, Cause, Cure, and Breathe!!! Three deep breaths.

"Fuck me, I am so fucked."

I viewed everyone in this place as a loser. I would never admit to being an addict or drunk. I could hold down a job and handle responsibility. Each of these tormented souls wasn't worth my time. This motley crew reeked of weakness. Fear raised my shield, and I harbored an undiscerning view of toward life on the ward's floor. My thoughts changed their design to fit the anxiety of my situation. I didn't open up to anyone, for it would be rude to speak my mind. I gave them this courtesy to be in my world. In a strange and odd sort of way, I sat with my back pinned against the wall, for I had no intention of joining the maladjusted demographic of this unit.

My situation wasn't going to change so I wouldn't let this place alter me. A prisoner of Reagan's war on drugs, I looked for an escape. Nothing strengthened me more than silence, and I wouldn't let others control me. My mind walked the halls a hundred times that night, looking for... I wrote some blank verses and searched endlessly for a way-out sobriety. I found no great consolation in being humble, for my pride served me well over the years.

I continued to walk over the miracle in front of me.

Every morning, the whole ward started out with a group meeting. There were thirty-nine lost souls and one radical bastard. Everyone identified themselves as an alcoholic or addict. I said, "My name is Larry, and I don't want to be here."

Every morning, the oppressive brainwashed group greeted me with a loud and thunderous, "Welcome, Larry."

"Fuck all of you!"

♥

Cold-blooded eyes with the instinct of a predator, confidence, and arrogance gave me the prowess to survive any hostile environment. My body aided and abetted my mind's existence. I listened to find a way out. I spoke when threatened, and I acted forcibly when I needed to. The pleading prayers of the patient's words made detoxing a horrifying experience. Addiction may be delusional, but delusion kept reality away.

In my small group, I looked at the faces of my fellow men with much scorn when they talked about how they felt. The vacancy in my eyes kept the weak-hearted at bay. The counselor always looked for ways to break me. "Larry, would you like to share anything about Joe's situation?" she asked.

"Nah, I think he's a big boy! He can figure it out for himself."

I looked at old men with broken teeth pleading for salvation. I watched the vanity of a dream not equal to those who dream it, and the wicked of the world became idle and fell back into humanity. I wore myself out listening to my fellow patients in group complaining and quarreling about their loved ones. I pretended to do nothing and planned my escape every day. After all, I knew I could play any part on the world's stage. I could become an acrobat, artist, a politician, or even a priest to survive.

Nighttime was the hardest time to be alive. All the little demons bounced around freely in my brain. I had no medication to put them to bed. My movie crypt played its classic horror flicks. Fist fights, my father's whores, sex acts and near-death experiences shouted, "There'll be no sleep for you tonight, Little Bastard."

I had not slept in days when they sent me to a shrink. The doc asked, "So Larry, tell me what's going on?"

"Well doc, I kept having violent nightmares and don't know why. My nightmares are usually about war and violence. Everything is okay during the daytime. It has been going on for days, now."

"After reviewing your chart and your therapist's notes, it is my opinion you suffer from Post-Traumatic Stress Disorder. I bet you used to medicate yourself to sleep every night. It is common to have nightmares or flashbacks in the first few months and years of sobriety."

"Doc, can you prescribe me a few beers in the evening to put my mind to bed?"

He looked at me and said, "Next patient please."

♥

I wanted to walk out and drink myself to sleep. The images from my past appeared in my head taunting me back to the world from which I came. Thinking I wouldn't kiss the hand of the mundane, for the battles I've won and lost shaped me into a trained and skilled fighter. Game on bitches! I'll let someone else idealize them as a god. I raised my game to win against these scalawags.

Each night, I regrouped and planned another day's defense. After all, I survived the brutal assaults of my childhood and being homeless twice. I felt no sense of obligation to belong to the universe at this time. I slanted my eyes to look for angles of my escape. I deployed my unforgiving blues eyes, and my mammal's instincts made me stronger than those in my presence. Attack, defend, I was fat with rage. I paced in my cage and drooled at the thought of being high. My infinite comprehension watched the therapist poke me with sticks. They wanted to get a reaction out of me and make me feel something. I wouldn't play their game, and my tactics paralyzed their strategies. I moved across the board to avoid being placed in checkmate. I sat still and smiled at the end of each session, for I walked among the ruins of thirty-nine lost souls and only cared about myself. I didn't know what the therapist saw in me. I fucking didn't care. When she stared back at me, I looked at her in pity for the compassion she felt for me. I fight and don't know how to surrender.

In a bankrupt state, sarcasm pushed back against the onslaught of theories they taught. With no filter, my creativity became a flame thrower. One evening, David and his wife visited me, and they brought me a pan of brownies. In defiance, I walked up and down the hallway and shouted, "Get your hash brownies here."

The staff quickly looked like a SWAT team in action. They confiscated the brownies, and the next morning the policy about visitor's baked goods on the ward changed.

My therapist sat down and talked to me about my behavior, "Larry, why did you parade up and down the halls like you were a drug dealer?"

"I am bored out of my mind in this place."

"Well, tomorrow we shall see how bored you are when your coworkers show up to the group."

"Who's coming?"

Out of the FIELD

"You'll have to wait and see."

That night, theoretically I was under attack by God. Cracked in half, one side looked at the other side all night long. I mumbled to myself all night, "I've got to get the fuck out of this place."

♥

The next day, a few of my coworkers, Dan, David, Tuck, and Paul showed up to inform the group of my behaviors. Once again, I didn't party with anyone at work, so no one had any dirt on me. From my castle rock, I looked down at them trying to assail my walls. The therapist tried to find something on me.

Swelled with pride, I avoided verbal interaction with any one of them. The risk remained too high, and it was more of a threat, to tell the truth. The secrets of my drug dependency kept me sickly strong.

The therapist asked, "Dan, you haven't shared yet. Do you have something?"

Dan arrogantly took a second to reply, "Larry is the kind of person who would bring you flowers one day, and he'll shoot at you with arrows the next day. I heard about the time he had a meltdown when I confronted him about his hygiene. He lost it one day in the back parking lot and danced around in a mud puddle."

A long and wicked smile formed on my face. My eyes spoke before I did. Like a Bengal tiger, I lunged at him, exposing my canines.

No one moved, except the therapist. She stepped in front of me with her arms open.

I shot burning arrows of chaos across the room and said, "Whatever you think!"

The therapist held me back at the end of the session, and she commented, "I like flaws, for they let me know who you really are."

"You don't shit." I turned around and walked away.

♥

That night, I licked my wounds. The brutal honesty of this place let a perfect stranger invest the intuition of theirs into anyone's life. Somehow suddenly, my mind realized I couldn't battle on forty fronts. I changed my tactics and decide to give them something. The end goal was to walk the well-trodden path of others to get out and use again. At the morning group, I introduced myself, "Hi, I am Larry, and I'm an alcoholic addict."

Everyone clapped and cheered. Everybody welcomed me to Club Detox. I played them like a mark on the street. Lying was an art form to me. I've done it all too well over the years. Openness became a smoke screen, and I hid under its cover.

♥

In a compromised situation, I looked for bold moves, but my thoughts drifted into compassion for another's misery. I'd evaporate into thoughts of the unknown. The patients' emotional drama fluttered like a pigeon in a meadow. Amidst the fury of ideas and loud cries for peace, I looked at the games being played. The patients ran in and out of darkness, and deliriums stole their blue sky. I witnessed that the dirty truth had to be accepted before forgiveness and living could begin. It was the loneliest moment of my life. All I could do was to stare blankly at God and make faces at Him.

♥

The patients dreaded Family Week as it was supposed to turn vanity into understanding and clemency. The acts of the wicked fell before the feet of their loved ones. Three families came together in one room and were treated at the same time. All group members attended to support their peers. I watched the subtle ways that people choose their words to hide their double life.

A soul slips out a conscious word to confess a confession it can't express. I listened to the tone and reflections revealed a lie. I heard utter silence kill by tearing a man's heart in two. Men who never said the word "love" shudder at the thought of its tenderness. I cheered for a tear that couldn't trickle down a cheek. Hideous psychotic fallout, detox drama, I wondered how sobriety would change me.

As my Family Week drew near, I had had no mind-altering substance for thirty days now. Jesus, I thought, what a terrible thing to be sober and in control of my thoughts. Sobriety was a bitter disappointment, and I had no remedy to fix it. This place reminded me of an old town bar. I saw every-

Out of the FIELD

one settle into the path of least resistance. They were herded like cattle, and the staff kept saying, "Don't forget to tell us about your feelings." "You can't do this," or "you can't do that."

Exhausted from boredom, I purposely chose not to verbally fight or criticize anyone. Keep it on the down-low, I infiltrated sober conventions and blended in with the other dope freaks as a ruse.

The way to make it through this confinement was to give the staff the general truth they would accept. I'd played many roles in my lifetime, and no matter what, the sweet spot of denial opened my imagination. The right words and gestures suddenly appeared out of nowhere, and I held them captivated by the certainty they felt inside. Their self-interest found in conformity was no match to my street genius.

♥

When my Family Week came, David, Steve, and Nancy showed up, and I sat and listened to how they described my strange behavior. They talked about my many black eyes, my unkempt appearance, and the apathy toward life. Only God knew how much I used. No one could talk about my drinking or drug use, for I hid it all too well. Just like my father, no one ever knew when I was high.

Lulled to sleep, I shut down and drifted away from the moral melee. Just like when I was a child, my fancy opened up, and I disappeared into the next something to make me feel free. My murderous inheritance of a thousand years and two hundred dead souls called me to use again. The vain repetition of my family history lived in me, and I sat in the terrible surge of silence in my mind and did nothing, just like they would do.

On the last day of Family Week, the therapist brought a boom box into the session, and she gave a lengthy speech about both love and family. She reached down and hit the play button. Debbie Boone's "You Light up My Life" filled the air. She went on to say, "As we leave here today, I want you all to remember why you are here. Please take time and listen to the words of this song, for you always will remember your loved ones each time this song is played in the future."

While the song began to play, she motioned for me to come to her. Confused at first, I sat and looked at her with a dumb frown upon my face. She motioned again for me to go to her. I thought, "What the fuck?"

I walked over to her. She took my hand and indicated she wanted me to sit on her lap. A lumberjack-sized woman, I looked at her and was confused. She offered me tenderness. She reached out and took my hand. The music played on as my walls crumbled away. She reached out and pulled me close to her heart. Cradled like her son, she whispered into my ear, "You have to learn to love yourself, my friend."

My eyeballs squirmed in my sockets.

Once the song was over, I stumbled through a lot of unknown emotions and realized I had met my match. My heart roared, "I'll never be defeated." I kept my sword drawn against the real King in this ward—compassion.

These bastards didn't play fair.

♥

With my Family Week over, I couldn't wait to be discharged and had no thoughts of ever staying sober. I saw many faces come and go and was the Senior Statesmen of Abstinence on the ward. I didn't want the leadership of the group meetings. A lone wolf, I protected my territory with howls of sarcasm.

A lone wolf can see through the lead wolf's bullshit, and she called out in the group. Two sharp minds processed each other's behaviors. Four piercing eyes stared. I met my match, and my posturing shriveled. The eyes of conviction never yielded. It was like she had to save me to payback her gift.

All the tactics she used against me only left me petulant, annoyed, and scared. Our next session, my counselor stared at me again. Punch for punch, I knew my draw was near, but she threw an uppercut through my defense, "Larry, I have decided you're going to have another Family Week. I want you to call your uncle Burney today, and ask him to attend our next family session."

Mad eyes never let one lose the ability to defend oneself. A crazy-eyed boy replied, "You're nuts! He won't fucking come."

That afternoon, I called my uncle and guessed right. Burney had too many business meetings to attend next week. I handed my counselor the phone. Her facial expression told all. She now understood my fall from grace was more significant than she had ever known.

She took a deep breath and said, "Larry, you always need a plan B."

Out of the FIELD

Two days later, she told me in the group, "Your uncle will be attending our next family session."

I mumbled to myself, "I keep getting my ass flanked in this place."

♥

At my second Family Week, Ethel and my uncle attended. Ethel talked about my abnormal behavior and inability to be emotionally mature in certain situations. I sat there doing cartwheels in my mind. A grin on my face, she had nothing on me. I didn't destroy a family with my drinking and drugging. I only continued to kill myself slowly, and that was the gift my family gave me. When it was time for my uncle to share, he said, "Larry, I knew about my father's heavy drinking and nothing more."

By being sober for over five weeks now, my senses came back to me. I saw a little man afraid of doing the right thing. He shut off his feelings, and it destroyed his sense of reality. He couldn't see he abandoned Robert and me, and he had no reflections of remorse in his eyes. His theory of my childhood can be summed up in four words, "It's not my problem."

Unnaturally abstinent, I looked at him and saw a counterfeiter, someone who forged love with compassion. As a poker player, I never showed my cards and just mucked them. I knew this man wasn't my family.

In the sunless place, reflection showed me my instincts to jettison my family was the right thing. My mother would be very disappointed in him.

He kept on telling the group, "His father had a good lawyer."

His empty words could never fill the hole of being unlovable. He never genuinely cared for Robert or me. Making money became more important than his two orphaned nephews' lives.

The counselor tried to build a bridge in a relationship and fasten the bonds of our DNA together.

She suggested, "I think it would help Larry's PSTD if I have some pictures of his mother and him. He seems only to remember the trauma of his life with his father."

My uncle agreed to send me some pictures.

I ran into my imagination to hide from my father, for no one ever came to save us. The men in my family were castrated dogs, and the women were merely ticks embedded into their skin.

I absolutely wanted to madly indulge in drugs and alcohol now. I couldn't wait to get released and pursue the pleasure of numbing my pain. I thought freedom was a day away. I had been in treatment for over six weeks by now. In Monday's group session, the counselor told me, "Larry, you will be with us for another week. I signed you up for a group session called Trauma this coming Saturday. It was hypnosis therapy for patients who suffered from PTSD, emotional shutdown, overreaction, and other behavior issues. The therapeutic arena of hypnosis is frequently used with trauma survivors."

"Do you think you're Jesus Christ and you can save the world?"

"Let's play nice, Larry."

"Okay, let's play nice," I smiled at her. "I can't wait until Wednesday."

"Why?"

"Wednesday is Salisbury steak night. I am addicted to Salisbury steak now, for we have had it every Wednesday since I have been here. You might have to keep me here and wean me off Salisbury steak."

The group laughed, while she sneered at me.

♥

As the week passed, I witnessed more people come and go and wondered if I would ever leave this place. One day, I sat in my room all alone, and the chaplain knocked on my door. After simple introductions, he said, "Son, why don't you tell me why you been here so long?"

A defiant smirk rose from cheek to cheek, "I guess the staff loves my personality."

He chuckled and said, "From what I heard, your hands are in all the mischief in this place. The staff listens to your comments about heroin, delirium tremens, and trips you have been on with drugs. You don't seem to follow the program here."

I smiled and nodded my head and laughed a bit. I replied, "Life is not very fun when you live your life for someone else's expectations. I haven't been much of a follower."

As he glossed over my comment, he asked me, "Do you believe in God, son?"

I stared into the distance and remembered the God or angel who came to my field. It examined my heart. I replied, "He visited me once, in the field I lived in, so yes, I do. We have kind of a dysfunctional kind of relationship, for we don't see eye to eye on many things."

I think my comments bothered him, for he took his time to reply. I believe he wanted to see some act of remorse or hear some sad words come from my mouth.

"Son, I have talked to you for fifteen minutes now, and my observation is you are a radical bastard."

I chuckled loudly, and the gleam of life poured out of my eyes. I said, "Yes sir, I wouldn't be here if I didn't know how to fight."

He smiled and said, "I have to get going now, but I will say a prayer for your relationship with God. I will ask Him to touch your heart, so the love I can see inside of you does not need to hide anymore."

As he left my room, I gazed off into the distance and quickly forgot his presence in my life. Sullen and slow, weak in my convictions, I only thought of being high, but life is unfair. It kicks you in the ass when it wants you to move in the direction deemed best for you. They kept flanking me. God was on my left, and my counselor was on my right. I emptied my pockets of all my tricks and maneuvers.

Truth be told, I found my soul pristine, beautiful, and bright as a newborn child. I looked at it in wonder. I was afraid to take it back. Failure was my alibi. No one man could resist God's grace forever, not even me.

♥

Saturday arrived, and ten of us trauma-ridden souls were loaded into a van. We were driven to the outpatient building. As I walked into the room, I saw a small-statured man with white hair and big, bushy white eyebrows repetitively utter the word, "Welcome."

He wore a white shirt, charcoal-colored pants, black belt and shoes. As I studied his interactions, all his movements were precise, and each monotone syllable he spoke kept everyone in the idleness of the unknown. His voice resembled Vincent Price's eerie tone.

Once he saw everyone was in the room, he assumed control and repeated welcome again. "You have all chosen to volunteer to be hypnotized to help you understand your past better and chart your future. No one will be forced to participate. It is important for you to know while you are hypnotized you will never do something against your beliefs. Hypnotherapy is a tool to help you change your thoughts, attitudes, behaviors, or feelings toward the event or events that have shaped your life. In other words, I will open your mind so you can see you have other options. I hope each one of you finds the answer to your fears."

Hocus-pocus, mumbo–jumbo, I waited for the Space Gypsy to wave a magic wand and make life disappear.

One by one, each patient volunteered, and one by one, every patient revealed their inner being. I only came to watch, but I soon realized this was my destiny. Would I play for stalemate once again?

I sat and listened to the Space Gypsy turn shame into the magic of acceptance. I heard the shrieking scream of being raped, and the sound of terror that echoes in a human soul. Angry faces turned red, veins almost popped out of someone's head. A man got down on his knees and begged for forgiveness for killing someone. I felt the slash from the knife cutting through my skin when someone talked about their suicide. He opened everyone's mind ever so slowly, and he probed into the subconscious mind like an angel working for God.

I sat back and took in the show, and I hoped he would run out of time. I did make an emotional connection with each patient. I sat at the table with the worst life had to offer. Everyone in the room had gone, when he looked at me and asked, "Larry, it's your turn."

I looked at him.

He smiled at me and said, "Larry, it's time."

My mind said, "Hold on," as I got up and walked over to the chair.

My broken memories dug in for the fight of their lives. A thought flashed in my mind "Would this Space Gyspy set the ghost inside me free?"

I stood before him a Supertramp extraordinaire, and I readied myself for battle like I did many times before. A rebellious smile found its way to my face as I thought of the chaplain calling me a "radical bastard."

His monotone voice spoke, "Larry we are starting now, and your eyelids will begin to feel heavy."

Something came over me. I battled it, yet it released me into blackout in seconds.

Blankness!

Blankness!

Blankness!

Blankness!

I don't know what happened or what was said in my trance. I awoke enraged like I had been in a fight. I stared at the wall. Simmering in rage, I sat in my space. Slowly shifting back to my conscious self, I staggered back to my feet and walked to the outskirts of the group's circle. There I sat down.

The Space Gypsy asked, "Does anyone have any comments or feedback for Larry?"

A long silence remained in the room, but someone did raise their hand to speak. A patient with long, wavy, red hair and two thousand freckles on his face said, "I have something to say."

I didn't like him before and hated him now.

As the whole room turned and looked at him, he said, "Larry, you're going to be just like your father."

His comment bullied me into reflection's silence, and I smothered the victim inside my soul.

That evening, I took the time to reflect on the grace of the miracle defining myself. I was my father's son. All I have done with my life was to survive incredible events. I reached out to touch the wholesome wind of time. The clarity of my inner voice gave me permission to dream beyond reality, and I quit living minute to minute. I found the courage to promise myself to never use drugs or alcohol again.

♥

A few days passed. A few more new faces came into the treatment center. On Salisbury steak Wednesday, my counselor told me I would be released back into society on Friday. That evening, the faculty had a ritual for the person leaving to pass down gifts or trinkets other patients gave them during their stay on the ward. I had a pillowcase full of items after forty-nine days. I felt like Santa Claus and made sure everyone got something.

I only brought one new thing to the party. My street colors. I embroidered a jean jacket with the Union Jack flag and the name of my favorite rock band, The Who.

I held out my jacket and paused and told everyone, "This jacket symbolized defiance, for it was my soldier's colors against the world. I wore it to concerts, drug deals, and keg parties. I even slept in this jacket when I was homeless in Bristol. I used it for a pillow my first night I slept in my field in Oklahoma City. This jacket was my armor against the world."

I smiled and paused to hold back the tears and told everyone, "God had touched my heart while I was in here. I will no longer look for the opportunities to get by in life. I will now look to be of service to others."

I gave my jacket to the loner who sat away from the group and told him, "Surrender doesn't hurt as much as you think it does."

Right before I left, my counselor told me I wouldn't receive my graduation medallion, and I would have to complete the outpatient program and stay sober one year to collect it. Some things never change, and I don't think anyone thought I had much of a chance.

"I'll see you a year from now."

I had always, essentially, been waiting. Waiting to become something else, waiting to be that person I always thought I was. On the verge of becoming, I walked out of the treatment center and into the sunlight bright with wisdom.

12
Blinded by Life

My first evening home from the treatment center I sat alone under the stars. My thoughts were like a baby hearing its voice for the first time. I sat and listened to the inner whispers of a lost soul found. I felt infinitely, wholeheartedly precious. My thoughts shifted back and forth between the duality that lived inside of me. I reflected on the miseries of poverty, abandonment, cruelty, and the fears of surviving life. I stood alone against this world with only the nobility of hope, and the thought that I was another deep inside my heart. The eyes of my memories stared back at me. You can't fight what you can't see. I saw the unseen puppeteer's hand who distracts us with fear. Yanked, swinging from strings, three hundred million puppet-people jerked together, snapped into conformity. Invariably, it was too late for them, not for me.

My walkabout turned silence into words, and I found a sense of worth came from acceptance. A crownless king, I stood among the pale shadows and forgotten names of society. Transformed by gratitude, the courage to change came from the graveyard of my memories. The moonlight spun around me, and my shroud lifted as I humbled myself before God. A serene and majestic presence overcame me. Sacred noble inclinations filled my heart. I was a survivor who did anything to find his fate. God made it hard to live without His unconditional forgiveness. His loyalty gave me a reason to believe in Him. His grace was mine, for I reached out and took what I didn't deserve. I discovered wisdom from the anguish, and from the dungeon of nothingness, I unlocked the invisible shackles on my feet. I dared to dream. I dreamed, and I dreamed like free men do.

My passion and sarcasm were gifts from God. My thoughts freely mused like a warm summer breeze through the flowers in a mountain meadow. Refreshed by enlightenment, I had no limitations, for I was an artist who drew freely upon my imagination. I could immerse myself in the shades of color or in the tone of words and held eternity in my fingertips. I spun in thought. Over! Under! Through! Born to create, I picked up my pen and scratched poetic prose and sprinkled it with emotion. I froze delusions into ice. Emancipated from addiction, I basked in the sunshine of self-love and left the judgment of others to God alone.

My past no longer made my future. My soul wouldn't settle into the herd of complacency. My thoughts couldn't be domesticated. I saw the blanked-out faces of the human race standing around. They were dressed in designer fashion and peacocked about in self-arrogance. Day by day, I began to solve the great riddle entangled within me. Nothing happens by chance, the light inside of me contradicted hand-me-down prejudices. I stumbled over the truth and found myself on my knees.

This world is only temporary, and my religion became kindness. I embraced the sweet stupidities of my family's legacy. Once a puppet shaken about, I cut all earthly strings. The great expedition to forgiveness surrounded my soul with angels. The years spent on the streets ministered to my mind's eye. The journey through virtual time and space finishes at the point of arrival. I've got many miles to go to reach my destination, and each day, I began to learn something new about myself.

I no longer wasted my life manufacturing a numbness, and I no longer killed myself to hide my weaknesses. Humility opened my soul to be stronger than mankind. I reprogrammed myself and cultivated the love inside my heart. I met a friend Bill W., and Bill and I spent many evenings together processing the thoughts of who I didn't want to be.

♥

Once a week, I had to go to outpatient therapy with Steve, Joanna, David, and his wife, Stacy. Within a few weeks, Karen and her family joined the outpatient group. I first met Karen in my last week in treatment. She was an unruly eighteen-year-old. The smoke from the unseen fire inside her heart burned bright, so fiercely, she never wanted anyone to forget her free spirit. She didn't take the time to think of anyone else.

One evening, out of the blue, she called me and wanted me to attend a meeting with her. I drove down to Moore, Oklahoma, and picked her up at her parents' house. I didn't take heed of the words one counselor told me, "Never date anyone you met in treatment and work on yourself in your first year of sobriety."

The red blinking lights in her eyes didn't keep me away.

I preferred to be alone, write poetry and swing from star to star. Abandonment never let me trust anyone. Sitting in the loft of my mind, I saw the world as a human comedy. Survival meant being a lone wolf. I never developed the self-worth to date. The toxic shame my family gave me maintained a constant vigil in my core being. Being a poet, I uncovered the lust's glow, sweltering in emotion. A dark planet once eclipsed by the sun no more. She became my new drug, and my feelings no longer lived in Switzerland.

I desired, wanted to catch on fire. Hidden deep in my soul, I traded love for lust. The point being, I didn't even love myself enough before I made my son. The baby inside my heart still screamed in the middle of the night for love and tenderness. I won't lie. The moment she started talking about baby names, my heart stopped.

I thought, "I'm no expert, but two children just brought another child into this world."

Smoke screens of denial pretended like this was nothing at all. Seven months without drugs or alcohol, I moved into my house, and I married Karen in November 1983. I tried to fill the emptiness in my heart with another human being.

It didn't take long for me to realize my colossal mistake. Isolated from the world, right or wrong, the fog of marriage made my life very unpleasant. Two plus two was five to me. I had committed the cardinal sin of lying to myself by marrying her. I clenched my fist and marched stupidly into the unknown puffing my chest with the pride of ignorance.

♥

A marriage made me feel part of the scenery, and my soul was trapped. I was born to be a writer, but I knew so little. Blinded by life, I couldn't help but spin in circles over and over again. I survived, never truly lived. My heart still showed me I was someone else.

♥

My complacent disposition reconciled me into doubt. My insides began to rust from my silent tears. I came home from work and smiled at Karen and played with my son. I became an actor once again. I couldn't give her what I didn't have to give. A coward, I didn't have the nerve to tell her. I carved out a portion of my heart and kept it for me. I hid behind my skyscraper façade.

When I did come out from behind my walls, a melody of boundless energy played in my heart. It was safer to hold on to the past and not judge yourself. I continued to deny myself, instead of listening to my heart. Most days of my life, I wore a mask. I was a non-believer in self, an under-achiever, and primary caregiver.

Sometimes God allows us to make a mistake to accomplish what He wants in us. The love I felt for my son became a vessel of marvelous thoughts. Into the wonderment of his being, my son's tiny fingers surrounded my pinkie. My mind slowed down, and it was there I felt the pulse of poetry bursting to be written.

♥

As a new family, we attended church between our verbal arguments. Karen wanted my devotion and understanding, but I gave her the anesthesia associated with a delusion. We had nothing in common except Joshua. I put my energy into being a workaholic. Out of rehab, my denial and self-punishment worked me into exhaustion. Caught up in the trap of my self-imposed ignorance, I gave way to the melancholy thoughts and the habits associated with surrendering into freeze-dried, double-wrapped, vacuum-sealed conformity.

I switched my addiction from drugs and alcohol to work and working out. I used "Fuck" every other word. I have been alcohol-tested, chemically-proven, and spiritually-formulated into a modern medical miracle. Being married bored the shit out me.

♥

A dry drunk, I passed out every night after I beat myself. The past was stronger than the present. A poster boy for the illustration of a human tragedy, I never thought beyond the day and never deposited anything into my future. I reaped no commissions from the world around me, for I lived the life others wanted from me. With a clenched fist, my Irish anger white-knuckled sobriety each day and shut down my heart.

I hung on to the promise I made in treatment never to use again. The power to choose and respond to change could never happen as long as I played god in my life. My ego was conflicted. Good versus evil, a civil war raged within me. I had to fight someone, so I joined a kickboxing club. We met every Saturday morning and sparred full contact. Being only an orange belt, I remember throwing down with blue, brown, and black belts. A streetfighter, I beat them to the punch every time. They practiced. I continued to fight my father. The ability to take a punch and move forward through chaos came with over one hundred fist fights to my name. City-resilient, hard-headed, mean, and nasty, I had the intangible. Something an instructor couldn't teach was the spit and grit from living in the streets.

I found a new way to attack and rise up against the absurdity of life. I would fight anyone. One day, I took on a professional kickboxer who hated other black belts. He was an undefeated contender in Oklahoma City. He beat me like the hands of God wanted to beat some sense into my thick skull. Round after round, I smiled at him each time he hit my face. It slowly became cut, swollen and red. I didn't know how to back down and charged in for more. It wasn't him I was fighting.

After we had finished eight three-minute rounds, he came over to me, and he said, "Thanks for the workout, man! You are tough enough, but you better work on your skill set some more."

I hugged him and walked into the locker room to get my stuff. As I cleaned out my locker, a black belt came over to me and asked, "Why did you continue to fight when you knew you were outmatched?"

With two black eyes, a swollen face, and my right eye cut, I smiled at him and replied, "How will you ever know what your limits are unless you test yourself every day? This is what I do. I know no other way to be."

♥

After several months of sparring, blood was always in my urine, so I took up running. I wanted to run twenty miles and did. A few weeks later, the newspaper had an ad for the Andy Payne Memorial Marathon. I entered the race with only the expectation to finish. With only two long runs to my credit, my weekly mileage barely hit forty-five miles.

As the race started, I started out a pace comfortable for me. I held my position the whole race, and at twenty miles, I remained in third place. Running on empty, the only thing I had left in the tank was my heart. Over the last six miles, seven runners passed me. I finished in tenth place in a little over three hours.

The next day, my hamstrings punished me, and I could barely walk, but I fell in love with the runner's high it gave me. I ran every day in the wind, rain, or sunshine. My weekly mileage went over one hundred miles a week. I found the perfect drug, endorphins, to make me escape who I was. A man on a mission, I planned to win that race next year.

I settled for life below my intellectual level. Time ticked slowly. I did nothing to nourish my inner soul and tortured myself daily by running ten miles before the sun rose in the east. After work, I picked up Joshua from daycare and helped him with his homework. I cooked and made dinner for us. I fenced off my inner life and closed my heart to its calling.

I leaped from star to star to ignore my soul's whisper. My life was a hybrid between discipline and insanity. My self-imposed blindness protected me from all my insecurities. Reality had won, and my life became a silent movie. I stood in the background listening to the dull and little people express their small ideas. All I could feel was the illumination of self-forgiveness seeping from my heart, changing me.

♥

The vines of vanity grew separately and in a different direction. Karen and I chose our lives apart from each other. The truth inside of us began to reach a point in which the powers of our actions began to speak the words we both repressed. My pride was adamant, and I hadn't lied to her. At least, I couldn't articulate my selective reality. From time to time, I saw the hurt I caused in her. A quick smile hid her tears. Her eyes revealed the tenderness of her need to be loved. I could give her neither my pain nor joy, so I remained silent in my self-imposed prison cell. I didn't know what to do and upheld the legacy passed down to me.

Karen couldn't take it anymore, and she moved in with her parents in January 1987. It was no more than a power play on her part, and she hoped it would make me think. Life behind the eight-ball meant I had no choices, but once she moved out my dreams reunited with desire. Physically, intellectually, and morally I remained in the small circle inside my brain. I was afraid of living, so I gave chase to the setting sun to catch God in the dust of time.

In May 1987, I entered the Andy Payne Memorial Marathon. I had just finished a thirty-mile run three weeks before the race. The day had come to let loose in my soul a monstrous desire to achieve. At the starting line, the confusions of who I was slipped away when the gun went off. With each passing second, my feet skipped beyond the scenes of my life.

The race was held on old, empty Highway 66. The frustration of each step was trying to outdo the last one. Dedicated to moving forward toward a goal, I felt the miracle of each breath inhaled. My heart filled with passion and burst with energy through each mile. I crossed the finish line, and the joy of my dedication overcame my exhaustion. I won that race and discovered virtually nothing was impossible, even if the newspapers printed my name as coming in second. I qualified to run in the Boston Marathon.

♥

I continued to train and push myself each day and saw Joshua on the weekends. As the months went by, Karen and I decided to give our relationship another chance. They both moved back home in November. Her first night back, I discovered the irrationality of my choice. My heart wouldn't let go of the thought I was another. I understood the value of forgiveness and the lure of reinvention. I would rather be alone than be with someone I couldn't talk to. We separated for our final time.

I looked at the ugly and mean side of a promise made. I married someone without being in love. I brought a son into this world and wondered what chance I would give him. I took in all my sorrow, and in my negative waking thoughts, I followed my heart's calling. I looked into my son's blue eyes, filled full of wonder. I knew the love between us could never be wrong. I taught him how to read, just like my mother taught me. I mused while he played on the floor with his toys, "My child! I will protect you from the silent legacy bestowed unto mankind."

Every morning, I told myself, "I hate you."

Every evening, I told myself, "I love you."

At a crossroad of insanity and conformity, the voice inside my heart called me closer. Pain always made me advance into the unknown. The nature of this family tragedy could have closed my eyes, but instead, compassion opened my heart to see how my actions affected another. I saw patterns emerge from the past, circle back, and recreate a variation of something new, yet old. The truth was ugly to see, and my past wouldn't let me be. Although it was my life, the shades of others colored my soul. The impossible could be achieved only if I came to grips with my self-inflicted mental paralysis. Something inside of me wouldn't let it slip back into obscurity. I could feel the angel nestled in my soul sprouting its wings. I dared to reimagine my destiny from the ruins of my dumb choice.

♥

Writing has always allowed me to see life's fairytale coincidences were related, and they were only explained through self-reflection. The truth was hard to see when my eyes were closed or focused on other things. The mediation of two hearts beating as one equals enlightenment. A wandering soul, I ransacked ideas and wasn't satisfied writing all day. Pregnant in thought, my muse gave birth to poetic mischief beyond our daily arrangements. Through recognition, patterns long-concealed, emerged. When I stand in front of you, why can't you see me? I can see through you.

♥

Searching, I started attending church again while I got divorced. Thought stripped me of all biases and judgments. I examined the evidence of my life, and in God, I discovered the law of possibilities. My altered consciousness destroyed any thoughts of being an ass-kisser. My sensitivity opened the colors and emotions in words. In a world full of flag-wavers and crazy zealots, a poet is armed with only tolerance and understanding. I stood back, and my eyes broke down disguises of self-importance. There were nights so long, I howled at the moon.

I put my faith in Him and trusted He would guide me to His vision of me. I began to embrace each day, and gratitude permitted me to uncover the Cracker Jack surprise meant for me. As I mused, mammoth grasshopper thoughts jumped out from my mind, and I found knowledge came from adventures under the sun. In silence, I heard the wisdom of the wind whisper to me. I kissed each moment, for I now knew how vital each second was.

Out of the FIELD

♥

One evening, I attended a church singles party, and life's beautiful colors deepened, danced, and twirled before my eyes. I observed a Southern belle named Dixie. My heart felt the splendors from her beauty. The elegance of this woman opened my eyes, and my heart followed. She moved without warning. I reached the core of my being when I talked with her. She smiled into my eyes, and the world fell at my feet. She wanted something, something different out of life. Our conversations opened our candlelit eyes. Her friendship made me experience a hundred new words each day. I reached down into the garden in my heart and plucked a flower to give her. I asked her out, and we spent endless hours talking and laughing as our souls coalesced.

I felt myself a better man with her by my side. As my mind's eye watched from afar, the binding effect of laughter and love began to make me feel whole. I felt connected to another human being for the first time. As the months passed, I couldn't imagine my life without her. My thoughts illuminated brilliant progressing prose, and I stretched out the sky and engineered the sunrise. I twirled around naked and stripped away all my shadows. I skipped the part about protecting my heart. One day, I awoke, and she was there. She came from nowhere and filled my darkness with galaxies of stars. Her love let me look at everything differently. I never saw anything more enchanting. Gorgeous! I spent each morning lost in the wonder of watching her sleep. Beautiful and unclothed, love suited me fine. All day long, I waved goodbye to loneliness. Her danger invited me to rescue myself.

On Valentine's Day 1989, I walked into the Oklahoma state office where she worked dressed in a suit and tie. As I made my way through the maze of cubes, all the women in the office began to follow me. They sensed the romance in the air. I had in my hand a single rose in a vase, and I bought a simple card. As I walked up behind her, all the women huddled next to the wall to see. I whispered her name, "Dixie" just loud enough for her to hear me.

She turned around, and her eyes brightly glistened in both joy and embarrassment. She said, "Honey, what are you doing here?"

I handed her a rose and told her I wrote something on the card just for her.

She smiled and opened the card. Around us, forty wide-eyed ladies gawked at us. I looked and thought.

"The rose is from my heart, and the card entitles you to lunch. I already cleared it with your boss. The gift on the back of the card is to make you feel special. The way I feel when you're by my side. Happy Valentine's Day."

She turned the card over and attached were two tickets to the opera. She jumped up from her seat and gave me a hug. I whispered in her ear, "Let's go to lunch. I am getting the creeps from these old ladies looking at me."

She slapped me with a smile.

♥

Happiness warmed my soul. Kisses, hugs, barefoot and naked, the nights we spent together suited me fine. I was happy and blinded by life. I believed in her and thought love had finally found me. We began to spend every waking moment together. I never looked back and trusted her. I introduced her to Joshua. Every other weekend, the three of us started to do things together.

As our lives began to become entwined, she insisted, "Larry, you're going have to get your GED if we were going to take the next step. I don't care if you make more money than I do. My family will not accept you if you don't have an education."

I hesitated and thought, "Oh yeah, your family knows what's best for you."

She went on to say, "I have never ever had someone love me as much as you do. I feel completely and utterly adored by you. I want us to be together forever."

I smiled and told her, "You're the one who frees me. I love you."

In April 1989, I took Dixie back to Connecticut with me, for I decided to run in the Boston Marathon. My uncle Burney let us stay at his beach house, for they were on vacation in Saint Marten. I showed Dixie the pieces of my past that I wanted to forget. We drove up to Torrington, and I got lucky and found Robert washing dishes in some restaurant.

As I walked through the back door dressed in a sports coat and slacks, Robert was dressed in a white apron blotted with the day's events. The moment our eyes met, I saw the haunting images of our childhood trapped in his eyes. I walked up to him and said, "Hey brother, how have you been?"

He eyed me. Coldly he said, "What are you doing here?"

I noticed anger tighten every muscle in his body as he avoided interacting with me. I scanned the room. All his coworkers were looking at us. I said, "I flew in to run in the Boston Marathon on Monday."

From the hole in his heart, he looked up and said, "You always liked to run, didn't you?"

"Yeah, I am pretty good at it."

He couldn't scream. He couldn't talk, and he still lived under the bed. I saw his stifled life, and it confused me. He crawled inside himself like a snail. Beaten and defeated, I could only wonder why I had been blessed, and why he hadn't been. I wanted to love him, but he wouldn't let me close to him.

Unable to make an emotional connection, he was lost back in our childhood. I asked him, "Is there anything I can do for you?"

"You can leave."

I searched my mind for the image of his innocent face, and my mind ran through all the nightmares we shared together. He couldn't find his way out of the maze, so he gave up. A tear came to my face. I turned to him and said, "I was sorry I didn't do more to help you. I didn't know how to help myself."

The words I spoke ricocheted off his armor and headed toward the moon. My presence merely irritated him. With each step I took toward the door, empathy overwhelmed me. I loved him and couldn't correct what went wrong. I was a boy seasoned in hell, and my brother morphed into something small beyond repair. He was still five years old and still sobbed endlessly in the corner. Fear smothered his life. The sight of hopelessness in his eyes told me the words he couldn't say, "Is this going to happen to me all over again?"

As for the rest of the trip, I was thrilled to be with her every day, kissing her in the morning and seeing the reflection of my smile in her eyes. I finished the marathon in the top five percent of all runners.

Once we were back in Oklahoma, Dixie told me, "My parents want to meet the man who took their daughter to Connecticut."

"Is this a good thing or bad thing?"

"Well, dear, we'll find out how they really feel about you."

♥

As we drove up to Owasso, Oklahoma, Dixie told me, "My father owns a few gas stations in town. My mom is a stay-at-home mom. She is highly devoted to church activities. We'll know if they accept you in less than two minutes."

"Oh boy, I cannot wait."

The moment we drove into the driveway their dog began to bark endlessly. Dixie's father opened the screen door for his wife. His scrunched-up face looked at me.

I thought, "No, I'm not ready for this. It's going to be a long day."

As we got out of the car, we walked over to meet her parents, she said, "Mom and Dad, this is Larry, my boyfriend."

"Nice to meet you, Larry," her mom responded. "We thought your son was coming with you, too."

I looked over at Dixie, and her embarrassment told me I was done. I kept my head up high, free and had nothing to hide. Locked in their judgment, their lack of faith overpowered hope and robbed them of common sense.

Her father extended his hand for me to shake. He squeezed my hand like an instrument cracking a walnut open. I didn't dare make a face.

As we engaged in small talk, it was hard for them to bluff their way through this conversation. I quickly read every card they held. They never intended to move their position, so I went all in and grabbed Dixie's hand and pulled her close. I slammed my lips into hers and said, "I love you, babe!"

My outward affection said, "Okay, goddamnit, she's mine."

The look on her parents' faces told each other, "You're right, he's a problem. He has to go."

The rest of the day, I watched the silent movie play out before my eyes. A thought is an irreplaceable spark to intense action. The reason I always talk to God is I wanted to learn how to accept human absurdity. Their judgment made them forget about Christ's teachings. I knew Christianity was the marriage between Christ and a human spirit, and they judged my life from the Christian caste system they created to feel like the chosen ones. I smiled often. I tried to stay active in the conversation. I lied to them when we left, "It was so nice to meet you, and I hope to see both of you again soon."

On the way back home, we talked about my insight into her parents' thoughts of me. I said, "I don't think your parents like me very much."

"They don't like you. It is because you are divorced and have a child. I told them that you have treated me better than any other man has, and I love you and want to be with you."

I smiled and felt the sincerity of her words. "You know I love you, too, and I want to be with you forever. You're my best friend in the whole wide world. You're better than ice cream on a hot summer day."

Her face warmed in tenderness. Her smile glistened like the sun warming the earth. She said, "I'm not going to let my parents dictate my life. I love you too much for that to happen."

I felt safe in the world with her by my side. As the days turned into weeks, I picked up on the deflation of her devotion toward me. My ears didn't hear the same bubbly passion in her voice. I sensed her pulling away, and it happened more and more each time she went back to visit her parents. Her tapping fingertips foretold the secret she hadn't yet shared.

I have known lonely times when I couldn't find a friend, but I always thought our love would still find a way to overcome. The lack of time on the telephone told about things brewing, and one day, out of the blue, she came over to my house. When I let her in, she wasn't smiling.

She took a deep breath and said, "Larry, we have to talk. I don't know where to start, but I have decided that it is best if we don't see each other anymore."

I thought, "Holy shit."

She just grabbed the Band-Aid and ripped it off. Her words let me hemorrhage, and I reached a moment in life where I even abandoned myself.

As she stared out the window looking for help to come, my mind wanted to sit this one out, but my lips couldn't help but whisper the words, "Your parents! They got to you, didn't they?"

My mind kept changing directions, and my abandonment issue gave chase. I felt completely unlovable and danced with a ghost named Rejection.

Her deafness made me feel like a meteor racing through the earth's atmosphere at Mach 40. Tiny dust particles, memories were being burned away. I reached out to touch her, but she pulled away. The absence of her love spun me like a top. I fell backward into the darkness which was filled full of tyrants, demons, and my father's voice inside my head, "You'll never amount to anything."

I couldn't hear a word she said and had no place to hide. I shook my head sadly and muttered, "No! No! No!"

She turned and looked at me crying, and she said, "No man has ever made me feel so loved and cherished the way you do, but I cannot be with you anymore."

My failing soul illuminated every suffering known to man, and the innocence of my love froze and shattered when she shut the door.

As she drove away, I caught a glimpse of the light before darkness instantly engulfed me. The wonderment of my discovery transformed back into my silent legacy. My mind knew I could survive anything, but my heart merely broke in two. My self-esteem depreciated, and the compounded daily interest I owed for daring to defy the odds bankrupted my soul. A poet and wise man stood before God, not with a pen in his hand. I fought for each second and found out I was a slave of my baptism. I cried for days. Blinded by life, I almost abandoned myself forever.

13

I'mpossible

I couldn't sit home every night, so I got dressed up and went to a bar. A drink of rum and coke sat in front of me, watering down from time. I'd look at it every once in a while. The bartender asked me, "Are you going to drink it or look at it all night?"

"I'm taking my time, for I may never find my way back home."

"Oh, you're one of those. How many years sober?"

"Over six years."

He said, "Let me give you some advice, son. You see that fellow over there in the purple shirt with two women next to him? He has been to treatment three times and can't stay sober for more than a month. His wife just kicked him out of the house. The guy sitting three tables to your right just got his year chip, and he's now off the wagon. I'm ten years sober. I see them come and go."

"Why do you work in a bar if you had a problem with drinking?"

"I'm God's helper."

I laughed and responded, "I got to hear this one."

"God has put me in your life. At this moment, you're shattered and lost. Your addiction has broken you down into arrogant impatience. At least twice a week, I share the same insights with other lost men who are searching for the answer to anything but themselves. Without a college degree, I can tell you a third of them never hear a word I say, a third of them aren't ready, and the other third gets it. Anyone with over six years gets it. Be careful not to let your shortfalls strip you of your wings."

"Don't!" my inner voiced yelled.

I scanned the people laughing and drinking all around me. It was embarrassingly clear I had a choice. I pushed the drink forward and said, "Not today, I'm not really in the mood right now."

He smiled and nodded back at me.

♥

As the weeks passed, my deepest fear muddied my thoughts. I lost my focus, and the images of the past made me an egomaniac who hides inside himself. I wasn't content in silence. A human soul shrinks or grows in accordance to one's gratitude. Small, there was nothing enlightened about me anymore. I fought the world around me once again.

One day while running after a snowstorm, I gave the driver of an automobile the middle finger. He thought he owned the road and didn't have to share it with me. The sides of the streets were piled high with snow. He turned his car around and headed back toward me. I ran in the middle of the road and gave up no ground. Like knights on horses wielding lances, we charged into the hellish powers of our egos. We both stayed in our lanes, but my fists pounded on the hood of his car as he passed. He turned around again. He stopped across the street. I told him, "If you get out of that car you will not get back in it!"

His wife yelled at him, "Leave him alone! He is crazy!"

"You better listen to your wife."

It was like I regressed to fourth-grade recess. I felt so alive, picking fights. I challenged men twice my size, for the power of rage made me stand ten feet tall with tusks made of steel. There was no heaven, only the coldness of hell in my heart. I traded gratitude for those old rusty, ugly, and meaningless behaviors. The madness I kept re-experiencing came from the abandonment buried deep within my soul. I've paid the price for trying to own myself.

The images of the cheap paint-by-numbers colored portrait of my family stuck in my mind. Of the ten thousand days of my life, I found in the billionth second my mother's memories shaped my life. She brought reason back from the dead. A white speck of dust against the blackness of a cruel world. I opened my mind. Bastard wisdom gave birth to a poet's soul. I didn't ask for my role and couldn't ignore it. I wished I couldn't see the dandies and chameleons. Life on autopilot de-evolved the human race.

The winds of time still chiseled and sculpted my life. Weakness made me feel, and it became hard to grow spiritually when I felt so inferior. However, the more I struggled, the more I learned. The ability to think heightened my self-awareness. I had the strength to reach far into the unknown parts of my emotions. Being a poet, my eyes stole what they could along the way. I made fire out of words to keep my heart burning. I found it again, eternity! Out on a tightrope, I experienced the choice of placing each footstep in front of the other, and in the imaginable, I found it was possible to walk on air.

♥

Jesus must love the idea of fixing something broken and unwanted, and then, He must like to watch it grow in the harmony of His love. He is an artist, inventor, and a soul mechanic all rolled into one, but his greatest quality was His humility. He had washed His disciples' feet before the world crucified Him. I remembered He once said, "No servant is greater than his master, nor is a messenger greater than the one who sent him." I smiled at the sunbeam of love I found in darkness. After six years of white-knuckle self-denial, I saw my old friend Bill W. walking down the street one day, and he invited me to a club on Western Avenue. I sat and listened to the insight of others. I looked for a sponsor who had street smarts.

After a couple of weeks, I noticed Mark crossed my path several times. His confessions often stimulated my thoughts. The design of God can only be appreciated if you see things for what they are, and if one opens his heart to hear the Author's words. He read the inner pages of my life without knowing me. I had come to terms with the One who shared my heart. I surrendered my will, or I would have continued to beat the shit out of myself.

After a meeting, I went over to Mark and waited for a few people to stop talking with him. I told him, "Every time you say some in a meeting, your words scratch open my wound."

He smiled and asked, "Why do you suppose that is?"

After a long pause, I replied, "I am broken inside, and your words pick at my heart. They invoke thoughts inside of me."

"Obviously, you have things inside your heart God didn't put there. Why don't you share at the meetings?"

"I kept my thoughts to myself. Hey, I came over to ask you if you want to be my sponsor."

"Come to the speaker's meeting on Friday, and we'll go out and talk after the meeting."

"Okay, see you then."

After that meeting, we drove to a twenty-four-hour dive diner. As we sat across from each other in the booth, Mark asked, "Why don't you tell me about yourself?"

My street sense knew I couldn't posture for position or even manipulate him. Not much of conversationalist, I began, "I started using at twelve years old. At times in my life, my profession was a drug dealer, a burglar, thief, an actor, and poet. I've been homeless twice and lived in a field for almost eight weeks. I've been sober for six years and not attended any meetings. I met my ex-wife in treatment."

"Didn't they tell you?"

Looking at the table, I said, "Yeah, yeah, they did."

"Oh, I see you're one of those who thinks he is different or even unique," he interjected. "A little about me, I too have lived on the streets and will call you out on your bullshit. I have been sober for six years too, and I have attended a meeting every day. It's my guess, you're good at just getting by."

"Wonderful assessment."

After we had stared each other down for a few seconds, Mark asked, "So you have not been to a meeting in six years, and you're still sober?"

I looked at him and didn't know if he was challenging me to something. I replied, "Yeah, why?"

Mark smiled and said, "You must have the will of Samson, but your self-will can only take you so far in life. Nothing in this world happens unless God wants it to happen. What do you want out of life? Do you want to just survive or learn to be part of life?"

Caught off-guard, my mind flatlined and froze. I eventually said, "I don't know. I deal with life as it comes to me. Make it up as I go. You know, I'm a freestyle poem."

"You come to me dressed in a suit and tie, and I can see that you have done very well for yourself. You have navigated your way through many obstacles in your life. However, are you really living? Are you the best person you can be? Do you wake up every day and know you are going to give life your best effort? What have you really done with your life? I am offering you a life you only dreamed of when you are alone. God knows your thoughts and desires, and I can see you are simply too afraid to venture beyond the thought of what you could be."

My emotions fluttered between being irritated and ecstatic. I didn't know if I wanted to fight Mark or embrace him. I thought and replied, "I am not exactly clear what you are saying to me. I'll talk to you later, man. I have to go."

He grinned and said, "Well, my friend, I am saying you can choose to challenge yourself and grow every day, or you can be captured by your fears. I will open your eyes to see that your disappointment and suffering are profound lessons, no more. You will embrace your failures, for they define your character. One should live his life in two stages. The first one, who you are now, and the second one, who you want to be."

My soul told me this wasn't going to be pretty. There would be no friendships made here. I could tell he didn't play fair, and the hardest thing would be to keep my mouth shut. He always was right! I had thought of the word freedom before I mumbled, "You're offering me freedom?"

"I offer nothing. You choose your own truth and honor what you already know. Break free! Break free from what has not worked for you. You did it when you walked away from your family at eighteen years old. That took some real guts!"

"You're a trip. You like to hear yourself talk, don't you?"

He ignored my comment and went on to say, "I can tell you my eyes see the miracle of each sunrise. Fear will shrink-wrap and smother your life. Your thoughts of being inadequate are powerful beyond measure."

"Everything I need is inside my heart. It has always worked for me," I snapped back.

Mark counterpunched, "Ah, you might, but have you honestly seen the moment God has given just to you? I'm mindful of my journey, and every person God has put in my life. I sense His presence every day. You can continue to deny yourself, and you will only survive. Is that the life you want? Will it satisfy the hunger inside you?"

I never had a problem with saying what I thought, "You're a witch doctor, aren't you? A fucking witch doctor."

He chuckled and replied, "I once could only communicate through sarcasm, too."

"I take that back. You're a smart-ass witch doctor."

I looked at him like he was crazy, but there was a stubbornness about me that was never frightened by words. I live and breathe inside of them and told Mark, "Hey, I have to go and will get back to you if I want you to be my sponsor."

"My friend, I will hear from you tomorrow."

I blinked, caught momentarily off-guard. "What?"

"I can see in your eyes the life that you've left behind already. Your eyes are full of wonder, even as you mumble words of disbelief at me."

I walked away mumbling, "Witch doctor."

♥

My eyes burned from the vision of explosive growth. I didn't want to punch a time clock. I wanted to be better than my family. Did God put the life I couldn't find right in front of me? The struggles of the half-life lived began to die. The deeper and darker the pain, the brighter God can make a human life shine.

♥

Humbly, I accepted the grace offered to me. I called Mark. "Hey, after kicking around the idea of you being my sponsor, I would like you to give me a chance."

A long pause ensued. "Why?"

"Aw fuck," I shouted out, "Not this witch doctor shit again! Okay! Okay! Your words speak to my heart!"

"You have a hard time sharing. Why don't you come over and tell me your story?"

Later that day, I opened up to him and found someone who understood and accepted me. It completely turned my world around, and I trusted another human being. Serendipity, a natural oasis, let me drink from the waters of friendship. I didn't know how to connect with people, but I did that day. I wasn't afraid anymore. The magic entwined in conversation changed the mundane into the profound. Self found its purpose.

My ensnared mind began to untwine. There were no spiritual centers, no gurus, no wise men, and no graduate degrees given. I spied on the world and its cruelty, but faith opened my heart to love. The quiet moments alone with God let me find the beauty inside of me. My inner voice cheered me onward.

Before I left for the day, Mark said, "We're going to rectify the situation right now."

"What do you mean?"

Out of the FIELD

"Your situation, Larry. We're going to start your training— with the basics," he said. "I want you to write down all your immoral acts and crimes against civilization. I want to know about the first piece of bubble gum you lifted from a store, you got it?"

"Yeah, I got it! You're on your witch doctor trip again."

Over the next two weeks, I wrote down all my dirty deeds and exposed the naked truth of my plight of survival. I never fully expected to be expunged from my past. I was wrong. The splendors of self-forgiveness gave me back my heart, and I found the likeness of myself in everyman.

A speck of dust suspended by sunlight, I hovered above it all. Compassion rid my soul of nonsense. I felt another's sorrow, and I immersed myself in a tear. I heard the voice behind the words spoken. Sufferings found wisdom. I pardoned myself and let each day begin with a smile. I appreciated my sensitivity for the first time, for it was the cornerstone of my lawless prose. I reached into the mindfulness of God and saw the mile marker in my journey to be another.

♥

Mark instructed me to attend a meeting every day, and he wanted me to share experiences in these sessions. A lone wolf, I kept to myself and shared every now and then. A few months after the pink cloud disappeared, I compared happiness to misery, and a foul mood followed. Several bad days later, my patience wore thin. I attended a meeting anyway and sat there waiting for the hour to pass. I made no eye contact with anyone.

Suddenly without notice, the chairperson called on me, "Would you like to share?"

A wicked smile spread across my face, and I said, "I don't even know why I am here. These meetings, all they do is cause me pain. I don't even like any of you people. I should go home and get my machine gun and fill this place full of holes. All I feel is the pain stuffed away from my past. I hate every one of you."

The chairperson looked over at Mark and said, "Thanks for sharing. Keep coming back!"

After the meeting was over, I tried to make my way to the door, but I was trapped by compassion. Twenty people came up and gave me a hug and told me, "I love you, brother! You're doing good work. Keep it up."

Mark looked on from a distance and laughed. He walked over and said, "Let's go out and get a cup of coffee."

"Yeah, let's go and get away from all these touchy-feely people."

At the café, we sat across from each other in a booth. He asked, "How many guns do you have?"

I laughed and replied, "I have a fully auto machine gun with a silencer, AR-15 converted to fully auto, a .44 Magnum semi-auto, a .357 Magnum, a 9mm Beretta, and a .380 for concealment. I have a few .22s for plinking. I make my own ammo, too."

"Why do you have so many guns?"

"Just in case I need them. You never know what might go down. I'm ready for anything."

Mark snickered and said, "If you truly have God on your side, why do you need a gun for protection? My trust in God flows out of my ability to experience His grace every day, not hide behind false security of a gun or a nation."

"You truly are a fucking witch doctor, you know? You had one too many acid trips, didn't you?"

He ignored me and said, "I found the greatest single cause of pain and suffering came when I denied Him. My strength comes from the capacity to let God do His job in my life. He doesn't need my help."

"Keep going, I don't have a smart-ass comment yet."

"I kneel down and humble myself to set myself free. I have simply been unmasked. When you discover the core value of your life, you'll freely trust God and be mindful of His grace. You will let God be God, and your humbleness will become a childlike trust that will exalt you. Nothing in this world happens unless God wants it to happen. Keep on knocking on the door, and one day, God will open it for you."

My eyes pushed him back, and my pride blew up like a pupfish. I replied, "Hey man, why do you push me so much?"

Like every great wise man, he took his time to answer, and he said, "You get it. You don't realize you have what it takes to do great things. You once were homeless, and you have found your way to gain material things. You have more things than you need, and it doesn't fill your heart. I see the story that you can share with others, and the souls you could save by sharing. I have watched you around people. You understand their emotions and their needs, I can see the love and compassion inside your heart. You can see beyond the immediate need and search below the surface. Some of these folks cannot make it through a day without using drugs or alcohol, but all you have to do is make a promise to yourself. You just fight everything and everybody in your life. A word of advice for you, a soldier either lays down his weapon, or he dies by another's weapon. Which one are you going to be, Larry?"

Every time Mark talked with me, I felt like I brought a knife to a gunfight. As his words bounced around in my head, I said, "Yeah, yeah, yeah, I love you too. You're still a witch doctor in my book."

He laughed to defuse the situation.

♥

As the weeks unfolded, I saw the truth was never far behind. I just had to look within myself to find it. One thing I learned about sobriety is you have to keep killing all those little pesky dragonflies that pop up every day. If you don't, they'll mature into an armor-plated, fanged soul-eater. I never stopped paying attention to the little things anymore.

♥

Mark treated me like a prospect. I trusted not in my willingness to do the task itself, but I sought the wisdom and experience from doing the task. He made me sponsor young men who had less than thirty days' sobriety. With each conversation with them, I tried to help these young people stay sober, and one by one, they fell back into their temptation using drugs or alcohol.

After the last one had gone back to using, enlightenment hit. I did "get it."

The key was in my heart the whole time. I entered the sacred space and found the wisdom to change my life. I once peddled dope and now dealt hope. It was when I used my mind to see others that I discovered me. Each day was a precious gift, and I saw the wonder and amazement of God's grace. I respected those who couldn't offer anything to me in return. I had untangled the many strings that kept me from growing.

♥

Mark kept me busy learning something new every day. I read a book a week. Individually, I rose above my petty personal concerns and began to love everyone the way God loved me. I looked at the war of self-interest raging everywhere, and in the battle cry of everyone's thoughts, I witnessed the illogical, unreasonable, and self-centered. The world was full of businessmen and idiots. Desire, greed, and lust destroyed one's capacity to love. We are who we are, from the choices we chose.

I fell into quiet revolutionary thoughts. I disarmed my old memories and gave myself an opportunity to envision godhood. As I stepped back in my mind, I examined my wounds and the truth about being disenfranchised. My whiteness allowed me to see how an outside appearance shut down someone's senses. A categorical mind draws battle lines and converses without embarrassment. Secret infidels, groupthink strategies, the truth, I found, we're more similar than different. My eyes displayed a kaleidoscope of color, shapes, and sizes. In the tumbling corridors of my empathy, we all performed the same movements and choose to create, destroy, love, or hate.

Humility let my soul wander among the blended red, orange, and yellow sunsets. I expanded my mind's eye beyond the moon's shadows, and the reflection extended my circle of compassion. I prayed for those who troubled me. I wrote down every defect on a piece of paper and placed a note into a bowl. Each morning, I pulled one out and worked on my shortcoming throughout the day. For example, "self-confidence," was written on one side, and the other side of the paper had examples written on it. "Introduce yourself to three strangers." It was when I set short-term goals God took care of the bigger picture for me. I became a parent to myself.

♥

I allowed myself to be loved, and it took courage to open up to a room of complete strangers. I analyzed every detail of my spiritual growth and was astonished by the power of forgiveness. I called the witch doctor and told him, "I think I am ready to share my story with others."

"Really! Why now?" he asked.

"Okay, I'll tell, but you can't say a word."

"Fair enough."

"I purged the pieces from my mind to free my heart. It won't be easy, but it will rid me from the ugliness inside of me."

"I'll set it up."

♥

I had an appointment to speak at a detox center. It was a ten-day program, and it offered hope to patients at the first step in recovery. Dressed in a suit and tie, scared to death, my palms began to sweat. I exposed my soul to the fear of public speaking. I looked into each of the patient's eyes as they introduced themselves to me. Compassion overwhelmed me.

My words found the spaces between us and entwined our lives. I am my brother's keeper and could feel each one of their lost souls searching. My mind was in its own place, and it was freed with a single step toward the podium to share my story. As I stumbled, courage led me to complete honesty without fear. Supertramp extraordinaire.

♥

That evening, I strolled through the meadow of my memories. I journeyed from the inside out and felt the coolness of His presence near my soul, once again. The noise of the world disappeared, and intuition spoke to my mind. Poetic images awakened my soul beyond the charming poisons of a once-mutinied life. Uninhibited by my faith, hope, and empathy, I witnessed the world through the eyes of God.

My spiritual survival depends on the awareness to see the strings attached to desire. The illumination of spiritual realities came alive in self-taught words. I extracted wisdom from suffering and sorrow. I fell backward through time and saw the inherited vice that once consumed me. I was once the king of deception, for I told ten thousand lies. I was once the master of all façades, for I deemed myself the greatest of all actors. I, now, became the greatest of all thieves, for I stole back all my sin and the knowledge accompanied with it.

I stood in a moment in time which I saw the riches of kings, poets, and visionaries. I saw the hand-me-down values and common thoughts worth two cents. I knew my life was now my own. I found a Father to love and please. He loved the wandering poetic kid the world threw away.

He opened my eyes and heart to every talent within me. I saw the world as my playground and grasped the love every person deserves. I remembered the toil and the blood of a life without a choice. I became every word I spoke, and my actions or lack of action defined me as a human being. Limitations made me think outside of the box, and struggle was wisdom waiting to be discovered. Empathy allowed me to feel the hearts of others and see the world through another's eyes. My tears dried in the sunshine of joy, and I found the capacity to forgive. I had a choice to love or hate. Madness led me to serenity.

I saw the truth that resides in every human being, and a life deeply lived expands the circle of love in which it both gives and receives. Love has neither color nor gender. Human life can be seen or even judged a thousand different ways, but only God can read the poetry one writes in his soul.

I took back all my senses, and in the respite from fear, I stepped out from the shadows of nothingness into the mindfulness of thoughts and feelings. I dreamed of spiritual ideas that were gorgeous, gallant, and made of gold. I embraced religion, birth, death, the past, the future and became part of the human race. I had the greatest advantage in this world, for I once lived in a field under the watchful eye of God alone. I wouldn't choose this life I had been given, and then again, I didn't win or lose it on my own. I came out from the places I hid and began to breathe, and the molecules of air allowed me to think, enjoy, and love. His grace found a way to my heart. His love was stronger than the hopelessness I was fed by the others. The beauty of His forgiveness now shined outwardly through my eyes, and I beheld the truth of my existence, within one body and soul.

14

The Spirituality of My Religion

I found myself when I had no one else to blame and stopped judging others. The gates of eternity opened when I surrendered my will. An artist, I drew from my imagination and encircled two worlds. Detached from the illusions others created, gratitude embraced simplicity. I reflected on what love I had given and what love I failed to provide. Every vision I'd imagined was at my fingertips. A broken-winged angel, hope healed my wings so I could fly. Religion gave me Jesus, and the light from Christ's eyes let me see all the tortures associated with slavery. I walked through the door of enlightenment and stepped into mindfulness. I saw the face of God in every human being.

Love cannot be divided or given incompletely. I put my heart back into my soul and saw there was no chosen one, no master race, and no absolute conviction. All of God's children were contagious in judgment. I immersed myself in my indifference and stood on the edge of life. I only knew one thing with any certainty—belief in God made me recognize there was nothing more Godlike than to love everyone. With the likeness of God in my heart, there was no place for elegance, science, or violence. My soul glistened, and I forgot all of my yesterdays and was knighted today. Passion opened my heart and let me give each second of my life the attention it deserved. Being alive was marvelous.

Redemption came from being of service to humanity, and acceptance of others gave me divine compassion. Transcended by acts of benevolence, awareness brought me to a place where I experienced the mindfulness. He was the Great Conductor. In the knowledge of both truth and goodness, I found the character to reshape illusions and trade my dreams in for actions. An up-to-the-minute substitute for a belief, my spirituality let me touch the one who walks among the breeze. In a greater understanding of God, I saw religion without spirituality was no more than a mob with an objective to control the world. In the realization of my own potential, I recognized kindness was the universal language of God, and happiness came from being humble enough to experience His grace. I lived to tell the secrets of my soul and found where real beauty lives. In my service to others, I volunteered at the detox center and embraced each addict that crossed my path.

Humility honored my former self with the nobility of forgiveness. In a world that follows blindly, I forgot all about this talk of Jesus coming back and began to live. It's a great balancing act thinking for yourself. Each morning, I stepped back and threw out my arms to hug the universe.

I changed myself, and the world changed with me. As my story got around, I was asked to be the main speaker at the Friday night meeting. As I walked into the club on Western Avenue, I saw one hundred and fifty souls waiting for me to share my experience, hope, and dreams. Before I took the podium, I took a second and reflected on my spiritual journey of forgiveness.

My mind flashed back to the child's prayer I said on Lovely Street that one cold, dark, snowy evening. My heart felt the warmth it created, and soon I realized everything I ever needed was inside of me. It came as no surprise that God had planned this all along. I couldn't imagine where I would be today if I could not feel all the colors, tones, and variations associated with words. The physical experience I had with words let me see one could rewrite his life. The secret of my success was the ability to see the smallest choices had the most significant impact.

Once on stage, my spirit took me through a series of natural emotions and memories. I remembered the simplest act of kindness that saved my life. I opened my wound, and the light of my compassion poured out. With no resentment and no hatred, I embraced the oneness of God in my soul. I shared the story of an abandoned boy who created a monster inside to protect himself from the adults in his life. I guaranteed each person listening would enrich their lives serving others. I closed with, "I weep not for my memories, but I weep for those who let life pass them by. Each day, I remember Him who remembered me, the one who lived in a field."

After I finished speaking, a dozen or so strangers came up and thanked me for sharing. As I observed each of them, shame held them hostage, but their eyes cried out for freedom. With the emotional range of the cresting sun, I could read a motive in someone's actions and sense a tear behind an eye. A blooming flower of thoughts and logic, I plucked the red, black, and tri-colored petals of knowledge and tossed them into the wind. I reduced the world down to a single word fighting to be heard. In my mind's eye, I illuminated the certainty with a pinch of empathy, and sympathy expanded my awareness. I saw each of us in our improvised costumes. I was hidden and wasn't. A poet's eyes spied on the ebb and flow of God's grace.

♥

The revolutionary thoughts of God evolved to no end in my mind. As I stopped and beheld church life unwinding before me, I couldn't help but wonder where God was in the sport of world religion. True believers raised His flag and proclaimed themselves the defenders of His faith. In their lukewarmness, they wasted their time talking about those whom they disliked and cared not to understand. It was a conversation that compared every human being to themselves and their superior faith. They judged others on what they saw, and they thought being saved gave them the solemn rule of the world and free speech without compassion. Learned behaviors one seldom regrets.

Every time I listened to them, I saw how all my changes flowed through Him. God's justice was discovered in the reflection of each of my actions and motives. All of us pass or fail in our choice to listen to Him. I had to die a thousand deaths to experience His touch upon my soul. I recognized truth through Him and understood gratitude had led to the acceptance of everyone. I lived the actual meaning of forgiveness in both myself and others.

Religion is based on the thoughts of God through man, but the spirituality of my religion was based on my day-to-day experiences with God. As I grew in both love and understanding, the risk of separation and being lost ceased to exist. Every breath was a simple gift, and each one reminded me of His loving grace. I knew God could defend His own flag, so I walked out into His world and began to embrace it like a child embraces the flowers in a field.

Unquestionably, the purity of religion can lead to a spiritual experience only compared with harmony. Enlightenment opens the mind to see the world through the eyes of God, but True Believers consider themselves too pure for anyone. The vanity of their beauty, and the dishonesty of their wisdom twist language, muddy clarity, and pull mankind into a freefall from God's intended grace. Their idolatry comes from their ability to hide behind quotation marks, and it portrays an us-versus-them attitude, pitting them against everyone.

♥

The eyes of God have no preconceptions, and I was freed from the appalling ignorance of others' religious interpretation. God's ambiguities were not poetic lenses for one to become a bigot and speak on His behalf. The anguishes I saw were abolished by my humble prayers. The freedom to forgive my neighbor came when I chose not to play demigod in others' lives. The evolution of consciousness came from my suffering, and grace was realized when I opened my eyes to see life as a spiritual journey back home to heaven.

A fenceless civilization, a walkabout to wisdom, I reached the core of all truths through prayer and meditation. I kneeled only to weep with His angels. I traveled to the sacred holy place in the idea that love is only achieved within oneself. He loved the world, so I too will love my brother. It was a child's broken heart that opened up the wilderness of Self, and it allowed me to discover the journey was filled with magic and keen insights.

An ignorant mind could not separate grace from luck. I saw most people had no moral obligation to ensure integrity or fair play. There were so many different versions of God out on the street, I wondered if religion was invented to see how a man would treat someone of a different belief. Individuals and groups cared more about their views of God than being merciful toward others. They paid attention to the sins of others in order not to see their own.

♥

An evil man takes more than he needs. I found a Christian man robs with a smile and uses a self-righteous arrogance as his gun. One day at work, Rich called a company meeting. It had been known for some time that Rich didn't see eye to eye with his partner. Rich had tried to get financing from a bank to buy the other half of the business, but he was unsuccessful.

As the meeting got started, Rich introduced Mr. Williams, his personal financial advisor. "Everyone, please be seated. I would like to present Mr. Williams. He is a man with a vision for our company."

Mr. Williams stood up with a jackass's smile.

Rich's voice began to crack while he told us, "I have called you all here today, for I have reached an agreement on buying the other half of the business. I have decided to take our retirement cash account and turned it into an Employee Stock Ownership Plan (ESOP). The benefit of the ESOP plan will provide each of you with ownership and an interest in our company. You, as owners, will take great pride in working for our business. You will be given shares equal to the value that you currently have in your retirement account. How do you like them apples, partners?"

He acted like a child at Christmas, for he schemed a grand plan to deceive his flock of workers. His eyes sparkled like silver dollars in the sun. Greed hollows out a human heart through the constant impulse of a lie to yourself.

As I looked at Mr. Williams, he reminded me of a street hustler with his neon-colored paisley tie and cheap pinstriped suit. I thought, he's a pimp with a shuck-and-jive vision on how to help himself. A puppet of greed, a sociopath, can never comprehend the word "enough."

I thought to myself, ignorance is indeed bliss.

Being raised on the street, I knew I was being played and had no options to foil his plan. The clarity of my vision saw a life of loneliness, a false face grinning from a hollow shell. The money he took from us demonstrated he served two masters. White-collar crime, legalized thievery, begins when you short-sell yourself and pretend to be someone else of greater importance. A man of God just sold his partners a hundred shares of nothing and the chance it might be worth less tomorrow.

I turned to David and said, "This is not a good thing, and I bet we make nothing on our investment from this point forward."

"You're probably right."

♥

Hometown cooking, everything tastes the same. Men, especially, close their eyes and make vain faces against the total rationalization of life. Women live their lives how they been taught. Hometown thinking never escapes the boundaries of being born in a small town. I've noticed that their minds were filled with home-grown indulgences. I came in from forever, and now, I have to go somewhere else.

The missing piece of my life was elsewhere. I'd ask myself what I was doing here. I grew beyond my coworker's hometown thinking. Every thought I had, I'd dug around in the mud to find the grassroots connection to God. I wrote each night and found inspiration in the brown rusted flakes of time.

My coworkers slowly turned on me. They wanted me to be just like them. It was the voice inside my soul that crushed the small-town vision of me. Things change. Friends leave. Life doesn't stop. Whose heart must I break to be me? What lies must I shatter to find freedom from this world? The red bitterness of love makes me a lawless scribe. It was back out into the wildness from which I came.

♥

Real friends are always honest, and when they aren't, it's a pain you'll never forget. Friends turned into enemies who looked like dwarfs with big insect eyes. I held a book over my eyes at lunch. Lost in thought, I read boorishly dumb books, philosophy and poetry, and it opened my mind to the truth. A life without boundaries leads Republicans to scream bloody murder.

My bohemian soul traveled beneath, over and around the emotions attached to words. I grappled in the marvelous undercurrent of life until a poetic vision formed. The blessing of each day expanded as I continued to walk farther from the hissing fires of hell. The evolution of my soul wanted a perfect ending—an angel freed from all earthly constraints. I felt the wholeness of my spiritual empowerment. Faith and prayer let me see beyond attachments of this world. With a childlike heart, I walked fearlessly forward and realized the distance between God and my soul wasn't infinite, after all. I dreamed of revolutions in morals, movement in race relations and a life without greed.

My Christian coworkers didn't like me expressing my new beliefs, and they made sure their future came from their past. The generations of de-evolving followed true to those who die without understanding the gift of life. They no longer screamed at the atrocities of the world or heard a silent cry for help. Comfortable in mediocrity, their indifference thought everyone should see the world through their eyes.

They began to tell me to sit down, stand up, and roll over. I could see the love of Jesus somewhere in them, but it was shrouded by visions of dead presidents and vacations in Hawaii. Awareness opened my eyes beyond the walking dead. It's a blessing to love life and be able to see the dead among the living. A slave to their thoughts, I couldn't express my spiritual awakening to them, for I would be deemed a pagan in a traditional Christian sense. In stillness, I understood silence was the music that brilliantly orchestrated reasoning. Silence, in some measure, let me get to know my own mind.

♥

In my morning reflection, I no longer lived in a sardonic destiny and chose my own path. I saw the motivational factors of love, fear, and greed that made most men mere puppets on strings. I stood still, vision clearing, and saw the air of a winter night sneak its cold crisp hands around me. A vagrant's eye wondered why? A frozen heart still yearned for love. Eyes full of color, yet vacant and dead. Faces brightly painted, real things became fake. I couldn't stop this knowledge populating through my poetic eyes.

I watched those who believed in Jesus stuff their pockets full of paper notes. Their repentance was paid for by the toil and sweat of others. Children playing in paradise, some wanted to be a baby god. Money imposes a monopoly on the mind. Attitude and actions, told everyone, "I haven't done anything wrong."

I taught myself to see beyond the cookie-cutter thoughts. In the disconnection from others, my heart became free. I stretched out my imagination from star to star and to seek the magic from discovering my inner soul. I no longer played the part others wanted me to play, so management began to time my lunch breaks. They took my company vehicle away. They changed my job duties and watched my every move. I grew, and others never moved.

One day, Rich told me, "You have no future here working for me, and you won't receive another pay raise."

I looked inside him and saw sealed and preserved, the freshness of past generations. He was a fool who thought himself a wise man. A smile shined from my heart before I told him I would continue to do a good job for him until the fall semester started.

Reflection births wisdom, and in what others marginalized, I found useful and insightful. One day, my soul spoke to me. Others accepted me for my whiteness. Some employees placed a broken ghetto blaster in the middle of the grassy median of a four-lane road outside our office. They laid and waited for a homeless person to stroll by and pick up the radio. After he had taken a few steps, the employees chased him down like a lion hunting a hobbled gazelle. They humiliated and threatened the homeless person until he gave back the broken boom box.

Silently, I watched the collective mind of the group, and they were socialist at heart, not from a political position, from a moral one. Each of them succumbed to a frictional force. It's there, and it wasn't. Part of something more important than themselves, consciousness vanished, and paralysis overwhelmed their minds. They refused to see the dimension of God in the less fortunate or someone of another faith. The mob trampled on the spirit of the man to avoid feeling despised by the group's innate longing for anger and hate.

I did nothing. The mob repeated this action several times until they got bored. They wore designer shoes and were nurtured in human stupidity. They used words like "niggers" and "wetbacks." They looked down on the unwanted, unloved, and forgotten in society. Their thoughts bore no similarity to Jesus's teachings which they worshiped.

The worn-out ideas of traditional religion were an essential part of developing my soul. I cleared out the fear-based fire-and-brimstone thoughts with love and compassion from eternity. Despite being self-educated, the essential substance of my ideas came from my spiritual intuition and visions.

One night, my inner eye created a silent movie that revealed what He expected from me. My hands held tightly to the ghetto blaster as my coworkers chased me down the street. Startled, I woke frightened, for I failed to recall the field God rescued me from. I dressed in a suit and tie every day and ate most meals at a restaurant. I worried more about what others thought than doing the right thing. Selfishness stifled empathy. Cowards follow. Leaders take time, so I expanded the circle of my compassion to include a stranger's soul.

Out of the FIELD

♥

He held me closer than I ever knew. It was the flaws in my own soul that drove the lore of the unknown. I came down from my self-made throne. Resurrected, evolving, and falling apart, I climbed, as I fell, back into His grace. An army of one had a dream, and I couldn't hide from the truth of my being. Anyone can sell out. Each morning, God let me know, "I'm not done with you yet."

♥

As each day passed, my coworker's actions muttered to my ear. "You're not allowed to think unless you ask us first."

I thought to myself, traditional values without reason and logic were the cornerstone of their lives. They had no beliefs or imagination beyond what they were told as children. They spent their lives walking in an endless circle chasing the comforts of this world. Each of them pictured himself as the wisest of all generations. I witnessed the resurrection of the dead transcribed by their repetitive actions.

♥

An ego is blind, and sightless men are resistant to the power of grace. I observed Rich's choice to promote his own financial convictions and disregard his employees. He wanted to buy his way into heaven, and he could afford it now. He used his employees' retirement money for his own advantage. He showed me that a person who validates themselves with the acts of selfishness seeks only their enjoyment.

Without a conscience, the Christians who gave me life began to push me out the door. Disapproving of self-education and spiritual values, each day became remorseful. The more they showed me who they really were; the more I realized sadness only belonged to me. With my daily admission, I let God have each minute. Until one day, Rich summoned me into his office, "Larry, please come in and take a seat."

Eyesight has always been my second method of gathering intelligence. I continually listened to my angel's voice who poked my intuition into a heightened sense of awareness. Nothing looked right that morning. An intuitive mind feels its way through the booby traps of the time. Internally, I felt the current of my life shift and greeted it with acceptance. I let go and welcomed the gift of my new journey.

Rich was a man who required so much and honestly gave so little. In an arrogant tone, he stated, "Larry, you have worked here a long time (eleven and a half years), and your job performance is not what it used to be. Ethel told me you shipped the wrong product to a hospital. I cannot have this in my company."

"What order did I ship wrong and to what hospital?"

"I don't have the specifics, but I can ask Ethel for them."

With my self-worth intact, I looked into the soul of the small hollow and stuffed man sitting before me. I blurted out, "Don't you think you should have that information if you're going to fire me?"

The paradox of my situation was narrow, and a selfish viewpoint set me free, and I remembered I could overcome any obstacle with a carpenter's belt filled with tools. The odds against me might have been overwhelming, but I smiled and got up and walked out the door without saying a word.

I had a moral responsibility to myself disobey the small minds of the world.

♥

Living life on life's terms meant wisdom could only be obtained through prayer and meditation. Against the backdrop of misery, every day was a struggle, but none were the same.

Enlightenment awoke me from a deep sleep. I saw no real value or meaning in following the assembly line of ideas. My spiritual path allowed me to see the yellow haze from the sun, and it illuminated the path I took. Against the backdrop of the cotton-ball blue sky, I stood among the red, yellow, and purple flowers and found every talent I possessed. With the sense of an explorer, reborn in reason, I christened each day and deemed the world safe. I hit the open road, and each step I took was a pilgrimage to discover Self and leave the shadowlands behind.

♥

After talking with an ex-Army Ranger, I enlisted in the United States

Army to become an Airborne Ranger at thirty years old. To do so, I had to pass my General Education Diploma (GED), for the army wouldn't take me unless I had a GED and fifteen college credits.

I recognized my gifts and started to develop myself. Self-education acknowledged no authority, only the truth. Overcoming my instincts to be alone, the ever-evolving idea I was another pushed me forward. I wouldn't let unhappiness be my god.

♥

As I moved forward, fate gave me an opportunity to barter brawn for knowledge. I mowed a teacher's yard every week while she tutored me in English grammar. Each morning, I told myself, "It's not where a man starts in life, it's how he finishes."

Only rich people die without scars. I realized it was impossible to have a victim mindset and move forward. I wouldn't allow my past to define me. I continued to volunteer and work down at the detox center. My testimony unleashed my feelings, dreams, and desires. Humility was the palace of wisdom. Faith gave me the courage to fight back my fears. I never let the world get the best of me. I smiled back at it, and I knew my day would come.

♥

After a few months of studying, I knew the time had come for me to take the GED test. I hated the fact I was responsible for my own happiness. No one could provide it to me. I had to love myself and let the joy of the day touch me. The depths of my contentment could be measured in the mindfulness of the moment. The ability to be tolerant showed my strength. The capability to be sympathetic allowed me to open my heart to another. Eyes wide open, enlightenment, changed my disposition. I pitied the ignorance of the self-important and the small cramped, dark place in which they live.

♥

With nothing to lose, I could be fearless, and the impossible made me brave. I broke through the cling wrap that smothers a life. I'd smile at the first sign of trouble and drew my strength from the presence of God. My heart would rise no matter what the occasion was. The rest of life was an illusion of the dream I dared to weave. The beginning of time started when I opened my eyes. My memories let me see my steps toward eternity.

I felt the emotion and color tied to every word in the dictionary, and the day came when I received my GED results in the mail. Nervous, I scanned across the page and noticed each category had a number over ninety across from it. My negative filter initially thought I got ninety percent of the answers wrong and failed again. The yellow warmth of the stars brightly passed through my eyes' knowledge.

I dared to be a fool who believed a human life can be revised. Optimism whispered to my soul, and it told the world not today, not me and not ever. By getting my GED, it opened the door to Oklahoma Community College. I began my studies with eagerness and soon discovered that college wasn't quite what I had imagined. The disclosures from those who thought they were wise revealed the disguises of education to me. Students, foolish in their lack of understanding of the world around them, faded into the drudge of the learned day. A poet thinks, muses, and interprets the real world. Wisdom honors those who cannot humble themselves. Education can make some people studious but stupid.

I enrolled in five classes, so I could be an Airborne Army Ranger and live the life of danger. I bought myself a computer without knowing how to even operate it. The quest for knowledge allowed me to leapfrog the monstrosities of the overeducated and pompous. Nothing worth remembering can be taught, for life must be experienced. I celebrated every day of living.

Once was exiled beyond human dignity, my soul was under constant reconstruction. The treasures I uncovered came from being an outcast and made my mind an outlaw. My love had no strings attached and was boundless. I aided and abetted every thought and pushed myself past dreadful skepticism into the grassland of tranquility. I dedicated myself to self-awareness. The deceptions of an impoverished childhood and an apprenticeship in survival gave me confidence. I received three As and two Bs on my first report card since the third grade.

Out of the FIELD

15

Rangers Lead the Way

Buying into the thought, "I could," allowed me the mindset to achieve. Life could have broken me. Nothing is ever simple. Pain opened up my heart to understanding. Inescapable suffering gave me intelligence. I wouldn't let another man drag me into their his thoughts. I'd pushed back the world and discover the greatness inside of me.

♥

At the end of the fall semester, I had less than a month to go before my induction at Fort Benning, Georgia. At thirty years old, I found myself involved in a revolution of my soul. All the good I'd done spurred me onward. Good deeds faded into old memories, but my heart never hardened.

An underdog who refused to be a sled-dog, gratitude opened a path through the illogical, unreasonable, and self-centered. Seared with scars, I realized my wounds empowered me with the strength of faith. There was an endearing voice in my heart, and it was in silence I heard the crowds in heaven cheering me forward.

Consciousness untangled my past, and acceptance opened me up to the love I deserved. Perseverance allowed me to cherish things most people took for granted. It took me thirty years to move past zero. Accomplished at living on the streets, proficient in the art of survival, I spent hours viewing false friends and real enemies in this world. This skill set couldn't be bought. My heart wouldn't rest until I became another.

♥

The day came when I sold my body to the U. S. Army. I caught a flight to Atlanta and took a bus with another recruit to Sand Hill, Fort Benning. As soon as the bus stopped, a huge black man in a brown hat started to shout orders, "Get your civilian asses off the bus, now!"

I looked out the window and saw a pack of Brown Hats of all races and sizes screaming at the top of their lungs. The young soldiers who accompanied me looked like stray dogs in the middle of an intersection.

Once I got off the bus, a smile overcame me. I was at peace in this human comedy before my eyes, for my father's Midnight Inspections made this look like T-ball league. One Brown Hat got in my face and started barking like a crazed dog, "What are you smiling at? Drop and give me 25!"

Once done, I popped back up with a smile on my face, the Brown Hat made me drop five more times. He said, "I'll take that smile from your face!"

I got back up every time and smiled.

The Brown Hat shouted in my face, "I see you're a smart-ass!"

"Yes, Drill Sergeant."

As the days unfolded, I mused on how a survivor doesn't have a victim's mindset. Words expose our deepest fears, reveal our inadequacies and are eternal in our lives. I held on to the emotions tied to my father's words, "You'll never amount to anything!"

I let go of the darkness associated with his comment, and it illuminated my path through hell. Words are creatures that need to be tamed, or they'll manifest insanity.

♥

Inside this war machine, they called it high command, but all they did was demand.

Out of the appalling mouths of the Brown Hats, the heart of filth exposed the dishonor of the politicians who proclaimed the world as their own. Sound the trumpets! Sound the horns! Sound the charge! My superman eyes saw the limits of each actor and exposed the anguish of conformity. I lived in an inferior tribe, stepped to the cadence, and remembered every day I was wiser than those who gave the orders.

♥

As I began to sort through the acronyms and the actions of these strange people, I stumbled into a new moral climate. The real genius of the military

Out of the FIELD

was to make people think less of themselves. The country came before God. The propaganda of ignorance was passed down by cunning, prosperous men who had their own agenda, and they sold the execution of their plan to the poor. Might interrupts right. Everyone wanted to be on the winning side, so God's world was constantly under attack by religious leaders, politicians, and dictators who wanted more than their share. Blinded by righteousness, they'll never experience grace's contentment.

Surrounded by stunted souls, they heard nothing and said nothing. Their torsos swelled from the military chants from all those non-peaceful things. They didn't want us to give up on them when they set the world ablaze. After all, the homeland was a precious, shining jewel. A rebellious skeptic, a revolutionist, my only loyalty was to my soul. I remained one thing, and one thing only, a child of God. It superseded the rank of any general or politician.

Touched by grace, my heart remained unscathed while being immersed in the control of every detail and thought. I beheld pride peacocking about, and it was a marvelous monster to watch in army green with its bayonet pointed toward God in the sky. I let them show me the artless arrogance that belongs to conformity. I perceived all officers to be in costumes, and their supporting actors voiced orders down a narrow, enclosed street. Onward, I marched. Onward, I followed blindly with my eyes wide open and saw the shadows that drove men from the beginning of time.

♥

In a world in which a single idea didn't emerge, I let my imagination stare off into the distance and found it possible for me to fly. I earned my jump wings in Airborne School after five jumps, and I walked my duffle bags down the street to the Ranger Indoctrination Program. Everyone imposes his own dream in the world, but the Rangers impose a steady and non-random process to break a recruit's heart. My heart had already been broken, and it was stronger than before.

My Ranger class consisted of two hundred wannabes. The moment I walked into the compound, the Dogs of War howled, "Let's get moving! March, drop, roll over, and low-crawl, you maggots!"

I entered the real kingdom of madness. My lungs burned. I thirsted, and still, the orders advanced. Black was the sunlight from which I rose.

Thoughtless, I stretched out in the mud, and my wide eyes were open while sleeping. Perseverence earned my next obscenity. Life didn't begin or end the way I thought it should. Every second was a battle. A true soldier fights not for what is right; he finds a way to survive.

By the end of the first day, we had already lost ten wannabes. The only time we had any peace was when they had to teach us something like tying knots, navigation, and other useful things. Late nights, early morning, they switched out the cadre twice a day to make life a living hell. They did know I walked out of hell to get here.

As my mind wandered at the pace of my footsteps, every single mile, I became someone else. Throughout the night, I stood or kneeled beneath the fair, round moon in a field unsown. A poet, it was in the long shadows of the trees I saw the bridge between earth and heaven. It was amidst all our human deformities and disproportion that the crisp, cold wind brought the comfort of His touch to me. My slumbering eyes never took for granted how God watched over all of life.

After six months of combat infantry training, I could see the end in both their purity and their fiction. I survived their mutual cohesion, indoctrination of thoughts, and a twelve-mile forced march after being up forty-eight hours straight. My inspiration came from the man who dropped his eyes before he quit. From the same wilderness, from the same night, men marched forward to discover the limits of their body and minds.

That morning, leaning against a tree, I watched the sunbeams toil, darkness crumble, and the earth awakens from its sleep. There's nothing more beautiful than sunrise after surviving man-made bullshit.

Once a battered child, the apprenticeship I served in hell made me humbly strong. What thoughts I had of my fellow Rangers. Out of the two hundred wannabes, our graduating class consisted of forty soldiers. After the ceremony, I was headed out west, Fort Lewis, Washington. I was assigned to the 2nd Ranger Battalion, Charlie Company.

♥

I reported to my duty station right before Labor Day, 1992. My first day they took me to the range to see my marksmanship. I hit thirty-nine out of forty targets and maxed out the physical training test, too. On my second day, the captain told us our squad had been chosen to be the opposition for

Out of the FIELD

Delta Force operations at Hanford Nuclear Site. There was no pretending with these guys. This was a tight-knit group whose camaraderie spoke of honor. Rangers Lead the Way.

As the newbie in Charlie Company, I had no doubts about my loyalty to my fellow Rangers. One guy could be a total jerk, but as long as he stood up for the brothers, we overlooked his shortcomings. The squad had a wolf pack mindset. Rank made you an alpha dog, but it also revealed your limitations. The wolf pack looked at the loner as a porch dog and passiveness was considered obnoxious and offensive. You invited yourself to join the campfire. This showed the pack you were one of them, and you would fight with them.

♥

I kept my lovely words to myself and concentrated on my tradecraft. Alpha dogs were merciless creatures who probed around for softness. One college graduate private just didn't get it, and he became entertainment for all of us.

A sergeant was instructing a recruit how to use a knife, and he asked him, "What would you do if you had an ax man closing in on you?"

The young recruit looked at the sergeant with suspicion. "An ax man? I wouldn't take on an ax with a knife."

"And that is why your college educated brain will be the first to die." The sergeant laughed. "Lee, what would you do?"

"Shoot him."

"Right answer! I can tell Private Lee will not run, hide, or overthink things, college boy,"

In a political gesture, I shouted, "Hooah."

The sergeant barked, "Lee, give me twenty-five and one for the Ranger in the sky."

♥

Army Rangers are trained to be the best professional warriors in the world, and they had an honor about them that would not leave a fallen comrade behind. My heart became whole and mighty under the stewardship of their wolf pack conviction. I packed myself into silence and unpacked myself in the imagination of words.

The Rangers regularly trained for war, and the 2/75th rotated on a national call status with the two other battalions. Their motto was, "Wheels up, anywhere in the world in twenty-four hours."

We trained and consistently conducted live-fire exercises. At the Yakima Training Center, I never knew you could dehydrate from shivering in a cold, desert night. I looked at the stars and tried to steal a glimmer of warmth from them.

Jungle Warfare School was in Panama and was a month long. I packed over 100 pounds through the jungle, slept in the mud and rain. I had to have my mates pull me out of quicksand. I held my M-249 high over my head, for it was always clean and ready to fire.

We trained all the time. I barely had time to read poetry, philosophy, and religious studies. I kept an eye on my mates, for I didn't stumble around drunk like they did. I never stopped dreaming that one day I'd have a home filled with conversation, laughter, and love. Sometimes, I walked in circles, but the path chosen for me was guided only by my spiritual instincts. Making my way through red tape and Cro-Magnon thinkers, I could tell no one ever strived to be a Rhodes Scholar. These guys kept saying, "If you're not cheating, you're not trying."

♥

One day, I was playing a practical joke with a friend, and we made lots of noise in the hallway. A twenty-year-old robustly built sergeant came out of his room and put me at parade rest. The power of his ego voiced a tiny mind, "Lee, what do you think about taking orders from someone over ten years younger than you?"

I stopped for a moment, and my superman's eyes saw his small ego. Somebody who wanted respect without earning it. I replied, "Well sergeant, it is my belief I can learn something from anyone in this world no matter what their age is, even from a child."

He wasn't smart enough to understand my words made fun of his lineage. His tribe, the oldest modern people, still walked this planet but never evolved. Stupidity always pushes back with rank or brute force. I had to pay the price for being a smart-ass. He made me low-crawl in the hallway. Proud and noble, a defiant smile became my shield.

♥

Most of the time, I didn't get hazed like the other privates. I stayed in my lane and took care of business and didn't give a twenty-year-old warmonger an opening. Every evening, I went for a ten-mile run after work, and on Sunday, I'd run twenty miles around the airfield and give my best even if the sergeant didn't deserve it.

One day, Fort Lewis had a ten-mile race that started late in the afternoon. In the middle of my Combat Infantry Badge training, I asked my first sergeant to run in the race, and he made sure I went to the front of the line on every drill. My testing ended about an hour before the contest. I put on my Ranger physical training gear and went over to enter the race.

The top three winners got an all-expense-paid trip to Washington D.C. to represent Fort Lewis in the army ten-mile race. I had been up since five a.m. and on my feet all day training. As the event started, I snuggled in with the second pack at a six-minute clip and kept the leaders in my sight. About seven miles into the race, I started picking off the runners who went out too fast. At nine miles, I was fourth, about fifteen seconds behind the leader. With less than a half mile to go, I made my move and put the hammer down. I didn't have an elite speed kick, for I was a strength runner, and my will to win was immeasurable. Tooth and nail, with less than two hundred yards from the finish line, I snuck up on the top three runners at full speed, and my Ranger buddies were so excited to see me they yelled at the top of their lungs, "Rangers Lead the Way!"

They ruined my ambush. Like scared dogs being chased by a wolf, the three runners mustered something from nowhere. I passed them only for a second before they passed by me inches from the finish line. I finished the race in fourth place, fifty-eight minutes and some change.

Little did I know, my company commander came out to see the end of the race, and he noticed I was upset about finishing in fourth place. He yelled, "Ranger Lee! Why are you so down on yourself?"

"I let those legs (regular army soldiers who walk everywhere) beat me."

"Son, you exemplified the Ranger spirit. You hold your head high. I am sure no one here trained all day for combat and then ran a ten-mile race. I am sure they sat around resting or sleeping. You are a Ranger because you go above and beyond what is expected of you. You hold your head high, soldier."

I looked in the eye and saluted him and felt the unselfish loyalty and dedication for every Ranger that came before me when he saluted me back. I belonged to a fraternity of men who gave me their name and let me earn a spot at their table.

♥

Little did I know, my company would be deployed the day of the race in D. C. Fort Bliss, Texas was my new home. We were training for a real-world mission this time. Our assignment was a snatch and grab of Somalia's war-lord Mohamed Farah Aidid and his advisors. Day after day, round after round, all we knew were the commands of war in the heat of the desert sun.

A Ranger and a poet, I turned to my brother-in-arms, and in him, I found neither happiness nor misery. By suffering alongside him, he helped me make it. I found the generosity in both living and dying for my comrades. Trained to kill, I lived to write about my face in the dirt, heel pointed toward the sky and fields of fire. We felt what it was like to die every day from exhaustion, only to be resurrected from sleep. We postponed God's will and revealed the wisdom of man in a few words, "Hurry up and wait."

After five weeks of intense training, we learned our company wouldn't be deployed to Somalia. The Department of the Army decided to send the 10th Mountain Division to pull security and the 3rd Ranger Battalion. Rangers always backup other Special Operations Forces or other Rangers. This decision was one of the major blunders in the Battle of Mogadishu in October 1993. The world and I watched my fellow Rangers make the broadcast news. I was proud to serve with men who would risk their lives to save mine, and I in return would risk mine to save theirs. Brothers forever, Rangers Lead the Way!

♥

Being thirty-three years old, I served two years in the Ranger Battalion and decided to seek an assignment with the regular army. I found a job working at the Fort Lewis Reenlistment Center. After being in a Ranger Battalion, the regular army was a just higher form of welfare in most cases. Undisciplined officers and NCOs who couldn't lead, women getting pregnant in order not to go out in the field, soldiers stealing a truckload of meals-ready-to-eat (MRE), drug use, drunkenness on duty, and even rape. In my new world, I just stayed in my lane and counted down the days until I was paroled (honorably discharged) by the army.

♥

An individual, I walked among the tribe and listened to words without meaning. I eavesdropped on the spirit of the world around me and found my voice in the whispers of the wind. A bandit, life's complacency pursued me. My eyes illuminated the falsehoods of mankind. I slipped out the back door when I felt conformity was near. I wrote like a saint in prayer. Burning words pardoned my soul. Mad in love, I howled back at those overwhelmed by the tribe. A conscript of good writing, I let the world blow up and examine each piece before I put it back together.

Ah, I have done it again. It's not my fault I can see. My bastard wisdom continuously tears everything apart when it's just held together by duct tape, lies, and hate.

I picked up a pen to defend my life against the arrogance of adulthood which devours all. The brightness of thought became my sword. Words dried on a page shouted at the deafness of the world. The ways of God seem to be very strange. I grew spiritually while camped near hostile tribes and watched their tribal rituals. I had nothing in common with most of my fellow soldiers yet resembled them in most ways.

♥

Tyranny observed, sharpened my eyesight. Among the smoke screens and rustled appearances of the day, I re-entered my soul and became invisible once again. I saw the shadowlands of time pulled at the downtrodden. The gentle winds of mediation transcend me in quiet grace. It was for the journey sake I never became overjoyed by the homeland, the village, or destructive perfumes.

Most of my life had been a high-wire act, and it was a delicate line between survival and disaster. I resembled a circus performer, juggling five or six items at one time. Every day presented new challenges as I struggled to become another. I removed myself from the poppycock. God had already given me everything I needed to be successful, and self-actualization was up to me. The illusion of freedom always seemed a million miles away, but once you get pissed off, you'll find it resides in your heart.

I lived and worked as if God didn't exist in this world, and at the end of the day, I paid homage to the experiences He let me have. Prayer and meditation let me see the center of my own ability. I cut my own path through the overgrowth of minutia, and it allowed fear to pass through me like an apparition. Gratitude uncluttered my mind and enabled me to entertain others without accepting their behaviors.

I carried God in my heart and was never without Him. I feared no fate and wanted no more than I needed. A humble soul hopes and a deceitful mind connives. The miracle of life kept me jumping from star to star. I learned to do without or make something up. It takes courage to handle what the world throws at you and change it. Three months before I got paroled from the army, I totaled my car and just had liability insurance.

Busted flat, broke down along the road of life, I was thirty-five years old without an automobile and no money in the bank. I only had a dream. This something inside of me gives me a chance to be.

Out of the FIELD

16

Climbing as I Fall

San Marcos, California, became my destination. I moved in with Big Mama, who rented his place from Kurt. I met them in basic training. Kurt was the father of one of my Ranger buddies. With no job, I packed up my U-Haul on June twenty-fifth and drove southbound along the coast of California. I had many hours to reflect on life and realized the ignorant could neither feel misery or love. My feeling will not be repressed. I ardently admire the fight in me.

Big Mama and I shared a duplex together. The college was a mile and a half from our house, so I walked to and from class each day. My unemployment benefits would only get me by until January, but my GI Bill would last for three years. With no automobile, it was hard to find a job. Living hand to mouth, in faith I promised God I wouldn't give up before the miracle happened.

One day, after talking to Uncle Burney, he got his bank to give me a signature loan so I could get an automobile. After my fall semester, I finally landed a job working for a yacht company. I started out as office help and worked my way up to office manager. Payroll, accounts receivable and payable, inventory, purchasing, and charting daily commodities reports in Excel were my daily tasks. I eventually began to work full-time and went to school full-time. All the days seemed to roll into one. I was loneliest when I had nothing to do.

As a poet, I pursued the best and the worst in every human being. In Mac, the owner of the yacht company, I saw the lies and gross conduct that came with the blessing of being a privileged child. He pickpocketed life each day and lived without consciousness. He enjoyed living off the labor of others. Each day came, and new workers showed up. Without apologies, employees quit. His past hindered him from appreciating the present. Conceit isolated him in the kingdom of his mind, and he never learned to share his cookies in kindergarten.

I smiled every time he asked me, "Would you go get me a smoothie?"

"Sure thing, Mac."

Once I got back, he responded, "What took you so long? I don't want it now. Put it in the refrigerator."

♥

Ugliness lives in someone who has money and assumes everyone else can be replaced. I nicknamed him The Chosen One because his actions degraded every man who worked for him and he treated them as servants.

Born into money, his father sold his printing company for ten million dollars, and he was fortunate to pursue his studies in England. Mac thought he was the master of the universe, so he borrowed two million seven from an older gentleman. The monthly interest payment was over eight thousand dollars. Mac farmed out his commodities trading to a brokerage house in Ireland. I had to decipher the numbers each day to show his profit or loss.

Mac had a huge desire to live big, and he pretended to someone to get his way. Appearances were everything to him. He wanted to build a yacht company from the ground up. All the profits from his commodities trading were put into making a prototype forty-four-foot yacht. He liked to play all day and party all night. He let his right-hand man, Eugene, manage the day-to-day activities. Piece by piece, his dream yacht came together at the rate of one hundred fifty thousand dollars per month. With no concept of money, he booked his vessel in a Florida yacht show.

Eugene had a hard time keeping up with the timeline for the completion of the yacht. Mac came up with the brilliant idea that they would have it transported by day, and the employees could work on the interior of the boat while it was parked at a truck stop at night.

When the crew got to Yuma, I got a call from Mac. "Hey, we forgot to load the radar system. I need you to drive to Yuma and bring it to us."

"I just paid all my bills and don't have enough gas to make it there."

"Money management, son, is the key to being successful. Take some money out of petty cash and get a receipt."

"What about the wear and tear on my car? It's four hundred miles round trip."

Out of the FIELD

I could feel his anger oozing through the phone. "Do you like your paycheck?"

"Sure."

"Then get the radar system here or don't show up for work tomorrow."

I shook my head and said, "Sure thing, boss."

All seemed to go well the rest of the trip, but being under pressure, the crew had to work and sleep under unusual work-rest cycles. Once they got to Florida, they hooked up the engines. Everything was a go. A friend told me, the day of the maiden voyage, Mac perked up like a proud daddy. As Mac, Jim, and the yacht broker motored out to sea, Jim sensed intense heat in the engine bay.

Mac wanted to maximize the twin 420-horsepower diesel engines. Jim noticed something was wrong, and he gave Mac a hand signal to kill the engines. His consuming desires just got bitch-slapped right across his face. A fire soon started in the engine compartment, and the vessel caught on fire and sank.

♥

After the ship had sunk to the bottom of the sea, it was business as usual. Mac decided to build another yacht. Except this time, his commodities trading lost over four hundred thousand in one day. His loss revealed his dependence on others. Day after day, his commodities account continued to plunge.

Without the status of money, he was numb and in a trance. He tried to stop the hemorrhaging, but it was too late. He had to borrow money from his dad to keep his brokerage account open and to fund his new yacht project. Each month, I considered all the factors in the budget and called his father. I let his dad know the monthly expenses. Monthly, he showed up with a check for over one hundred thousand dollars to keep Mac's company going.

Fate always reveals a man's shortcomings over time, and arrogance shows dishonesty by deceit. Hypocrisy is a bitch. I couldn't take it anymore, so I quit.

♥

I had to work to feed myself and pay my child support. I landed a job working for an electrical headhunter who contracted with a California electric company. This owner couldn't communicate what was expected of me, so he let me go three weeks after I started.

Unemployed for months, the simple physiological needs for the basics like food, drink, and shelter brought back the demented shades of my abandonment. Walking down a dark staircase, I stretched out my heart to look for a safe place and found no one to talk to. Fear pulled me backward. The monster I created as a child broke loose from his tether and began to turn on me.

"Damn, damn, damn!" my soul screamed, "Here we go again!"

Isolated pain is the beginning of self-cannibalism. Negative thoughts found an opening like the Vandals who sacked Rome. The fear of being homeless drove my actions. I legally stole and lived off my credit cards. Poverty dispelled all my efforts and eclipsed the sun. Blackened by fear, the marsh of mediocrity began to swallow me whole. Cold and stagnant, I couldn't reason and only could compare.

My ancestors let me know, "You don't deserve to be loved."

All alone on Christmas, the burden of being poor and unloved was so uncomfortable. The days never changed. Fear and stress ran over the guardrails into the vale of depression. I looked back and never got an opportunity to do more than survive.

Life's invasion left me with only $89.06 in my checking account. With no hope of employment, nothing seemed extraordinary. I blocked out the vision of looking my son in his eyes and telling him why. A thousand embarrassments came from the lack of being able to meet my basic needs. I knew people's view of poverty could only change if they become penniless.

Sorrow made me vain. I came under attack from frenzied angels in black. My world inverted. Armed with anger, monstrous memories assaulted me. Childhood terror rose from the dead. Black angels swarmed around in my head. I couldn't find my own compassion, and I stepped back into the confines of my father's abuse. Caged without a key, I shut the door on the world and prepared to strip the radiance from the sun, and surging darkness flipped the world upside down. Everyone had always left me. I was no more than a meal for a fly. The fury of abandonment spiraled and expanded the hissing fires of hell.

My heart continued to weather the storm, and it fought back while it could, in a world that didn't even know my name. The thought of God's love wouldn't leave me. Abandoned! I had no dreams. Trampled by thoughts, family memories kicked around in my head. Pauperized, silence turned into white rage. Pain assaulted my heart. Legions of black angels swarmed around me like locust ravaging a field.

Hour after hour, I was slowly being kicked out of my mind. Hauled through the air, I cut the telephone line to heaven to end it all. I couldn't even shout "Jesus" to save my life. I could have been a success, and I could have even written a great spiritual book. Simply put, I was a sober mess.

An acrobat tumbling through space, the destructiveness of my character had only hours, only seconds until the revenge of my love became the vengeance that set me free. The clock of life stood still and watched from afar. I kept throwing punches in the air, hoping to land a haymaker to free myself from God's nimble angels who defended my soul. Angrily preaching words of venom into the air, I fought the will of God and began to die from weariness, but something in my heart couldn't expel all human hope.

I should have died many years ago. I wanted to kick down the doors of heaven. So much for my salvation. I just didn't give a damn. My fingertips grasped the edge. Tossed from here to there, I never let go.

Climbing as I fell, the changing light in my soul tumbled endlessly until my spirit arose. I staggered back from an unusual and unreliable death. From judgment to acceptance, from pain to forgiveness, an illusion can be shattered. Kingdoms will crumble. I was just a pedestrian in this world, no more. I surrendered, or I surely would have died. For my will was not His will, and my way was not His way. I cried on the floor and said, "God, there has to be a better way."

This was all I was. His outstretched hand comforted me and whispered the promise of something better to come. It waited for me just around the bend, the miracle that would change my life forever.

♥

The purity of my heart has shed more tears than God required for sainthood. They brim and ripple out of my eyes, "Dammit, I am!" I am more than the horrifying limitations of my feeble existence. I am, so I'll be.

♥

I still had some unfinished business to take care of, for I volunteered to coach nine teenagers on a San Marcos youth basketball team. Our team was undefeated halfway through the season. I revisited each Christmas Day and the pain of being all alone. Tears rolled out of my eyes when I looked at my Christmas bacon sandwich.

It's only after I'd lost everything that I became free to do anything. There was nothing wrong outside me. It was all inside of me. Things already looked promising when I'd decided to try something new. Circumstances and events didn't determine who I was. After all, I wasn't in charge of the universe, only the treasures inside of me.

One cannot truly taste freedom unless you were once held captive by something. I found love was a mere shadow we all try to grasp. Understanding life became difficult when your survival depended on a salary. People lived blindly, sold themselves out daily, and they supported Reaganomics.

The next morning, I saw the eternal morning sunrise of hope, and my heart told me everything would work out fine. The best I could do was forgive myself and let God indoctrinate my life, again. I knew faith sometimes gets lost in a single thought. Humanity sometimes seems like one big parade full of clowns, bankers, and CPAs. One should always move forward until one cannot move at all. How endless time appears to be in our short time here. Our lives are characterized by the things we create and by the things we destroy. Ambition creates a void and success makes hustlers of us all. I tested my faith. Truth be known, I wanted it to fail, so I could stagger back to obscurity.

Illumination let me see generation after generation afraid of truly living. I'd surrender only when it was convenient for me. I'd give back my will when I longed to escape the pain I created. My many scars came from my attempts to change an unfair world, and in the light of my life lessons, I wrote a dissertation of broken thoughts, and I found the story untold in my soul. It was now safe to let go.

I spoke these words over an empty shoe box, "God, my dignity was assaulted and cruelly mocked every day of my life. I have fought those who wronged me. I realize the burden of wrongdoings, and it was the pain that held me back from being someone else. Surrender means I cannot do this without You. I'm not sure that I'm capable of yielding even one second, nor am I even worthy of being someone else. I humbly ask You for no more

Out of the FIELD

than fate would allow me. I completely surrender my will to You."

I began to drop pieces of paper with family members' names written on them and a letter that would never be mailed. The collected memories of abandonment, drug addiction, and poverty dropped, dead to me. I placed the box in the hole and covered it with the earth. I buried my past and was nothing at all.

I uttered, "Sweet Jesus, look down upon me and help me make a stand."

♥

The story of my life thus far was I avoided much contact with people, angered some and loved no one. My thoughts wandered wondering what I could be. Would God transform and help me? I am what I feel, see, and hear. God has given me only one life, and it was up to me to make another. We are one, God and me. I liked my odds against the world.

♥

A soul moored to immortality can run like the wind. I dreamed of writing monstrous living prose, dragon-breath poems, and a book that would make a lame man dream. My ears heard the prolonged echoes through the infinite expansion of time. My thoughts chased the morning sun. Curiosity fueled my existence. Enlightened beyond the shrinking insecure. Part of the universe, I expanded my heart's compassion and found forgiveness opened my eyes to see nature's beauty all around again.

Being unique, I tapped into the portable magic inside my heart and sutured my wounds shut. My scars let me reflect on my journey. A deeper instinct coerced my compassion. Forgiveness let me reach for the love I deserved. Courage through toughness let me know there were many more days to come.

Every job I applied for I was told, "You're overqualified," or "you're underqualified."

It was the basketball team I coached that helped me fight through being unemployed. I told my players, "You have to struggle through adversity and find a way to win."

I was self-coaching myself through each day. All my bad experiences helped my players discover the champion inside each of them. We won the

LARRY A. LEE

first fourteen games and lost the last game in overtime by one point. My top two players fouled out. My kids took on all comers, and they inspired my passion.

A rookie coach, I grew up exploiting the weakness of the other team. Once I gained their trust, my defense created insanity on the court. Before our first playoff game, I heard other kids talking trash about our team in the lobby. I huddled up my team and looked each one of them in the eye. I said, "Who remembers how it felt to lose our last game?"

Each of them murmured, "I do, Coach."

"Good, I don't know about you, but I don't want to lose again. You are the best team in this league, and that's why all your friends want you to lose. You choose your own destiny, so let's take what's ours and play like champions."

We won all three playoff games, and as the clock ticked off the last seconds of the championship game, I smiled at God and said, "Unbelievable."

♥

I continued to go to school and look for work and had no luck. With the need for money, I answered an ad for an office clerk and was offered the position. It was a Buddhist Pagan Novelty Store. Rodney, the owner, beat his wife, smoked dope, and shouted at his employees like they were servants.

One day, he burst into the office like my father did on his Midnight Inspections, and he said, "I got complaints from a few vendors that no one shipped their order while I was gone. Did anyone show up for work? What did you do while I was gone?"

The three ladies in the office sat back and took it.

As for me, I asked him, "What time did they call, and who did they talk to?"

His face turned red, and he blurted out, "Get the hell out of my office!"

I went to my desk and began to pack my things. A few minutes later, the ladies walked out of the boss's office in tears.

He yelled, "Larry, get in here!"

I walked into his office and responded, "Yes?"

Rodney said, "I like the way you handled yourself. I would like to let bygones be bygones, so why don't you and I go out to my car and smoke a

Out of the FIELD

few bowls of weed?"

Deep down inside, I wanted to get stoned like I once did, but I said, "No thanks." Then I asked him, "Why do you treat your employees that way?"

"No one has ever challenged me like you. I deal with them that way to get the most out of them. I want them to work scared, so they earn the money I pay them."

With nothing holding me to this job, I said, "You don't gain their loyalty by yelling at them with untruths. You make them dislike you. They probably give you less each day because of your actions. They are afraid of you, and I am not."

He looked puzzled. "I will get my things, and I will leave," I said.

Just like any other bully, he wanted to be my best friend now. He jumped up and said, "No, you can stay if you want to, and I appreciate your honesty. Anytime you want to get high, let me know."

Before I closed my eyes at night, my mind wondered where life would take me. Each day, I let go and let God do his thing. The promises I made to both my mother and God remained in my heart. A promise was everything to me, for I was part of each of the words I uttered. A promise means you will never forget that moment in time. The devotion of those heartfelt words became my shield of honor in an unforgiving world. That commitment gave me the ability to become a self-made man. It will forge the creativity that unleashed all the love and passion in my heart and made it impossible to be discouraged in an unjust world.

17
Team 2

Abandonment enabled me to see the lies passed down from generation to generation, and it made me wiser than the herds that just grazed the earth. I had to believe in myself to succeed as the loner.

♥

Deprived of being part of any tribe, my experiences never let me completely trust another human being. I resisted the mainstream thinking and saw the majority misled by their thoughts. Collective thoughts collapsed inside my brain, and I saw the disfigurement of hate and fear from other beliefs. I kept reverting back into the minority, and it kept freeing my mind from people who secretly ganged up on others. Groupthink stifled human life into the security of conformity. I couldn't bear the thought of being lost forever in someone else's idea, so I pushed back the encroaching world.

Born again, each morning I opened my eyes, and the wisdom of a thousand past lives rushed in with the light of the new day. Self-reflection stumbled through the dull pains of unconsciousness to find only gratitude. Understanding became my religion. Angels whispered against conventionality. In the sunshine of the human spirit, dignity didn't calculate, yearn, or plan. Compassion is the only mechanism to salvation. Once I accepted that destitution was part of my journey, I beheld the splendors of a soul detached from the world.

Maybe this time, I thought I might get it right.

♥

Every day I went to work, my boss called me into the office to talk with him. "Larry, you do an outstanding job processing orders. Let's you and I go out and get a few drinks and smoke a few bowls the rest of the day. You deserve it."

I looked at him and smiled before I said, "I gave up partying many years back, for trouble kept calling my name."

"Oh, you couldn't handle it. How long have you been sober?"

He invaded my personal space. "I've been clean for over fourteen years now. I have to get back to work now."

He always had to have the last word and said, "When you want to get off the wagon, give me a call. You'd be a cool guy to party with some time."

In my mind, I shouted back, "Not in this lifetime."

The next week his wife came in with a black eye. She was frail and shaky when he walked into the workplace. After five minutes, I had to go into his office to get a signature on a check. He asked, "Have you ever been married?"

"Once," I replied.

"You know the trick to getting everything you want from women is to make them think everything is their fault." He looked at me and said, "I can tell you want to say something. Go ahead."

"I'd rather not."

He roared, "She's my wife!"

I couldn't help myself. "She's a human being, too."

It hurts to let go and let God do His thing. My boss was selfish, impatient, and very insecure. He was out of control most days, and at times it was impossible to work for a self-aggrandizing bastard.

♥

Each evening, I took off my mask of composure and let God feel my heart beat. The petty prejudices of the silly human race disappeared when I prayed for others. Emotions and words cascaded out of my heart, and it allowed me to come to grips with the fact that I wasn't inadequate. Enlightenment doesn't shrink. It expands into knowledge and grows into patience. Suffering turns wisdom into empowerment.

It took courage to challenge the majority, and I realized relationships were essential to my success. When my path became burdensome, I clung to the memory of my truest friend, my mother. The thought of her always obliterated the shadow of fear and brought a smile to my face. In a world that is full of judgment-stamped days, I saw what others disregarded, and that was what gave me a chance to be. I held on to the thought I was another.

Temptation attacked my mind, "Let's get high and nod off into space."

Ignorance slowly blinds a human eye. Prayer was my daily prescription, and it provided enough to one who had little. In the struggle of each asthmatic day, I worked and waited for the miracle to change my life. Knowing I was the keeper of the Keeper's heart, it gave me the strength to look past the numbing pleasures. I blew a kiss to each morning sunrise, traveled through small spaces, ancient times, and heard the whispers from beyond the veil of time.

Each morning, I asked God for a miracle, and each evening, the day told me, "No." I'd say to myself He was setting up the pieces for me to succeed. I marched around those whose only intent was satisfying themselves. In a world of distrust, greed, and pettiness, I saw others sell their soul for pennies. A human heart vies against itself in its need to survive, and reflection can turn misery into love. Surrendering my will, I began to fly without wings. The terrible lessons of my life taught me humility, strengthened the power of a caring heart, and the wreckage of my past made me empathetic.

My life experiences served me well. I slept in the mud and dried myself off with the crime-infested air I stole every day. True enlightenment permitted me to see how a choice rippled through eternity. I ripped back all the strings stretched from the blackened abyss. Freedom at last! The certainty of who I was wasn't subject to interpretation. In the battle for my soul, my mind was armed with a descriptive, moralistic flair. I possessed the truth among all the salesmen, the magicians, and the lawyers. No man knows when the winds of fate will change his life, and no one man knows the time of his death. Oppression opened my eyes to see and understand the miracle of human life.

True happiness accepts the mediocrity of others and finds a way to maneuver around it. Excellence dwells in a man's heart and treats a stranger as a friend. The idea that one man can stand by himself against the world has caused more harm than good. The importance of valuing each human being reunited my soul with religion. The theme of my life found its way to my heart as a child when I sensed I was another. Overcoming weakness, I had to deny the world a foothold in my heart. A believer of great things, the depths of the human soul couldn't be measured, for it can evolve beyond

Out of the FIELD

the adornments of human stupidity.

Perfection in progress, the road well-traveled had no meaning, no challenges and was filled with generic shopping experiences. My choice was simple, and I felt the sensations of one world seeping through the cracks of another. Each day, I built on my previous ideas and themes, and I dared to offend the shadow-watchers. I deepened my personal idea of God, and it opened my eyes to the selfish, ulterior motives of others.

Every day the owner stumbled into work, I saw that the aura of his drug use dragged him backward.

I asked him, "Todd, are you all right?"

"Did you know my wife left me?"

"No, I didn't. Sorry about that. Why don't you call her and speak from your heart?"

"Hey, do you want to go smoke a bowl?"

"No, I am good. I have to get this shipment out."

When I observed the tragedies in someone's life, their ego sadly always divided and conquered them. I'd experienced this many times myself. Humility allowed me to balance tragedy with grace. Every evening, when I looked for Him, we ended up playing hide-and-seek. I cannot find where He hides in my heart, but every time I embrace Him, I feel so alive and free. Prayer and preparation give me the chance to be. My clothes may not be new, but they weren't dirty. Somewhere, beyond tomorrow, the purpose of my life awaits me. I walk there carefree like a child running to his father enshrined in the sunlight of grace.

Life is an exercise of free choice, and even though I tumbled down many chutes, I never could turn my back on Him. My finest moments made me feel uncomfortable, left me unfulfilled, and made me look the impossible in the eye. My thoughts and feeling separated from the rest and helped readjust my tactics along the way. One never sees the miracle unless one mirrors their journey. One foot in front of the other, each step was an act of faith, and down through the air, I moved forward and found the rungs of a ladder to the stars.

No one knows exactly where a miracle starts or ends, but with God on my side, grace opened doors I couldn't open by myself. Creating a life out of nothing was nothing to Him. The life I chose shunned store-bought logic. Contemporary wisdom and scornful professors endorse the universe of self. God said, "Let me show you the beauty of My soul."

Leaving the dream and stepping into the miracle, I took a long, deep look into my senses and never doubted I was another. My thoughts weren't my own and were destined for happiness. The calling of my fate let me journey through loss, abandonment, addiction, and shame. Self-empathy let me see the lengths I went to distance myself from Him. With nowhere to run, every whisper turned into a confession.

There was something in a human heart, and it resides somewhere we can't imagine. I found my starting point to become. Better than I could ever imagine, I never underestimated God myself. Nothing happened by accident.

♥

Finding the hero inside of my heart meant I overcame many tragedies. I reached out from inside every day to change my world. In August 1999, I interviewed with the United States Forest Service, and accepted an entry-level position in human resources. What a blessing, my employment came with health insurance, a 401k, sick and annual leave. When you have so little, it's easy to see the jump-up-and-down-out-of-your-mind-miracle.

I traveled through the thickets, briar patches and stood at the edge of the meadow. The light from eternity caressed my face. Powerless without Him, I couldn't help but think His plan would have happened despite myself. My distorted perceptions were no match against the force of the Spirit.

God never took my rejection of Him in the likeness of hatred. He let me understand if everyone is important, they're always important. I was free to feel any feelings, disapprove and reject anything but myself. Mindfulness gave me the strength to center me in a lopsided world. Refreshed by sorrow, my struggles made me a genius. I was now completely aware of my existence in a simple reality that made no sense. The power of my memory and the awe-inspiring mystery of my God flourished in me. In my mind, self-made from my thoughts, I closed my eyes and still could see.

Having survived self-genocide of living off credit cards ($25,000), now it was up to me find out who I really was. The disappointment of bankruptcy actualized my soul. Freedom expanded into hope and expectation. Chapter Seven freed my mind from the tricks I played on myself. The power of shame and despair always results in isolation.

♥

Life without a tribe made it nearly impossible to survive. I wanted to change my name and hope my life would miraculously follow. All I've done was survive and walk past the anxious voices that said nothing at all. I wasn't the same person. Perhaps, everything hadn't been entirely wrong. Principles arise from a struggle.

As a child, I saw the other me inside my heart and rejected the world's complacency. Reflection helped me gather strength. In the conventions of events, letters, and syllables, the perfect sentence began to write itself, and the whole paragraph followed. Transcribed thoughts became my tribe. My heart reconciled itself in the losses of the day, and my clenched fist cracked open.

In my spiritual partnership with God, the words I lack to become Another inside my heart, and they slowly transcribed the next chapter. It had already been written by the choice I'd made long before. Life freely drifts among us, and I've learned not to resist it. I've seen the damage done when you hold on to something too long. All my tomorrows started today. A suspended soul in midair, I had no landing in sight.

♥

My new job blessed me with many friends. The dignity of belonging to a tribe began to heal me with joy. I stood back and watched God work in my life. All of my coworkers grew up in loving families. Equal but different, our friendship was born out of the fun, joy, and secrets. Friendship without laughing isn't friendship. Our time spent together was often interrupted by work, and by the intruding and disagreeable patrons of the world who demanded everything "now."

♥

The fire bell rang, and these men and women flocked to the wildland fire raging in the forest. They were stimulated by pink retardant, backfires, and the dangers associated with fire. I listened to their stories about saving houses, cattle, and little old ladies in trailer homes. The fire militia put aside their personal beliefs and formed an army. Fighting fire became an individual commitment that created a group effort to rise up against a monster that roamed through the timberland. Firefighters protect those who could not protect themselves, and they value each human life and the animals that lived in the forest. Wildland firefighters' hands are never clean.

My boss, Debbie, oversaw a staging area, Hotel Basilone for hand crews. Each crew consisted of twenty persons, and we housed and fed them before we shipped them off to the large forest fires across the state of California. I stepped up and taught myself how to do personal time and logistics for up to four hundred people. Fire support called my name, and I listened. It created an expectation of me, and it manifested my destiny. I got a fair chance to prove my worth and let myself join a community. Every day, I felt more and more satisfied. The overtime gave me the ability to buy new clothes and a plane ticket for Joshua.

♥

The following year in May, my first full fire season started out in Cloudcroft, New Mexico, at the Scott Able Fire. The complexity of this fire was a Type 1 incident, for sixty structures burned to the ground. This was the first time I worked with Team 2. Don Studebaker was the team's incident commander, and he was a legend throughout the fire community. Studebaker looked at a map, threw pieces of grass in the air and determined which way the forest fire was going to burn. He picked an anchor point, like a small town, to defend from the monster's path. A natural born leader, he inspired the firefighters under his command to kill the monster that wandered the forest trying to kill Bambi. A firefighter's best friend, he was the guy next door with mustard on his shirt telling a story to make new friends. He spoke his mind, challenged the leadership above him and had a keen eye for undeveloped talent.

He handpicked everyone on his team, and every team member became part of his extended family. Team 2's motto was "Quit competence," but more than anything, it was the camaraderie that inspired the teammates to merge into a force of one. The command and general staff, operations, logistics, planning, and finance chiefs adopt a family atmosphere that every team envied. I stood at the edge of a new day not knowing I found a family of friends.

There was no legal document between Robin, Patty, Patrick, Loni,

Roger, and Steven issued that proclaimed our friendship, no fancy words spoken, or money collected in dues. The cold nights sleeping on the hard, unforgiving ground and lousy food created a bond that wasn't of blood. It was formed from out of the freedom to embrace both our differences and cherish our similarities.

Each of us played our part, and each of us was a groove in the key that unlocked our lasting friendship. As our lives became forever entwined, we opened ourselves to the truest alliance that would last ten thousand and one years. Our friendship was like a piece of art. It embellished the brightest color of life. In my new friends, the real reverence of a relationship brought the warmth of a smile on a chilly morning. Their friendship restored my confidence and ability to adventure back into humanity.

♥

After the Scott Able Fire, I went back to work for a couple of weeks before Team 2 activated to the Manter Fire. Robin called me to join them in the middle of the Domeland Wilderness. After a three-week assignment there, I went home for two days, and Robin called again. He called me his "utility player" and put me on the team roster.

The trauma of being both homeless and poor made me work harder to keep my seat at their table. I would do any job that needed to be done. A quick study, I learned every job in the finance section. Robin loved that he could plug me into any position in finance, and I would rise to the occasion and get the job done.

♥

After two days off, Team 2 headed to Missoula, Montana, to manage a complex of fires called the Thompson Flat Complex. I fell in love with the Big Sky Country's thick forests and the rolling mountains. The team spent a month living in Montana, for timber fires do not go out until September's rain comes. In good conscience, I would rather sleep in the rain in Panama than the cold rain in Montana. We all were cold and wet, but our spirits were warmed by a friendly word or passing smile for a mate. I finally was accepted.

After every fire assignment, Team 2 had a celebration of friendship that made them rich. Robin invited me to stay over with the team in Coeur d'Alene, Idaho, to celebrate the end of the assignment and the fire season. The spiritual energy of every soul danced in the celebration of the joy of being on this team, and I saw both men and women of character not of circumstances.

As I stood back and looked at the genuine love that flowed between beers, I saw a family growing together, and it opened my heart. I saw each of them laugh, cry, and love each other. I didn't see an angel among them, but they had a soul just like me. Team 2's mission was a lifetime bond in a two-week assignment. The love they had in their hearts for each other made my boot heels stop wandering. Some team members could tell you that they loved you, and others would show up when you needed to help the most. They would get their hands dirty and leave before you could thank them. I saw an unwritten code among these team members, "All we have is meant for each other, for the birth of our future together."

This code wasn't just in some of them, for it was in all of them. This team reflected Studebaker's huge heart. I stood back and took in the events of the Coyote Court laughing until I almost cried. The Coyote Award was given to the team member who wandered from the trail the team was on, or they had the biggest screw-up on the incident. Just like a coyote, the recipient of the pink backpack that stored the coyote would howl until the yellow dawn of sunlight broke through the night.

♥

My very first fire season was over, and I had spent over two months sleeping on the ground. I made several close friends and tallied over eight hundred hours of overtime. With two thousand dollars to my name, I didn't have to think twelve or twenty for hours ahead. The pressure of poverty no longer loitered around me. My soul expanded outward into light only darkness can make. An unremembered peace found its way to my heart.

I told God, "I wish my life was easier."

And my heart whispered back to me, "What use would that be to you? It's your choices that set you free or enslave you."

♥

Out of the FIELD

It doesn't matter how many times I got up off the ground in the fight of my life. It mattered I got up. A vagabond mind scrawled inner thoughts of freedom. Over and over I reached deep into a place where I couldn't hide to find myself. Until my mind's eye snatched a glimpse from now to then. My memories make me old, but my heart keeps me young. Down the lonely road, I traveled until my heart found a home filled full of love.

♥

My genius came from continuously outpacing the generations of shadowed hunters of lastingness. I walked forward, sideways, and crawled under things to lose them. A prisoner of shame my whole life, empathy emerged from my scars and the stitches of the grace that held my life together for a greater purpose. Sensing the angels circling above, I felt them cheer me onward helping me to unlatch the impossible. I never, never, never gave in to the negativity of my birthright.

I let go of blame that once made me powerless over my past, and let God make my life into a miracle. Once my physiological and safety needs were met, it allowed me to do more than exist. Friendship brightened my soul and helped displayed God's diversity. The idea of forgiveness illuminated my heart, and gradually, gratitude opened the borders of my heart. Love wrestled with my demons, and the cheering from the angels empowered me to overcome.

Only a helmsman, the winds of my muse let me travel to the far corners of the universe. With no envisioned destination, my thrusting fingertips grasped the lessoned learned, revealed the nuances of values, and displayed the motivation behind words. Unrestricted thoughts broadened my understanding of humanity. I plucked light from darkness, and my x-ray vision looked past the busy day and pushed aside the narrow-minded in search of my truth.

18
A Child's Heart

I sorted through layers of the English language to expand my knowledge of writing. My unspeakable torments gave me superhuman strength. No one ever taught me how to write a single word, but dammit, I tried to cultivate my soul rich in wisdom. The changeover between the dream and the miracle expanded my vocabulary to include the word "love."

♥

A singles ad in the *San Diego Union-Tribune* assuredly reached an unknown part of me, and I met Jada, an African-American. A sculptured life, I obeyed the intellect my heart sought, and the parts of me aligned with the Architect's design. With a click, my world opened up. It seeped in without me knowing and began to free me.

Jada and I became friends through our many phone calls. After she had moved to San Diego, I met her and decided we would be only friends. Jada tested my patience. An experience all her own, she saw less, wanted more, and she never had enough. This woman kept explaining herself to me repeatedly. She never listened and rarely came up for air between sentences. We were just friends, and we shared a laugh every now and then.

One day, Jada was in the neighborhood and stopped by to introduce me to her son, Justin. His father was Caucasian, so his skin was light brown. He was barely three feet tall and weighed thirty pounds soaking wet. His hair was braided in cornrows. Jada should've had a daughter, for his mannerisms were shy as he held on to his mother.

He looked at me, and I winked at him. My actions drove him closer to his mother.

"Hey little man, would you like a Reese's Peanut Butter Cup?"

His eyes got big, and he smiled before saying, "Yes, please."

I went to the refrigerator and pulled one out and asked, "Do you talk much?"

"When I like you, I do."

Jada screeched, "Justin, mind your manners."

I just laughed.

From that point on, I saw him occasionally and always gave him a candy bar.

♥

Life has always been a curious thing to me. Observing isn't passive, for my mind creates from what my eyes see. My heart inflates with the onrush of emotions when I feel someone's frustration, love, and dreams. Observing for me is understanding the essences of life all around me.

♥

Only a child could open my heart to its fullest potential, so I watched Justin from afar. I felt a tender curiosity about him. Something in the air pushed us closer together. Like a drifter who found a home, my heart sensed the freedom associated with love.

His actions made me forget about my life. The mystery of life was a puzzle he tried to solve by asking thousands of questions. He had an inquisitive mind, and his dreams were alive and bouncing around inside of him. He had no biases or hatred, and the sunlight of innocence flowed outwardly through his eyes. Innocence flourished in my heart just watching him.

I almost felt human, but almost actually means, "Not so fast buddy."

♥

Frozen in time, abandonment made it hard to make any emotional connections, for love required trust. I had to open up to become vulnerable. Time after time, everything got ripped away from me. One day, Big Mama started using methamphetamine again and simply vanished. He called one day and left a message, "Hey Larry, some bad things are coming your way. I started to use drugs again, and I am involved with the Tijuana drug cartel.

I owe them lots of money, so do not answer the door, whatever you do. It was nice knowing you."

Big Mama's message stabbed me with an invisible sword. I looked up to God and said, "Really, I'm obsessive-compulsive and have an Irish temper, and you get under my skin like no one else. You act like you hate me at times, and then you string me along waiting for a miracle. I never get anything right, and I don't deserve you, but I fucking love you!"

I went out into the street and dropped to my knees and screamed, "Why?"

My bright blue eyes looked up to the darkened sky toward heaven. My mind stumbled across the mountaintops to find an answer. My thoughts crawled back inside me, and I wanted to lay down again. A one-in-a-million survivor, I felt myself being dragged back to my old friend, Fear. Down in the most horrible blackness, hope pushed back. I stretched out my prayer from the surrounding rooftops, past the mountains and then willed it to the gates of heaven, like a morning newspaper.

♥

I got burned straight up, down, and even sideways. Scrambling, I wasn't amused about being the center of the universe, ever. It always felt like my life hadn't begun. Next week never came. The months passed by like the sun. Fuck, the more I tried, the more I went backward. Poverty stalked me like a jilted lover. I asked God, "What are you waiting for?"

With no money, a tiny blinking moment entered my mind, Jada. It was a disturbing thought asking for help, but I called her anyway, "Hey, Jada."

"Larry, long time no talk to. What's been going on?"

"Well, Big Mama started using drugs again. He told me not to answer the door, for the cartel is looking for him."

"WOW! What are you going to do?"

"I was calling you to see if you know anyone I can rent a room from? You seem to know everyone."

"I have an extra room you can stay in until you figure things out. I will be in El Centro for this week, but I'll leave the key under the mat for you."

Fate's absurdity left me no other option.

"Thanks, I appreciate it."

Out of the FIELD

♥

As I was moving my stuff out on the weekend, Kurt stopped by to see his place. "Hey Larry, have you seen Big Mama?"

"No! I hear he is using again," I muttered as I walked by him moving things into my truck.

"Why are you moving out?"

I paused, but I still couldn't catch my thoughts as I said, "Let see, Big Mama is using, he says the cartel is looking for him. I suppose you want me to say here and pay the full rent?"

I looked at him and said, "Yeah, I thought so. Here is the key. I'm done now."

Driving away, I thought I don't trust people who tell me what is best for their life.

♥

Shortly after moving in, Jada and I entered into a relationship. Sadly, the emptiness in both our lives allowed us to be partners. I didn't want to be her lover. Unanswered prayers led me to her. The multi-colors of personality made her larger than life, and her boldness drew people near. She dreamed big and talked louder. Jada pushed aside any boundaries for her personal gain. Often, she often told me my best quality was, "You go to work every day."

I looked at her and saw a red flag burning in the night sky. She had a magical paranoid presence that drove all her actions. In all truth, we didn't function very well together. Our relationship broke and fell apart each week, and every day we put ourselves back together with superglue. We became numb from hurting each other's feelings. I never met anyone quite like her. I left a blank check for my share of rent and utilities, and she would empty my bank account while I was on a fire assignment. She paid me back eventually, but I was no more than a means to an end for her.

The price of admission came with irresistible urges to jump up and down. I used the word "fuck," more than I ever did. Her lifestyle gave me Tourette's. I had been horrible at relationships, for the open wound of my abandonment liked the unnatural sense of autonomy. I pivoted back into myself, and I gazed upon Justin.

With me as a free daycare provider, she spent all her time shopping, socializing, and going to school. We looked at each other and thought, "You too."

As the days passed, I spent more time taking care of him, and slowly, the immense void shrunk from finding the purpose of my life. I smiled more, worried less. There was never a time when love made me whole, but it happened now and then. Accidentally, a child's heartbeat flashed an unconditional love from his eyes. I felt so vulnerable to love anything.

For thirty-three years, my thoughts were scribbled words on pieces of paper, and those words inspired me to rewrite each day. All my life, God kept me molding for this moment. I kept fighting for him, and I didn't even know his name. As I liberated him from his fear of being alone, his presence helped me find the child in my heart. It was right where I left when I was seven years old.

Happiness blessed me. A simple man, I co-parented Justin, and when he tagged along with me, his heart opened more and more. He marched up like a warrior, and he wanted to leave his mark on the world. The signature of his words impacted me as they rose up and declared, "Love me."

He just did it in a funny sort of way, for one day he walked up to me, and he said, "You are old, so when are you going to die?" with a jesting smile on his face.

The sparkle in my eyes made me feel safe. "In due time, my son."

"I am not your son, and I will never be."

♥

I admired the spunk in his little heart, and it made me travel back to a moment in time when I felt completely loved by my mother. His heart held more emotion than his small body could hold. A human pinball, he bounced around the room as I tried to read a book, for his mother never took him with her. She was too busy for him.

I was always amazed at the words that came out of his mouth. His little heartbeat pushed his love all around me. I saw no fear in his heart. All he had was love in his heart to give someone. The fragments of his life were passed around from family member to family member. No one person raised him. His teenage cousins seemed to be the ones who took the time to care for him before me. I could see the stars in his dreams, and

Out of the FIELD

his actions painted the colors of joy in other's lives.

In the openness of his love, I dreamed what Justin dreamed, and I regained my lost childhood. He gave me a gift no other person could have. My dreams no longer passed me by. Love was a riddle I couldn't solve, but his actions showed me I couldn't locate the meaning of my life alone. I couldn't walk away, for the dream I thought I'd never find looked me square in the eye.

He acted as a double agent when I was around. It was simply impossible to stay behind my walls. The spirit of this child was ablaze in the purest joy of living I had ever seen. Around him, my pain lessened, and I forgot about my ugly scar tissue. The love I once felt as a child rekindled. The more time we were together, the more I began to discover fulfillment beyond infinity. He kissed all my pain away.

As the days turned into memories, the weeks whisked by, and I noticed every time Jada would leave, Justin would run to the door and cry endlessly on the floor. The damage had been done, for in his mind, his mother kept searching for something bright, shiny, and new. I experienced his initial abandonment firsthand, and empathy dictated my actions.

She popped in, and she popped out of his life. Life began to pass him by at the age of seven. One day, as he was throwing a crying a fit at the foot of the door, I grabbed my basketball and stepped over him while he cried on the floor like a mama's boy. I opened the door and looked at him. I asked him, "Are you going to cry all day or go shoot some hoops with me?"

From his position on the floor, emotions filled his heart like a helium balloon, and our friendship began to dry his eyes. The love in his laughter spoke the words he couldn't say to me. An abandoned boy helped me pass through my childhood as an adult. I knew exactly what he needed. From time to time, he just smiled. He jumped all around like boys do. He couldn't shoot, dribble, or pass the ball, but none of that mattered to him or me. He was somewhat clumsy in his sandals, but he was overly excited to be running around under the sun with someone who wanted to play with him.

I noticed each day he sat closer and closer to me, and love began to free both of us from the families' abandonment. Capable of surviving the greatest sorrows known to mankind, I turned back the clock to when I was born. A child's love countered every grief I had.

♥

My mother's inspiration evolved beyond generations of conformity. My childhood allowed me to find my artistic genius, and I saw life for what it really was. Humbled by my experiences, light without darkness preserves the sightlessness, and rarely do others take the time to see beyond the traditions of their forefathers. Conventional minds seek only the safety of this world. I dared to discover the value of my life.

♥

Everyone is unique and has a story inside of them. Observing Justin's frustration helped me see nothing could replace a parent's love. Jada's and my relationship existed in the illusion somewhere between the twilight and nightfall. We forever would be linked by the things we weren't to each other. It was easy to be a couple without each other around. I had no other place to go or enough money to move.

The life I wanted to make and the parts of the world found each other. It empowered me. The paradox of my life in poverty and abandonment broadened my viewpoints. In a world with small-minded men with no character, I braved each storm and merely existed, and it was the memory of my mother's love that let me fear no fate.

I never forgot my heart was forever apart from Jada. She could do what she wanted with her seven-year-old son. Until one day, I came home and saw her holding him by his arm. He had just pants on, and she was beating him to the rhythm of the syllables that she angrily shouted at him. I looked at Justin's terrorized face and saw fear in his young brown eyes. I had seen terror immobilize and strip a child of conscious thought once before, for I remembered my brother, Robert, who stood in the corner crying relentlessly from the dread of my father beating my mother and me.

From somewhere deep within me, I stepped out of the thoughts that hindered me from completely loving another human being. In a place where my heartache lived, my infinitely precious soul drove me to act. For I knew, there was no other world in which Justin could live, and I knew he didn't have the resolve I had. His heart was pure and kind, and his unconditional affection opened my eyes to a love that had lain dormant within me. I could clearly see the evil passed down from generation to generation,

Out of the FIELD

for the nature of the tortured is become the torturer.

In a place where the past and the present coexisted, my mother's courage gave me the strength to extend my hand. I stepped out of the shadows, reached out and grabbed him. I pulled him close to my chest and wrapped my arms around to protect him. Each heartbeat felt like a bass drum. As I turned in Jada's direction, I looked into her eyes and saw someone else. She was a photocopy of the lives lived before her. She raised the belt to hit both of us, and I said, "No! No! No! You're not going to hit me with that belt."

The child in my heart stepped out to save another child. I walked past her with Justin in my arms. We went out and sat on the couch. I let him catch his breath and dry his eyes before I uttered, "Justin, I love you."

I spoke those words to make him feel at ease and to stop crying. Love holds a secret ingredient, and it can make anyone whole. The tone of my voice resonated the melody inside my soul. A simple choice to extend my heart forever changed me. I didn't know the effect those words would have on him. The fragments of my life fit together that day like the pieces of a puzzle. The tragedy of my life brought me to a moment of pure grace. I always have, essentially, been waiting to become something else. My dream was on the verge of becoming real as Justin adopted me.

His actions opened the door for me to love another human being. His eyes knighted me his hero, realizing I was the only one who had ever stood up for him. As his fear subsided beneath my arm, my fear visualized the love I wanted to feel. I looked over my walls at him. I had always found a way to survive and live life alone, for the shadows of my childhood inside of me. I learned to hide them well, and now realized I had been so afraid to let someone love me. I built my life around the show others wanted to see, and I lived between the distances I imposed on others to keep them away. My heart found its home.

I looked at this child's loving look, and the sweet, surreal thoughts that sparked change flew through my mind like chasing sparrows under the sun. They flashed the freedom I deserved, and the love meant for me, and my mind began to coalesce with my soul. I remembered the field God found me in and every breadcrumb of grace along my journey. I never knew my brother, and I never had a family to call my own. I roamed this earth every day paying back the pain I thought I owed. As the barriers of my denial began to crack, I still pretended to be oh so strong.

Justin's façade-piercing smile opened my heart so we could belong.

The sweet disposition of God's loving grace swarmed my barricades, overwhelmed the fortress surrounding my heart and took no quarter upon me when Justin said, "I love you too, Larry."

19
The Power of Love

Life undoubtedly had thrown itself against me time and time again. At least in part, I believed in the visionary company of love. Its voice drove me to overcome, even when little changed. The essence of love had been suspended by an invisible dimension. I couldn't know when it would come, nor could I avoid my heart's yearning. Yet, each day I was transformed by my beliefs. When it called my name, it touched my heart, and a great wink from eternity let me know I was home.

♥

The decision to let someone love me changed my life forever. The granite barriers I built to separate me from the free-grazers crumbled into dust beneath my feet. I placed each brick into the wall for a reason, and it gave me a chance to be someone else. I'd made my mind up as a kid to never let them take me alive. Only another child could find his way through the fortifications I built as a child. My memories spiritually inflated, and in the onrush of emotions, I took a deep breath and whispered to myself, "I am, I am loved."

♥

As a youth, I never wanted to blend into the loitering mind of the community. I saw everything as imitative, biddable, and uninspired. Ideas are genius provided by a sixth sense. Followers sell out for so little. Everything can be overcome with skill and resourcefulness. Being an orphan, I skipped the class on being part of the great American donkey train. I never wanted to see the world through someone else's eyes. Imagination creates. Love forgives. Love has no memory, no fear, and only hope. I found my salvation in loving another.

And so it was, I entered the world filled with love. Its voice soothed my soul. The journey of ten million miles had ended, and I held love in my hand. I welcomed its sparkle. My instincts let me know it had assembled this moment just for me. My heart beat boom, boom, boom.

♥

My life lay silent and tiny under the blue-black sky, and a child's admiration was the very last thing I'd expected to exalt me. Justin was the vaccination to the infectious insecurity that hindered me from calling any place home. I looked back at the written pages of my life and saw the mysterious penmanship of Another. When I empty myself of all thoughts, I can see the way the earth is kissed by the sun, the elegance in a human heart and kindness is the religion that can change the world.

Once a troubled boy who lived life as a double-dare do-or-die, I never let my life be detained by factory reason or the carbon copied logic of others. Circumstances defined my virtues. God gave me only one life, but empathy let me climb inside a million human beings. Compassion helped me connect to others and let me see there was no answer without listening, without seeing the other side. The greater the heartbreak, the greater the love and understanding. My bastard wisdom allowed me to recover my childhood at will.

♥

I suffered exceptionally well, and in the eyes of man, my life would be deemed a failure by most. I had no earthly possessions, degree, or fancy title, but love overwhelmed my past and gave the present its future. A vagabond kid blossomed in distempered society. Under the sun's rays and the moon's eye, I found out life hurts if you live it well and not standing behind the asses of others. Scars gave my soul strength. I let life be and worked on me. Being loved gave me wings to catch up with the time I had lost.

Every day, I got to look into a child's eyes and felt him say, "I'm here. I love you."

Every one of his actions shouted, "Look at me! See me now! I'm yours, forever."

Out of the FIELD

♥

The boy in my heart never cried again, and my soul never forgot what I'd learned. Love needs an accomplice. Our paths didn't cross by mere chance. It was like an old-time classic movie. We both knew we would co-star in each others' lives. Love is the most powerful emotion in the world. I got schooled by a boy, and love turned an outlaw into a child's hero. Emotionally secure, he knew his best friend would always stand up for him. I found a lifelong playmate, a continuous supply of high fives and bear hugs.

♥

The best moments in life came when I came across a thought, a feeling, and a different way of looking at things. It happened a lot when I gazed upon my two sons. I now understood the responsibilities of mentoring a human life. The thought of my sons' love pulled me upward and onward to make them proud of me.

Most people spend their lives following in the footsteps of others, and miracles pass right in front of their dull eyes. They go to high school, get a job, or go off to college. Real adulthood sets in with a house, kids, and the loss of self. On the contrary, the road to nowhere led me to fail with wit and grace. The story of my life is I always saw the daily miracles to survive. I earned an EhD (Extreme Human Development) degree from the University of the Divinity. I elevated my education all on my own. My studies had no syllabi or evaluations, only my own self-made laws of human dignity.

Since I couldn't change the hearts of others; I changed the way I viewed them. My heart finally knew peace, and it came from knowing my memories feed my imagination. I banished the dark parts of my soul with the illumination of love and forgiveness. I opened myself up to the unimaginable and found the powers beyond human measurement. As for the world, the invisible splendors flowed in and out of mind, and they weren't weighted down by the strings of designer fashion or the fog of old perceptions.

♥

Ah, my childhood. I ended up viewing it as something sacred and holy, for it showed me there was Someone there when no one was there. My life was nothing but a series of several mistakes. I choked on it! I screamed from its terror! I camped outside of the gates of hell. I even raised my middle finger at God. I have known anger, debauchery, and insanity all too well. In the ruses of my life, I lived as an entertainer, a vagabond, an artist, a criminal, and now I am a missionary of the faith. The pure innocence of kindness now makes me weep.

A common man with uncommon thoughts. I never planned my life, and it was lived like a freestyle poem. Forty years of disappointment led me to success. I never gave up. Fragments coalesced together, and self-reflection let me see redemption resided inside the human heart. The more I loved, the more my past was absolved. God gave me this child to spare me from being a martyred slave from antiquity.

My soul had always been a bird in a cage, and it waited to fly off. With my life resurrected, someone loved me. I looked up to the heavens and asked, "Why me?"

♥

Justin's innocence stripped away my personal space, and it gave me an understanding of how important parents are in a child's life. Leapfrog hugs and wet kisses on the cheek set my spirit free. The more I let life be, the more I changed myself. A deep sense of belonging came over me when he proclaimed me his "Dad." The love inside Justin's heart quietly opened the door for us to do more than exist.

Every day, I created the capacity to love out of nothing. Never knowing my father or what a father should do, I did what was right in my heart. After each fire assignment, I brought him a fire t-shirt. He wore those shirts every day of his life and told the world, "My father loves me!"

♥

Love made me dig deeper into my own thoughts. There are fragments of me I cannot begin to fathom. The condition of love was essential for dismantling my life's disorders. God loves me, real or not real? I tell myself "real," and that makes all the difference in the world to me. I tell myself

Out of the FIELD

I can be another, and my story just begins. From the corners of my mind crinkles a deep thought, the longing for the impossible helped find the miracle inside of me. Most humans are already passively dead, and they live their lives like a kitten in the wilderness.

♥

No man had a more significant effect on my life than my father. One day, I received a voice mail message from my uncle Timmy that he had passed. As I left the comfort of my life, traveling back in time, I counted on one hand, the times I'd seen or talked with him since he walked out on us. I still had a couple of fingers left over. Both my father and relatives violated my basic human rights. They produced a negative consequence. I became a criminal to live. My relatives were the cruelest people I ever met.

My father showed there is no excuse for not doing the right thing. He assisted in the birth of every one of my thoughts. I watched and listened to every one of his actions or words, and by doing so, I saw the generations of monsters scavanging his soul. My father's cold, cruel world shaped my entire life. I wouldn't have slept in the cold of winter's night, learned to steal like a thief, or found the voice clutched in my heart to stand up for the meek. The bright rippling muscle in my mind created the strength to never return to the place where my destruction started.

The price of my family's indifference bankrupted their souls. They were merely bobblehead figures. As a child, I didn't need anyone in my life who merely nodded and smiled. Their eyes were vacant. They never saw me or responded to my screams for help. I questioned, could they have a soul? Maybe not. I guessed it was worth a phone call to see.

The next day I called back to Connecticut. "Hey, Uncle Timmy, it is Larry."

"Hi, Larry. Hey, I am sorry we haven't stayed in touch over the years. I wanted to let you know your father didn't die alone. Jimmy, Richard, and I were at his bedside when he passed."

I had no feelings for him but politely asked, "What did he die from?"

"His liver shut down."

I thought to myself, "That poor bastard lived hard and died harder. He self-embalmed his own body."

"I got a hold of Robert, and he committed to showing up at the funeral services. It would be nice for you to pay your last respects."

The word, "respect," triggered a multitude of emotions, none of them good. As I remembered every step of my painful journey, in milliseconds my mind rehearsed each failure, hardship, and fistfight I had with darling Dad.

In my delusion-free mind, I recognized my father had co-authored my fate by making me unrecognizable to him. I flashed back to the darkness, and two scared eyes looked back through nothingness at me.

My memories transmitted his voice shouting "Little Bastard," at me from the other side of life. Sensing his cold, dark fish eyes looking at me, a long, slow, warm smile stretched across my face to say goodbye.

It was my decision to fight my father that saved my life. An outlaw child, I fought for every inch of my life and became everything he wasn't. I reacted to my uncle's request, "I am sorry for your loss and know you idolized your big brother growing up. I was never part of your family. He never did one thing in this life for me, so why would I come back to pay respect to a man who never valued me as his son."

Forgiveness doesn't hide from the facts. It allowed me to speak from the place of truth, honor, and love. A voiceless child became a man of integrity, something my family will never know.

He hung up the phone on me. That was the last time I ever heard from any member of the Lee family.

♥

A few months later, I received a call from an attorney, "Hello, Mr. Lee, my name is Jeff Jacobs, attorney-at-law. It seems that your father had $35,000 in his bank account at the time of his passing. I am sorry for your loss."

I couldn't help myself and said, "I'm not."

Mr. Jacobs paused and kept talking, "Your uncle Jimmy gave me your number, and I need you to sign a few papers, and the whole thing will be yours after the probate court takes their share. Your brother, Robert, cannot take a dime. Otherwise, he will lose his disability benefits and be homeless again."

"I guess the Lee family couldn't figure a way to steal this money."

At first, I didn't want to take a dime, but thoughts of Robert made me think beyond myself. He was forty years old, busted flat, broken down, and permanently disabled. I found out Robert lived in a senior citizen's home in New Britton, Connecticut. The only income he had was his disability Social Security benefits. My father and his family fucked him up real good!

I called my uncle Burney (twelve thousand was nothing to him) and told him I would send him a check for twelve thousand five hundred dollars so Robert could get cash under the table for his needs.

Through my short conversations with Uncle Burney, he told me Robert tried to commit suicide several times in his life. The Veterans Administration Hospital used electroshock treatment to try and kill the demons that still haunted him from our childhood.

My uncle gave me Robert's telephone number, and I called him, "Hey Robert, it's Larry."

Just like my father, he blurted out, "What do you want?"

In a soft tone, I replied, "It's been a while, so I decided to give you a call. Did Burney tell you I sent him a check for you to use Dad's money?"

"Yeah, he told me. Thanks," he snapped back. "It's time for my nap. I've got to go."

"I'll call you again in a week."

All I heard was a click.

There would be neither a relationship nor amends if I didn't commit to loving patience and lots of persistence. I kept calling him once a week and slowly made it past the walls he erected to protect himself.

Compassion will tear your heart in two if you allow yourself to completely embrace another life. I did just that. After all, he was my brother. Knowing the Holiday family lacked any emotional intelligence, I kept inching my way into his heart. Through our short conversations, I could tell he never changed his perception of me.

Our tragedy started when adults traded their values for the blank stare of apathy. Failure to act tells a child, "You're simply nothing to me."

♥

Making amends was the highest form of respect I could pay my brother. My broken life was held together by Band-Aids, superglue, and prayer. I reached out and tried to inspire his life, and I felt both joy and sorrow at the same time. The act of humility trades pride and selfishness for modesty and purity. My words kneeled, and my heart opened itself to be a big brother. No words could change what had been done, only the actions of love could show him I had changed.

Through our weekly calls, I discovered the choice that defined both our lives. Our families' abandonment seared into our core being, and Robert elected to live a defeated life. It stunted him, but it inspired me.

♥

Born an angel with broken wings, words scribbled on a piece of paper let me dream of another way. I felt, thought, hoped, and became the color and textures of sounds. I armed myself with a pen and wit. No one knows the limits of my heart, not even me. I would never let anyone strip me of my power.

I thank God for my tears, for they're the strength of my love. A fated journey with no direction. It changed directions many times and surged through the immensity of life. The purity of my heart awakened me to see each person as fraternal. The mindfulness of God archived in a mere mortal's mind only offended the ghosts of time. No more a secret dream, I got the chance to pardon myself and make amends to my brother. He decided to visit me when I bought a three-bedroom condominium in San Diego.

On the drive down to the airport to pick him up, the mirror in which I viewed myself helped me remove my defects. With humility and self-forgiveness, I learned to trust and to act on my faith. Many times, I have turned my back on religion, but my chattering voice couldn't speak or write without feeling the chi of God associated in words.

I thought, to live without forgiving is unforgivable. Would our shared suffering find mutual sympathy? Fate has given me a second chance to love my brother.

After parking my car, I went in to wait for his flight to arrive. God must have liked to see me sweat, for the plane had to circle around the airport for thirty minutes. The marine layer was thick as soup.

Once I saw Robert, my memory of him went from sixteen to sixty years old in seconds.

I had winked twice, shook my head. My eyes made a beeline to him. I whispered, "Ugh God, I'm going in now."

He looked lost in the mass of people. As I walked forward, I thought, "Lots of opportunities, plenty of possibilities."

Out of the FIELD

About twenty feet away from I raised my voice in the crowd. "Robert! Robert! I'm over here."

He looked over my way and didn't smile. I thought, "Oh shit! What should I do now?"

I doubled down and gave him a hug, and his inflexible disposition let my arms fall off him like rainwater. I couldn't help but remember the start of my journey, all those church ladies hugging me.

He felt so uncomfortable, he began to squirm away from me and said, "Yeah, it's good to see you too, Larry. Now please give me my space."

I found it hard to hide my tears.

We both sat silently on the car ride home and watched the world around us pass by. This event had taken a lifetime to happen. It seemed odd to be in the same space as my brother. Neither one of us felt content, nor did we want to be caught showing our feelings. The silence was fucking creepy.

Crazy memories stored in one's mind indeed drive perception. I shouldn't have all those years back. Crazy, how silence poked my conscience closer to my heart. The great paradox inside me always pushed me to evolve.

To change the situation, I'm going to have to change my perceptions. I told him, "Just want to warn you, there is a boy named Justin at home. He's a bit messy, hyperactive, and knows no boundaries. Everyone is his friend."

Once we got home, I opened the door, and Justin ran up to my brother and shouted, "Uncle Bob," as he hugged him.

Robert looked over at me, and my eyes said, "I told you so."

Looking inside of him, I saw he never learned to cry, forgot how to learn, nor could he open himself up to love.

My heart cried for my brother who couldn't cry.

♥

Throughout the week, we showed him around Southern California, and we even took him to Camp Pendleton, his first duty station in the Marine Corps. Slowly, over the week, he opened up, and he brought a thought to my mind, "The past will dictate the future, only when one rebels against the spirit inside of us."

He couldn't see the ghosts that influenced his life, and he didn't know he was the only one who could set himself free. His soul was a ball of yarn knotted. He couldn't listen, comprehend, and grow. Ignorance prevails if one believes they're cursed. He held onto the anchor of hurt so long; he accepted no ownership for his life. The memories he couldn't forget conjured the cell walls in which he chose to exist. Unrecognizable to himself, the hands of a stranger have slowly smothered his life.

♥

He gradually opened up to me, and through our conversations, I saw the two years between us made all the difference. He wasted his heart on a family who didn't value it.

He told me Uncle Timmy called him the day after our father passed. He let loose his real thoughts as he told me about his conversation, " Yeah Larry, Uncle Timmy calls me and tells me Dad passed. I'm thinking, like I care. Timmy kept pressuring for me to attend the funeral."

"Why did you give in and go?"

"Timmy kept saying it'd be good for both his sons to be there. He told me you were coming."

"I told him to take a hike."

Thinking to myself, "I couldn't believe it. In life as in death, my father still controlled his family."

"Larry, you always were a bastard," Robert replied as he laughed.

"No, remember, I was a Little Bastard."

We both lost ourselves in laughter, and our brotherly love found itself.

He went on to tell me, "I had to be around the person who molested me has a child."

Stunned I said, "Back up a second."

"Yes Larry, I was sexually molested as a child by a family member," Robert quantified as he looked down at the ground.

I skipped the part about me, and my heart dropped and put my arm around him.

I saw the tears form in his eyes, as he said, "Goodbye," and crawled back in his shell.

He opened up when he wanted to share his real family. Like when he told me, "Do you remember the Stoppani family?"

"Yes, they're the family you lived with after Dad split."

"Did you know Grandma never gave them any money for my support?

They paid out of their own pocket for me to live there for five years."

"No, I didn't know, but I'm not surprised by anything the Lees didn't do. I guess that means the two years after we left her house, she pocketed that money too. I went hungry for those two years, while Granny fattened her bank account. Robert, we lived like dogs who roamed the street in search of a meal. The Mack and Zoef families fed us most days."

Robert smiled every time he talked about the Stoppani family from Harwinton, Connecticut. His love and admiration sparkled out of his eyes for them. He was an adopted son truly loved by their parents. The smile he had on his face when he talked about the brothers, Tom and Bill, brought his mind back to happy times and family dinners. I listened to him speak of the realities of living in a small town with a family.

The Stoppani family knew every child needed a caring adult in his life. Mrs. Stoppani, a nurse by profession, exhibited both charity and wisdom for an orphan born into a non-caring family. The willingness for her family to give from their hearts made them rich. As I looked back at both our lives, I saw God does send angels to care for those who cannot care for themselves. The fact that one cannot see them doesn't prove they don't exist, for the hype to prove they do exist is contrary to their mission. They're the reason I'm still alive.

The Mack, Stoppani and Zoef families were blessed with compassion for those who were less fortunate, and they demonstrated humanity's greatest accomplishments which are to love a stranger as they love themselves.

That evening, my muse let me see Robert was unaware of comprehending the events and realities into which we were born, and he never questioned our upbringing or family members' actions. To a child, a family is everything, and it is the groundwork for adulthood. Destroy a child's trust, one has destroyed their beliefs and hope, and it's replaced with the awful suspicion no one can ever be trusted.

Reflection helped me understand my past, and it strengthened me to leap over recurring obstacles into the future.

My heart was ready to make my amends to my brother. The time together helped me understand our childhood. I asked him, "Hey Robert, let's go for a walk. I've got to tell you something."

"Why don't you tell me here? I'm comfortable."

To keep my humility, I had to take three deep breaths and said, "Please come outside with me."

"Okay! Okay! I'm coming."

Looking him the eye, which made him look away, I stated, "Robert, I'm sorry for all the cruel and mean things I did to you while growing up. Survival made me do a lot of things I regret, and you're the last amends I need to make. Truly, I never thought I'd ever make this one."

Robert rarely ever spoke and often just stared into space. He kicked the dirt and looked at me out of the corner of his eyes and replied, "It is all right, Larry. I'm happy you made something out of your life. You should be proud you are clean and sober now. You used to be a meteor heading for a collision."

Modesty overcame me as I told him, "I am sorry I didn't keep in touch with you over the years. Mom wanted me to look after you. I didn't know how to deal with our house of horrors. We were betrayed by not only our father but also the Lee and Holiday families."

Lost in a maze of memories, my words bounced off the hardened armor of his denial. Looking deeper, his invisible wounds were left open and never healed. I made no attempt to hide in the awkwardness of the moment. I lifted my weighted feet, moving closer. Sympathy let me put aside self-inflicted ignorance and problematic overthinking. I gave him a little man's hug while beating him on the back and said, "I love you, Robert."

He mumbled back, "Let's not get too carried away, Larry."

Within seconds, Justin opened the door and ran over to Robert and gave a child-mauling hug. It was a connection made with the heart and affected him positively. Justin uttered, "I love you, Uncle Robert."

No matter how much time has passed since our childhood, the yearning to be loved and accepted still affected him. He never paid attention to the past, so he never knew what to do with his life. The days of my life linked me with forgiveness and compassion, and it grounded me in humanity. Loving my neighbor gave me the capacity to be transformed beyond the pleasures of the day.

It made me happy to see Robert smile when Justin hugged him. The secret longing inside his heart rose up beyond its self-imposed restraints and belonged to the moment. My mind's eye flashed back and recalled Robert chasing bubbles around the yard with my mother at the age of five. I tried to tell him to take his foot off the brake and let the journey begin. He held on to the hurt my family gave him until he passed away at the age of forty-two.

Out of the FILED

20
I Am My Mother's Son

About one year later, my relationship with Jada officially broke down beyond repair. She never listened to or respected my personal boundaries. The five years we had lived together weren't meant for either one of us. Jada got her own apartment, and she brought Justin over to pick up the last of her things. Out in the parking lot, Justin stated, "Mom, I want to stay at Larry's house."

"Babe, we have our own place now."

"I want to come over to Larry's house after school. He's way cool."

Probing his eyes, I saw there were no forbidden questions, no matters too sensitive to share, and only the sacred truth of love stood before a father and son. The certainty of Justin's trust moored him to my soul. His young brown eyes helped me discover the truth of who I was meant to be. Love found us, despite all my differences. Once I accepted the responsibility for his life, something rare and beautiful was created. For me, every moment we spent together helped remove all my limitations. I became the man I was meant to be when I said, "I'll pick you up tomorrow after school."

His smile blacked out the sun.

♥

It was the great onrush of a child's love that had washed my soul clean, emptied me of self-pity, and helped me find the strength in my indifference. To feel loved made me realize freedom wasn't being average.

♥

I asked myself, "What are you going to do with your life now?" Love began to help me rewrite every day. Line by line, relationship by relationship, my imagination and skill found the courage to risk failure and rejection. I lived like a hero in a Greek myth. The world made me wise, and my seasons in hell made me cynically honest.

♥

Each of us comes and goes in other's lives, like passing clouds in the sky, my chariot of thoughts circled around and around the sun. The fourth dimension in my mind exposed my journey through the wilderness into the Promised Land. My photographic memories saw the blessing that came from the hollow, meaningless faces along the way. Empty words can't disguise the mold that remains in their hearts.

There's no love without listening, without seeing, and without understanding the tangled passion of the billion lives. The sum of all my choices created my destiny. The idea of life interdependent on one another allowed me to find the end of the rainbow. As a poet, my failures became my successes, for each one of them, led me to discover something about myself and humanity. Suffering freed me to evolve beyond the limits the world imposed on me. I read every road sign my guardian angel left for me.

♥

It took no bravery to stand up and do the right thing and be Justin's father. Loyalty and devotion created a bond of love. In his eyes, I saw the forever love words can't express. A child is born with an enormous need to receive affection, and it a terrible thing to deprive them of it. My mother's love served me well through my struggles, but a child's love healed my soul and let it soar.

Miracles happen every day. I just happened to never give up on myself, and once everything fell into place. I got a third chance with my son, Joshua, when he moved from Oklahoma City to San Diego to live with me. Wisdom cannot come without boundless compassion and brutal honesty. The marvelous love I dreamed of as a child, started to flourish in my home life.

Every night at dinner, our lives were filled with stories of trying new things, making mistakes, challenging ourselves and lots of laughter. The all pieces of time and intimacy I doled out from boy to boy made me

Out of the FIELD

whole. I didn't need to look around for anything else. Love blessed my life.

♥

Joshua, like his father, didn't get his license until he needed to. Once he got out here to San Diego, I had to teach him how to drive in the big city. Everything started out well until he turned the ignition and pressed on the gas. At our first corner, the tires screeched in pain from the speed he took it. I couldn't help myself, "Did you hear those tires? Do you think they are telling you something?"

"What are you talking about?"

"It's obvious to me you took that corner too fast."

Joshua snapped back, "You're freaking me out!"

"Well, you are scaring the shit out of me, so slow down!"

♥

Little by little, I trusted Joshua's actions and decisions. The more I let him be who he was meant to be, the more I found we had in common. We didn't need moral victories in our relationship. Respect came from doing the right thing. One day, I shared with him, "You know you're the reason I stayed sober and continued to push back at life. I wanted to give you a better life than I had."

♥

Being a parent, I learned silence doesn't mean that they didn't hear you. Silence helped me remember wisdom comes from struggle, and their present lives clung too acutely to social unawareness in teenage boys.

♥

As we stumbled through days of getting reacquainted with each other, we both found we needed each other to be complete ourselves. Our progress might not have happened all at once, but I knew my journey would end one day with my son going his own way. I didn't want to stunt our time together. From afar, I admire my son's compassion for those whose lives were less fortunate. He was a special education assistant in Poway school district. The joy he had on his face when he talked about his kids at school was genuine. Joshua didn't try to be different. He wanted to make a difference in people's lives.

♥

As a father, I took great pride in the accomplishments of my children. There are many ways to be a father, and many thousands of dads don't know how to interact with their children. I found my Father while I was homeless, living in a field, and the more I mirrored Him, the more my empathy expanded to reach out to the world.

Compassion opened my heart and helped me become a father. My sons' enthusiasm kept me grounded. Justin reminded me daily there always was time to change. Children keep life unwrinkled and full of zest, and their laughter knows no end when they are loved. My kids were blessed, for they didn't have to camp near hell and wait to die.

When I looked in the rearview mirror, the universe was in constant transition, and I found meaning in the meaningless. I may have seemed lost most of the time, but each day was an opportunity to experience the unknown, a lesson learned, and a chance to grow. I defined my standard and transformed the sorrow into joy. A wanderer, a dreamer, and poet who never entertained the thought of joining a pack of wandering hyenas. I determined Paradise or Perdition. A humanist, in his moment of surrender, foregoes all religions and social demands, only to discover the practice of humility. The ray of sun that shines through the rain enlightened my mind.

♥

It is when I looked deep into imperfection, I find perfection in my thoughts. Jada never allowed herself to be a mother. As the days passed, she let me raise Justin without remorse. He moved into my house full-time only weeks after our break-up. He never understood why his mother had no time for him. I witnessed his suffering torture him numb. From time to time, in her hyper-emotional responses, she beat him with a belt. She misunderstood situations, and she retold the event to make her look good in others' eyes. She could not adequately regulate her own emotions, and

Out of the FIELD

her failure to cope with her feelings made her rage at her son. Everything she did had a price tag attached to it, and she manipulated all the facts to justify her actions. She made him feel so small and irrelevant. She only used a small portion of his father's Social Security entitlement for his care. The rest she spent on herself.

I knew firsthand the internal banishment that came from being abandoned. I found wisdom in the ugly things that made up Jada's life. Most men would have walked away from a child that was not theirs, but because I have suffered like him. I find something inside of him that inspired me, and I have something inside of me to help him heal. It is in the essence of gratitude I can see the beauty of life, find forgiveness, and love the unloved.

♥

I cannot diminish the gifts associated with dignity. Love is a dignitary, and its noble intentions let me discover every talent I possessed. Never recognizing the limitations placed on my life, the race against time started. There was so much to do. I woke every morning and said, "Believe, believe and believe," in the mirror.

There was another life that I might have had. A chance was what I ask for, and leaving nothing to chance made me better. I paid myself first and invested all my overtime. The seed of self-love was planted and grew. The best way to improve my life was to be of service to others. I transformed myself into a commodity, and my endless energy reaped the highest profit. Dependable, straightforward, and honest were the words I lived by each day.

♥

Life has no goal for me, except for the one I make, and in principle and fairness, I exchanged myself in the open market and experienced a million moments. I never took one second for granted and quantified each miracle in my life.

In a world filled with man's façades, name brands, and cookie-cutter education, I walked a million miles to find peace, and God came down from His throne and walked beside me. Anyone can change the world they were born into, one must want it bad enough. In my case, I walked straight through hell for a second chance given to me by strangers.

Life can be cruel, and it moves forward against everyone with no mercy. Angels save us from situations we cannot see. We hold our lives in our very hands, and we choose everything we receive. We can opt to be the architect of our own dreams, or we can live in the nightmare of those who came before us. The key to life is being blessed with the charity to see the reflections of our actions in other lives.

♥

One day at work, I stopped by my friend's office to visit with her. Emilie, with a gleeful smile on her face, said, "I thought of you last night while I was reading the book *The Glass Castle*, and it reminded me of your life. I think you should write a memoir. No one knows how far you came. It will be inspirational to others."

After a very long pause, I said, "I have done nothing special with my life."

Emilie passionately replied, "That's where you're wrong, buddy. Look what you have overcome and done with your life! The stories you have told me. You even used to cope with life by writing. It will be a must-read. Oprah will love your book."

"You're crazy! No thanks!"

A thought is a curious thing, and it either dies or entwines itself in one's life. I put the idea of writing a book down, and it kept readjusting the way I viewed my life. One day, I stopped by Emilie's and told her, "I'm going to do it. I'm going to write the book."

It didn't take but a few seconds when she said, "You have to go back to Connecticut and do research for your book. You have to go back home."

My fate had been fated by the choices and promises I made. The most defining promise made was to my mother before she passed. "Yes Mama, I will grow up to be a good man."

♥

In June 2011, I returned to my home state of Connecticut. It had been over twenty years since I had seen the Holiday family. I took Justin back with me to distract me from the Holidays. On the plane ride back home, I reflected on the evolution of my soul and pondered how I escaped.

What would I have accomplished if I not been discarded by my family and been disenfranchised by my school and town? Possibly nothing at all.

The difficulty of my life never let me plan for this moment. I smiled in pleasure thinking of my mother. Compassion transcended and enlightened my soul. Suffering brought me the mental ability to focus on words. I am only a letter or a vowel in the world's essay, and apart from others, I can form no words on my own.

I learned the term "family" includes the whole world, and miracles start in the human heart. A self-disciple, I didn't come to God. He came to me, but I chose to listen. I discovered spirituality can be taught, and it is the science of truth, love, and forgiveness.

I opened my mind to the thousand ideas that lived inside of it, and I found happiness, a noble heart and too many blessings to count. To think I once stole clothes to cover my body, but now, I was upper middle-class and lived next to CPAs, businessmen, doctors, dentists, and yes, idiots too. As a finance section chief, I've helped manage some of this nation's largest disasters: the Space Shuttle *Columbia* disaster, Deepwater Horizon oil spill, hurricanes Katrina and Rita, and several large wildfires.

A voice for all those who were born without a chance, self-dignity and courage let me push aside the world of predatory greed. I listened to the story inside my soul, and I became everything I want to be. Wisdom brought me to forgiveness, and a writer's soul remembered every lesson it was taught along the way. All I can live is the life I've been given and write about the moments of truth in a world of lies and fake news.

♥

"Long time, no see. How you doing Uncle Burney? It's good to see you and your family."

"Yes, Larry, it has been a long time. You're looking good, too."

Later that evening, we all sat down for dinner, and the conversation seemed to circle around about me every now and then. My uncle made a comment, "Chief, you were pretty rebellious as a teenager."

I smiled and said, "I will always treasure the radical bastard inside my heart. It was worth more than money."

Silence overcame the table.

I quickly turned the conversation to Robert and asked, "How were his last days?"

Alice didn't waste any time telling me. "Every night he'd sneak downstairs and steal a few beers. He wasn't supposed to drink anymore, but he did."

Her statement hit my soul like a jagged piece glass, and I replied, "He did. Did anyone ask him why?"

The table became silent again, and I grew reacquainted with my devilish smile.

Some people never change!

♥

A misfit and rebel, I lived in a world of thoughts, feelings, and humanity, not wealth, prestige, and power. Later that evening, I asked myself, "Why is it those who have always stand in judgment over those who don't have?"

I could quote them, and no one would be surprised, for the world is full of people who speak empty words and think stupid thoughts. I looked past their disguises and saw a family ghost moldering in their remains. The actions of the father shape the future of his children unless you're resilient enough to become your own man.

♥

The highlight of my research was on June 21, 2011, when Justin and I took a road trip. Our first stop was the Patriots Hall of Fame in Foxboro, Massachusetts. The Patriots are Justin's favorite football team. Our next stop was Storrs, Connecticut, and we visited the University of Connecticut. The men's basketball team had just won their third national title, and Justin got his picture taken with freshman power forward, Roscoe Smith. Our next stop was my hometown of Unionville, and there, I took him to my mother's gravesite.

Justin had fallen asleep a long the way. As I drove through the town of Unionville and past 23 Lovely Street, frozen moments with my mother flashed inside my mind every few seconds. Once I entered the gates of Greenwood Cemetery, my mind became still as I parked next to the Lee family's gravesites.

Staring into the tree line, my spirit whispered to me, "You feared no fate, and here you are."

Opening the car door, I smiled and walked over to my grandmother's headstone first. I gazed at her name for a few seconds before I shook my head and said, "What kind of grandmother steals from her grandchildren and leaves them starving?"

Shuffling right a few steps, I focused in my father's headstone, and I began to speak, "I really didn't like you very much and still don't, but I learned to forgive you. Forgiveness allowed me to feel your pain as well as mine. The sadness of knowing your sadness is what gave me the strength to forgive you. I'm no longer crippled from your actions. I can take you or leave you. I'll choose to leave you under the dirt."

I turned and walked toward my mother's and brother's gravesites. Like a lost child in a mall, I couldn't find her. My heart began to ache, and tears began to flow from my eyes. After a few moments, I found them and kneeled before my brother's headstone and said, "I love you. You're my brother, please forgive me."

As I rose to my feet, tears began to flow freely from my eyes. My thoughts went back to my mother and teacher. It was her natural state of unselfishness that taught me to look deeper into the world around me. As I looked over at the automobile, I noticed Justin's head moving about, so I returned to the vehicle. I asked him, "Hey little man, would you like to visit your grandmother's gravesite?"

A child of few words, he replied to my offer with, "Sure."

Once back at her headstone, I paused and silently basked in the glory of victory. My heart silently shouted up toward the heavens, "Mom, I did it! I kept your promise."

It didn't take long for me to start crying. Justin looked up at me and put his arm around me, and he said, "Why are you crying?"

I caught my breath and replied, "I am crying, for I am happy. My mother would love you so much. She would make you feel like you could conquer the world."

My silent thoughts connected the two worlds, and on that gray overcast day, God opened the sky for a few seconds. The lines between heaven and earth were traversed. The sun brightly flashed through an opening in the clouds. Instantly, my heart warmed with the endless possibilities of being my mother's son.

♥

Months after returning home, I tapped into the angelic and poetic passion that has always walked beside me. I cannot see it, only sense it. It has always been there, and it has always kept me away from harm. It has allowed me to look past reality and see the hidden motives in others. In my mind's eye, I can see adversity has taught me humility, and when I am humble, I can see the virtue of God's love unfolded throughout mankind. In the remission of all my emotions, I can detach from this world and can forgive all those who trespassed against me. Forgiveness is the companion of compassion, and compassion is an act of understanding our humanity. Humanity is the light of an unburdened soul changing the world through Christ's love. I once was lost, but I found God in a field.

CPSIA information can be obtained
at www.ICGtesting.com
Printed in the USA
BVHW071452221119
564533BV00009B/184/P